Yolanda Harris

THE LONG JOURNEY HOME

Copyright © 2019 – Yolanda Harris

All rights reserved. This book is protected under the copyright laws. This book may not be copied or reprinted for commercial gain or profit. The use of short quotations or occasional page copying for personal or group study is permitted and encouraged. Permission will be granted upon request. Unless otherwise identified, Scripture quotations are from the Amplified® Bible (AMP), Copyright © 2015 by The Lockman Foundation.

Used by permission. www.Lockman.org. All rights reserved.

Publishing Services by

EVANGELISTA MEDIA & CONSULTING

Via Maiella, 1
66020 San Giovanni Teatino (Ch) – Italy
publisher@evangelistamedia.com

For Worldwide Distribution.

1 2 3 4 5 6 / 22 21 20 19

> *"'For I know the plans and thoughts that I have for you,' says the Lord, 'plans for peace and well-being and not for disaster, to give you a future and a hope'"*
> (Jeremiah 29:11 AMP).

God has always said to me, "Home is not a place; it's a person." Maybe with all the searching that I've done; the person that I was meant to find was me.

Yolanda Harris

DEDICATION

This book is dedicated to all of the veterans out there. There are many things that we go through that no one will ever be able to relate to if they aren't a veteran. Post-traumatic stress disorder (PTSD), Military Sexual Trauma (MST), the effects of war and friendly fire are all very real situations that we have gone through or know someone who has. Always know that you have someone praying for you; praying for your health, wealth, and well-being. I pray for divine connections; that someone comes across your path that can help you with whatever you are in need of to endure this civilian life. Know that God will give you beauty for your ashes (Isaiah 61:3 NIV).

And for everyone out there that has lost their way, try putting God first. He is the way, the truth, and the life (John 14:6). He will make sure that you find your way…your way back home!

MAIL CALL

In boot camp, one of the most exciting times for us was when we got mail from our loved ones. It was the highlight of our week and made us feel good that we were not forgotten. I would like to provide letters to those that have impacted my life as well as those who served alongside of me.

Dear God: Thank You Daddy God for birthing this book out of me. Although I ran from writing it for three months, when I came back to put pen to paper, You were right there with me helping me with every word written. I'm forever grateful that You chose me to help You get a message to the world. I'll do what You want me to do; go where You want me to go. I live for You and I thank You for dying for me.

Dear Matty: My Dook. I love you with every fiber of my being. I pray that you accomplish everything that God created you for. You are such a talented, smart, eclectic, fashion-forward, beautiful, God loving, happy young lady and I hope that you stay that way. Always put God first and everything else will fall into place. I'm here for you always, no matter what.

Dear reviewers of my book: I thank each and every one of you ladies for taking time out of your busy schedules to read this book and give me your feedback. You have no idea what that means to me. Your love and guidance are what living is all about. God never intends for us to do life alone and I'm more than blessed to have you all in my life. We never know where life will take us, but you will ALWAYS have a place in my heart.

Dear shipmates: For those of you whom I've had the pleasure of serving alongside, there is not a day that goes by that I don't thank God for the opportunity that He gave me to meet each one of you. I carry you around in my spirit, and I pray for peace, prosperity, and longevity for each of you. Some of you have become family, and that's something only God can do. He's awesome at divine connections and interventions, and I truly believe He brought me to the navy to meet you all. Know that I will always be praying for you and that the impact that you've had on my life has carried me through some dark times. Your lives have enriched mine and I thank you forever for it.

Dear veteran brothers and sisters: While there are some of you whom I have never met, please know that you are still prayed for. With military communities, we normally connect quickly and easily because of the job at hand. It's one of those communities where once you're in, you're in for life. I thank you all for your sacrifice and your service. For those that weren't able to come back home, you've made the ultimate sacrifice and I'm forever grateful. I pray for peace and comfort for your family and loved ones. I also pray that they keep your memory alive as we will never forget what you have done for us all.

RECRUITING STATION

The recruiting station is where those that are interested in the armed forces come to gather more information about what it takes to join the armed forces and what they have to look forward to. The recruiter outlines the process and creates an attractive picture of what their time in the services could look like. Welcome to the recruiting station for *The Long Journey Home*. Allow me to be your recruiter and give you insight into the journey you are about to embark on.

From almost being killed in the line of duty, to an attempted rape on the ship, followed by an event that would result in threats to her life, Payton had to endure things females her age should never have to endure but nothing could prepare her for what those events would ultimately do to her mentally, spiritually, and emotionally. PTSD in the military is a very real thing and not knowing how to deal with these emotions would leave Payton in a state of utter despair. Would she go through with killing herself or would she allow her emotions to force her to kill someone else? There's only one way to find out and that's by following Payton on *The Long Journey Home*.

Listen to my other comrades on what they have to say about *The Long Journey Home*.

⚓

What an incredible journey! Talk about twists and turns. Lots of hard work that you've done, and this was so interesting to read. Thank you for trusting me with something so important to you. God got this and you!

Leslie Etheridge
Wife, Mother & Close Friend

The adversity and heartbreak that Yasmine has to overcome give you strength and confidence in your own life. There are some stories that move you so deeply and so unexpectedly that you end up shedding huge tears in the end because you feel so much. As I read through this amazing book, I could barely see the words through all my tears, because nothing prepared me for the sheer emotion running through this stunning, gem of a novel. I don't know how Yolanda manages to create such authentic, heartfelt stories and to leave us utterly breathless and incoherent in the aftermath, but I do know that this book is on my favorite list.

Aquila Scott
Book Reviewer, Editor & Confidant

Yolanda's gift of storytelling captivates her readers by using her life experiences to help readers along their own personal journey. As a veteran and a mother, she seeks to help other veterans achieve the peace that they deserve. With unwavering faith, Yolanda and her daughter, Madison, travel the world spreading muster seeds of hope, determination, and love to those that need them the most. While this book caters to the journey of her fellow veterans, readers of all walks of life will find shiny beacons of light that may help them along the way.

Azhia Cotton
Sister Friend

The honesty and transparency of the author are impeccably unmatched. Yolanda not only has a way with words, she fragrantly knows how to capture the true authenticity of what it means to live aloud. Unapologetically, she neatly constructs her message and then dissects the grim subtleties of what it means to persevere through some of life's most debilitating moments. As the reader, you can expect lessons of triumph to be woven into the very fabric of *The Long Journey Home*.

With such attention to detail, I am always in expectancy because I know that I will not be robbed of a remarkable journey to strength and resilience. Her life is a miraculous testament and it is nothing short of a beautiful gift to experience bits and pieces of it through her artwork. *The Long Journey Home* has challenged me to search the depths of who I am with hopes to embrace who I was always destined to become. A book worth unfolding, a journey worth taking.

Terah L. Davis,
Ph.D., LPC, NCC
Professor, Licensed Counselor & Close Friend

CONTENT

Foreword 11
Introduction 13

HONOR
Alpha 19
Bravo 37
Charlie 55

COURAGE
Delta 75
Echo 105
Foxtrot 135
Golf 151
Hotel 177

COMMITMENT
India 203
Juliet 223
Kilo 247
Lima 275
Mike 305

FOREWORD

The Long Journey Home is unlike any other book that I've read because as a fellow veteran, it touched me in a way that is very relatable. This is a book written from the depths of the heart by a female veteran. It's not only for veterans but for civilians as well. It serves as a connection of two different worlds and therefore makes the title very fitting. The experiences described within will leave you feeling a range of emotions. You'll find yourself in tears, hysterical laughter, and deep thought at various moments as you flip through the pages.

You may notice that with a lot of the movies and books about military life out there, a lot of them are coming from a male's perspective. Their main focus is the action of wartime events—shooting, bombing, and killing—but they don't deal with the emotional sides of war because as soldiers, we are told to bottle them up, keep them in, and continue with the task at hand. What makes this book stand out is that it is coming from a female soldier's perspective. As women soldiers, we deal with things that are different from our male counterparts. Our experiences come from more of an emotional standpoint. We deal with rejection, being silenced, sexual abuse, and abandonment just to name a few. While female soldiers may be looked at as the weaker sex, we prove time and time again that we can endure and accomplish just as much as our male counterparts.

Both sexes will have to deal with the emotional effects of being in the military, but we may deal with them in different ways. All soldiers must understand that it is ok to talk about the emotional side effects of wartime events and that PTSD is not a bad word. It's something that we endure, and it's something that we can't go through alone. It's not something that will ever go away. We will endure this for the rest of our lives, but if we talk about it more rather than keeping it bottled up, then we will affect more lives in a positive way because it allows others to realize that they are not alone. There're others that are going through the exact same thing that you are. It's time to talk about it. It's time to share it. It's time to deal with it.

The Long Journey Home represents a journey within many journeys that could be experienced by anyone whether you are a "lifer" in the military or never served a day in your life. It is certainly a relevant reading and will be abundantly helpful to anyone who picks it up because it allows people to know that they are not alone but are very much connected to each other in ways they don't even realize. Yolanda shows her audience that although life may get tough and some unwanted situations may have to be endured, anything is possible, and you can get through them and identify the positive side of it. The journeys within showcase many twists and turns endured to get back home. The only thing is, you can't always see where you are stepping as you place one foot in front of the other, but you must keep moving forward and keep on the path set before you.

Yolanda is one of the most intelligent, compassionate, and honest women that I know. She has been one of my closest friends for over eighteen years, and I have observed her go through the many trials and tribulations in her life with an enormous amount of grace and, unexpectedly to me, a smile. She always manages to see the positive side of any situation thrown her way. I don't know how she does it, but she has been an inspiration to me. Keep smiling, my friend. Keep smiling!

Sharmon Lawrence,
Former OS2. Current RN, BSN
Fellow Veteran & Ace-Boon-Coon

INTRODUCTION

"Shut up recruit!" I heard someone shout.

"What are you looking at boy? Don't you dare eyeball me!" said another.

Who would have thought that I'd be here after spending a year and a half in college? This was not the plan. I was on the fast track to becoming an accountant. I would spend two and a half years in school, graduate, and start working at a fortune 500 company with a corner office all in less than 4 years but look at me now. I'm standing in this cold, gray hallway, scared and alone with what seems like hundreds of people all around me. I hear some people screaming and others crying uncontrollably. My recruiter didn't prepare me for this.

Just a moment ago, I was at the Military Entrance Processing Station known as MEPS getting sworn in. At MEPS, it was cold and sterile. It was created to process you in and send you on your way. This was not a place to get comfortable and start making life goals. This was a place where you were sworn in, gathered your newly signed documents, and loaded up on the bus to only God knows where. It was a way to get out of a seemingly no end situation and start a new journey. While I didn't know where I would end up, I knew it had to be better than here.

As we waited for the bus to come and transfer us to boot camp, I nervously smiled and laughed with this officer telling him all about my decision to join the navy and what I planned to accomplish while

I was there. He listened to what I had to say but also remained alert for the arrival of the bus. The bus arrived around 11:30 pm. It was a big bus with clothed seats, a weird odor, and a feeling of dread but that could have been because we all just made a decision that we couldn't take back. It was about thirty of us waiting to see what this decision would truly mean. The ride wasn't a bad one and the officer kept talking as if he was trying to make the silence less quiet, and for a moment it was working, but that would soon come to an end.

It seemed like we drove for hours and then the bus stopped. I was seated in the front because I always liked to be first. I was in the top ten percent of my graduating class in high school, always sat in the front row in school, and was normally one of the first people picked for important projects. I had no idea that being first, this time, would change the course of my life.

The officer informed us that we had arrived at our destination. I got up, grabbed my bag, and headed toward the door. As I reached the first step, I heard, "Hey, recruit." I turned back and looked at the officer, who now had this weird grin on his face. "Good luck." "Thanks," I said with yet another nervous smile.

As I got to the last step, I saw guys in fatigues standing still with these cold eyes and blank stares. From the time I touched my feet to the ground, I knew I wasn't in Atlanta anymore.

"What the fuck are you looking at recruit? Grab your bags and let's go! Yo mommy ain't here to save you this time!" "What did he just say to me?" I thought. My eyes got as big as a deer in headlights. I thought for sure he was going to grab me and knock me to the ground.

"Aww, are you gonna cry? Do you want your mommy?"

Now, my dad was ex-army turned cop so I grew up in a household where every other word was profanity but that was just how he talked; but this was different. This guy didn't even know me and he was cursing at me. I did want to cry. I did want my mommy but at this moment, turning back was not an option. I grabbed my bag and ran toward this open door of light. It was almost 1 am by the time we got to this place so seeing the light was a little refreshing, but I had

Introduction

no idea what I signed up for. No idea that being in the military would mean that someone would try to rape me, or that misplaced drugs could mean the end of my life, or even that being drunk at the wheel of a ship could mean the lives of hundreds. Yeah, this was different and definitely not something that my recruiter could have prepared me for. This one decision was about to change the whole trajectory of my life in ways I could not even begin to fathom but the decision was made. It was time to move into a destiny that only God could save me from.

HONOR

Honor yourself enough to know,
when the time has come to go!

ALPHA

"Get up! Get up! Let's get motivated!" I heard my dad say.

Every morning he would say the same thing and this morning would be no different.

"I said get up! Don't let me go get the water bottle!"

If we didn't get up, he would spray us with this water bottle that he kept beside his bed. We knew when we heard that, it was time to jump up like we had been awake the whole time. My dad was ex-military turned cop and you can say growing up in our household was…interesting. We were raised to get good grades and stay away from boys, but as teenage hormonal girls that wouldn't last long. There were two girls, my sister Lexy and I, and our brother Deonte. Deonte always got to do whatever he wanted because he was the only boy and there was always a double standard in our household with girls versus boys. Girls had curfews and Deonte came in whenever he pleased. Girls couldn't go on dates but with Deonte, it was well, boys will be boys. It was very frustrating seeing that I was the oldest of us three and you would think that the oldest had more freedom, but not in our household. Deonte had all the freedom and some, but you learned to deal with it and find loopholes.

As a cop, my dad would work the night shift so that meant that we could ask Mom if we could go out as long as we were back before Dad got home. He tried to pop in some times to catch us in the act but Mom would always call us to let us know he was on his way and we needed to hurry back. Sometimes, we would get home right around the time he walked in the house. Mom would lead him into the bedroom and sweet-talk him long enough for us to sneak back in through the back door, get our pajamas out of the dryer, put them on, and sneak back into our beds before he came and did a bed check. It was so funny because he never caught us. We would laugh under the cover and talk all night long about how we got away with it again. Ah, the good ole days. But today would be different. I was finally graduating from high school. Today, I was excited to get up. Probably because I was too excited to ever go to sleep in the first place. To finally be out of high school and on to college was a big deal in my family. Not everyone in my family had gone to college, so there was a lot riding on me graduating. There were so many decisions I had to make about this new adventure that I was to embark on, but they would have to wait until tomorrow because today it was all about walking across that stage and getting my diploma; Advanced Academic Diploma that was.

School was a means of escape from home. I would go to school early to do my homework and stay late sometimes to help out in the library. I hated going home because my parents were always fussing and fighting. It wasn't always that way, but it seemed to get worse the older we got. Maybe it was always that way but as a child, you don't recognize it as much. Either way, my schoolwork was my outlet to be free—free to get out of a chaotic situation and do something that I wanted to do, and it paid off. Graduating with a 3.83 grade point average was an awesome feeling and I was ready to let the world know just how hard I'd worked.

"Ok, ok! I'm up! I'm up!" I yelled as I had my head still under the cover.

"Wake up my daughter. You're graduating today," my mom said as she came into my room. I think she was more excited than I was. I got up and headed to the bathroom, but my brother saw me and ran in ahead of me and slammed the door. We lived in a three-bedroom, one-bath house and if someone was in the bathroom, you may as well go to the neighbors' because it was going to take a minute before you would get your turn.

"Deonte! You saw me! Get out! I got to get ready!"

"You should have thought about that before you go five extra minutes of sleep, Yasmine," he said laughing.

"Ma! Get Deonte out of the bathroom! I gotta get ready!"

"Deonte, get out of that bathroom! You know your sister has to get ready!"

"Ma, I can't. I'm on the toilet."

He would always say that anytime he beat us to the bathroom. He would make an excuse and say he was on the toilet when in actuality he was sitting on the toilet reading comics and smiling. He did this all the time but not today. I was getting in that bathroom one way or another. I decided to pick the lock and when I got in, there he was sitting on the toilet, pants still up, and reading a comic and yeah, you guessed it, smiling like he had just won the battle but today he would lose the war.

"Hey, get out of here! Can't you see I'm in here?"

"But you're not doing anything. Get out!"

"No!"

"Yes!"

"No!"

This could've gone back and forth all day and I was not about to take his mess. I ran toward him and pulled him by his shirt. He tried to take his shirt back, but I held on. We tussled a bit but I was able to throw him out, slam the door, and lock it behind me. He was so mad that he started beating on the door. By that time, my dad had come back in the house from getting the yard cleaned up a bit for the barbeque that we were having later on after the graduation.

"Have you lost your damn mind?!" my dad yelled at Deonte. "Do you pay any damn bills around here?"

"No sir," Deonte said with his head held down.

"Well you better stop beating on my damn doors before I beat on you!"

"Yes, sir," Deonte said as he walked back in his room to get his clothes ready for the graduation.

"VICTORY!" I said to myself. I was finally able to get in the bathroom at a decent time without interference. Well major interference anyway. Today was going to be a good day.

⚓

We all got dressed and loaded up in the van to head to the church. It was such a nice breezy June morning. We wanted to arrive around 9 am since the graduation was set to start at 11 am. I was just happy to be graduating. On the ride there, I rolled down the window and heard birds chirping, bees buzzing, and my brother and sister were fussing about who would get to hold the camera.

"Will you both just shut up?!" I yelled. "What does it matter? Neither of you can see anyway." I liked to mess with them because they both needed glasses, but my sister was the only one who actually wore hers.

"Oh, you shut up geek!" Deonte shouted. "Ain't nobody talking to yo ugly self anyway."

"All y'all shut up before I get this belt on yo butt." Dad always had the belt ready. No matter how old or young you were, if you were acting up, he was pulling out the belt.

We arrived at the church around 9:30 am because we wanted to make sure we got there early enough to save the latecomers some seats. We all jumped out of the car because we saw some of our family members standing outside of their cars. My cousin, Shonice and I, were both graduating from the same high school. We were thick as thieves growing up maybe because we were only about a week and a half apart in age. You would have thought that we were twins because we never wanted to leave each other's side. It was so bad that in kindergarten, we had to be separated. We started off in the same class but because we wouldn't play with the other kids, the school thought it would be a good idea to separate us. Good idea to whom? Not us! We were fine. I can remember it like it was yesterday. We were playing with our puzzles at the group table. The classroom was loud as always and the teacher was trying to get Mike out of the fish tank. He was always trying to catch the fish with his hands when all of a sudden it happened. There was a knock at the door. It seemed like everything started to move in slow motion. The teacher's assistant went and greeted the principal and our parents. I knew something wasn't right. Our parents only came to the school in the middle of the day when we had an honor roll program, and no one was getting an award that I was aware of. I knew this because my mom didn't dress me in the fancy dress with the huge collar like she always did when it was time for an award ceremony.

Our teacher calmly walked over to us and explained what was about to happen. Immediately, the waterworks started and my cousin and I grabbed each other, vowing to never let go. The principal came to try to talk to us, but we were not trying to hear what he had to say. All of a sudden, our parents grabbed each of us and started pulling us apart. What did they think this was? A tag team match? We were not having it. You would have thought this was a scene from *Color Purple*. I was not going to say goodbye to my Celie. It was as if I'd never see her again. Eventually, they got us apart and we screamed and cried and screamed and cried until we couldn't see each other anymore. It was like walking a green mile: my cousin would only have to go across the hall, but for a kindergartner with little legs it may as well have been a green mile. I sat by the classroom door for the rest of the day. I was going to be as close as I could to her. We were truly inseparable. But then life happened. We grew older, got our own friends, and things slowly changed. Oh, the games life can play on you sometimes.

By now, everyone had taken their seats in the auditorium and we were lined up getting ready to walk in processional. One good thing about graduating in the top ten percent of your class was that you didn't have to wait in a long line for your name to be called. They recognized the top ten percent first and then called everyone else by their last name in alphabetical order. This was one time in life where doing your homework and getting good grades actually paid off. I was glad that I used school as a means of escape instead of sex, drugs, and alcohol like some people did. I mean, there was some sex and alcohol, but everyone was doing it. It was hard not to when all of your friends were talking about it and all their advice made it sound so good and the only thing your parents said was not to bring any babies in the house. So, I listened. I didn't bring any babies in the house. Win-win for all of us. I had only had sex with one person, Eric, but that didn't mean that this didn't come without any consequences. No one told me that once you opened Pandora's box, that it would be almost impossible to close it. Maybe if I wasn't looking for love in all the wrong places, things would have turned out a little differently, but I was graduating at the top of my class, got into college, and had a plan. Yes, I had daddy issues but that didn't seem to get in my way of making plans for my future. I was looking forward to starting college and finally getting out of my parent's house. It was time to leave the nest and I was ready to fly.

At the end of the ceremony, everyone assembled outside of the church and waited for the graduates. It was like trying to find Waldo. Where was everyone? Where were we meeting up? It seemed like I would have to search forever, then all of a sudden, I heard a familiar voice.

"Congratulations, baby."

"Congrats to you, too!" I said with this huge smile on my face. Eric had found me amongst the crowd and showed me where my parents and family were waiting for me. He was my high school sweetheart. We had been dating for four years. Yes, we had our ups and downs, breakups, and fights, but we always seemed to get back together. We had been together since the 9th grade and he was the only thing I knew. I just knew we would be together forever and no one could tell me otherwise.

"I'll see you later. I have to go meet my mom and her boyfriend."

"Ok," I said as I gave him a hug and started on my way to where my family was gathered.

Everyone was so happy and excited. We were all going back over to our house for the barbeque. Our house was always the hangout spot because we had such a huge yard and we were located in a central place for everyone.

"Congratulations Sticks," my auntie Annie said. She called me *Sticks* because I was so skinny. I didn't know why I stayed skinny so long because I could eat any dude under the table but because my metabolism was so high, the food never stuck to my bones. Whenever anyone would ask me why I was so skinny, I would tell them that I was allergic to weight. We also got a good laugh out of it. When I was younger, it really bothered me because I looked at it as a problem that I no longer wanted. I was tired of getting picked on at school and having to have my clothes specially made because nothing fit me properly. It made me feel like an outcast, but what are you going to do? God made us all the exact way that He wanted us to be. We just have to learn to love what He loves about us.

After we took what seemed like a million pictures, everyone went to their cars and decided to meet back at our house around 4 pm. I was going to stay at the barbeque for a while and then head out because Eric was having a night party at his house and I was definitely not going to miss that seeing that a friend of mine told me that there was this chick that she'd been seeing him with at the mall whenever she'd work the late shift. I'd asked him about it before, but he always denied it; but about six months ago, things started to change. He used to answer every text, call at least five times a day, and always said, "I love you," when he hung up but now things were different. He stopped calling as much, texted maybe one time a day after I texted him first, stopped saying, "I love you," and started saying things like, "ditto," or "me too." I'd never caught him cheating but I was surely going to get to the bottom of it tonight.

Everyone arrived at our house around 6 pm, right on schedule. If you want people to show up on time, you have to tell them two hours prior to the actual time you want them there or else you will have a lot of time to kill because they wouldn't be on time. Everyone arrived with what they were responsible for. Some brought collard greens, baked beans, and coleslaw, while others had the meat to put on the grill, cabbage, potato salad, and drinks. My mom always made cakes. It didn't matter what kind of cake you wanted—lemon pound, red velvet, pineapple upside down, strawberry—she made them all and she always had to make at least two banana puddings. One thing was for sure, we were definitely going to be eating all night long.

We all had a great time. We played bad mitten and spades while the kids played in the water hose and got in trouble for it. Kickball was always a family favorite because it allowed the whole family to play while the more mature generation stayed in the house under the AC. We had activities for everyone, and the party was destined to last all night long. My uncle showed up with a box of DVDs and candy bars. He was the type of uncle that sold everything, from puppies to catfish plates. If you wanted it, he could get it for you.

"I got the latest movies and my son is selling candy for the band. How many do you want?" He never asked if you wanted to buy anything. He just assumed you would, cut out that question, and went straight for how many did we want. We were the type of family that supported everyone, so he'd find someone willing to purchase one or both. Shoot, I was bound to watch one of those movies tonight.

"What movies do you have Uncle?"

"I got all the movies that just came out within the last three weeks."

"You better stop bootlegging them movies and bringing them to my house," my dad said. Obviously, my uncle didn't care that our dad was a cop. He figured we were family and family didn't lock up family. If it wasn't for my mom, he would have definitely been locked up.

"It's all good, Carl."

"Yeah, it's going to be all good when I'm dragging you down to the station."

"Why do you always got to go there? Always trying to lock somebody up."

"Not somebody, just you. I have told you to stop bringing that mess around here, but you keep doing it."

"I'm just trying to make some money. I know you want to see these movies and from the looks of it, you want some of these candy bars too."

My uncle always teased my dad because he was about 280 pounds and he was a cop. He used to say there was no way he was chasing down anyone if they were to take off running. We always got a good laugh at that joke.

"Well make your money away from this house. If I see it again, I'm taking you in."

"No you're not, Carl. Leave him alone," my mom always intervened. She was not going to let our dad arrest anyone in our family while she was around. That's why they knew what they could get away with but out in the streets, they better keep their distance because my mom wasn't there to save them.

I knew our party was going to last all night long so after about four hours, I decided to dip out for a while and head over to Eric's house for the after party. I arrived at Eric's place around 10:30 pm and there was barely anywhere to park. There were so many people and it looked like everyone was hanging out outside drinking and smoking like always. I headed in to make my rounds and that's when I saw her laughing and giggling with her hand rested on top of Eric's shoulders. It took everything in me not to go and cut that hand off of her, but I politely walked over with this big grin on my face like it wasn't phasing me at all.

"Hi, everyone."

"Hey boo." I gave Eric a big hug and an even bigger kiss. "You missed me?"

"You know I did," he said as he motioned to everyone to give us some space. "How was the cookout?"

"It was fun. You know how we do. Everyone is still there so I slipped out to come see what y'all where up to. So, what is Nikki doing here?" I said with this look on my face that said, "And don't you dare lie to me either!"

"Oh, she heard about the party from one of her homegirls and decided to come through."

"Under whose approval?"

"I didn't think it would be an issue. Man, don't start any trouble."

"The trouble started when I came in and saw her all up in your face with her hands on you. If you don't want no trouble, then tell her to keep her hands in her pockets."

"Man, aight. Steve is acting up because he's drunk and here you go."

Steve was his mom's boyfriend. He didn't like Eric too much, but he'd been in his life for almost thirteen years. You would have thought they would have ironed out all of their issues by now but nope. It seemed like the older Eric got, the worse their relationship got and when I came into the picture, it seemed that he didn't like me either, but I didn't care because his mom loved me, so Steve was just going to have to deal with it.

"I don't have anything to do with Steve. Just tell that girl to keep her hands to herself."

I walked off to go see what everyone was doing outside.

An hour went by and we were all talking about the graduation and what we were planning on doing next. All of a sudden, Eric ran out of the house and started walking up the street. Steve walked out of the house after him and was yelling, "Back talk me again! You don't run anything in this house. I'm the man of this house." Eric's mom was crying and running after Eric. We were all looking confused because no one knew what had happened.

"Eric, sit down! Sit down!" his mom yelled through her tears.

"Naw. I'm going to kill that son of a bitch!"

As I got close to Eric, I could see something on the front of his shirt. I thought maybe he was eating a hot dog or something before the fight broke out between him and Steve but the closer I got, I realized that it was blood.

"OMG! What happened?" I yelled.

"This mother fucker stabbed me!"

"Stabbed?!"

"Yes, they started fighting and Steve grabbed a knife and stabbed him in the chest," his mom said as tears continued to pour down her face.

I couldn't believe this had happened. What in the world would possess him to pull a knife and stab him? Oh, I know, built up anger and alcohol. Those two are a deadly combination.

Not too long after, the police showed up and started questioning the group. They eventually took Steve to jail for assault and took Eric to the hospital for further observations. I couldn't believe that a night that should have been the happiest time in our lives became one of the worst.

The next day, I called Eric's mom to see if he was still in the hospital and she said that he was now home. They had stitched him up and released him a couple of hours ago. I decided to go over to see how Eric was doing. When I pulled up, I noticed a familiar car in the driveway. "What is Nikki doing over here and this early in the morning?" I said to myself. I walked in and was startled at what I saw next. Steve was sitting in the living room watching TV and Eric's mom was sitting next to him. "How did he get out so soon? Who posted his bail? And why is he still here?" So many questions ran through my head but now was not the time.

"He's in the back," Steve said without even looking in my direction.

I walked to the back and saw Nikki holding Eric's hand and talking to him.

"Excuse me! Am I interrupting something?" I said with a stern voice.

Eric pulled his hand away almost immediately.

"Na Na No!" he said stuttering.

"Doesn't look that way to me!" I shouted.

"I think I should go," Nikki said with this smirk on her face.

"Yeah, you should."

As Nikki walked passed me, her eyes said, "He's not yours anymore."

I immediately walked closer to Eric. "What do you think you're doing and why is she even here?"

"Calm down, Yaz! It's not what it looks like."

"She was holding your hand. Don't tell me it's not what it looks like!"

"Baby, calm down."

"I'm not your baby apparently! I came over to see if you were ok and I find you here with her. Do you know how that makes me feel? No, you don't because I would have never put you in this predicament. You know what? I'm done! I'm so over this back and forth with you. Since she's who you want, now you can be free to have her!"

As I stormed out of the room, I heard Eric scream, "Yaz! Yaz! Come back! We can talk about this." With tears streaming down my face, there was nothing else to talk about. I wanted to get as far away from him as I possibly could.

I rode around for what seemed like hours trying to figure out what to do next. I mean, I had planned a whole life with this man in my head and now I'd have to find other plans. Where did I want to go? College? Travel? I didn't know now. All I knew at that moment was that I just wanted the tears to stop before I got home. I didn't feel like hearing, "I told you so," from my dad. He never liked Eric anyway. Like the saying goes, "Ain't nothing slippery to a can of oil." My dad was a cop and grew up in a house with all boys. He had seen and done it all and he recognized early on who I was dealing with and he didn't want me to have no part with him but of course I didn't listen. I loved him, so I'd thought.

I remember when we first met. We were in the 9th grade homeroom together and he never said a word and because I was always the loud one and liked to mess with the quietest boy in the class, I gravitated toward him. We started talking and then hanging out together after school as we waited on my bus to come. He lived close by, so he could walk home yet he waited with me. Soon we would become boyfriend/girlfriend, as much as that could mean in middle school. Yes, we went through our share of ups and downs once we got to high school but this last year was the worst. I didn't know if the universe wanted to separate us because it knew we had separate places to be in our lives or what, but I sure wish it had held back some of the punches. This year, I had to deal with girls, drugs, and guns but I was over it all this time. I really wanted to just get away and start things over, but I had no clue where to start.

I pulled up to my house, checked my eyes in the mirror to see how much damage to my mascara these tears had done, cleaned it up as much as I could, grabbed my purse, and headed in.

"Oh look. The geek is back," shouted Deonte.

"Deonte, I am NOT in the mood," I said as I walked straight to my bedroom and closed the door. Eric had called me like 50 times and texted even more. Why couldn't he catch the hint? Maybe because we had been here before and I always took him back, but not this time. I was not calling him back. It was as if something in me just clicked and I was truly over it all. It was time to get my thoughts together and get a new plan in place. Since college was still on the list, I knew it would soon be time for me to go and register for financial aid and get my class schedule for this semester. At least there was something I could look forward to, but for right now all I wanted to do was sleep. I felt drained and the only thing that could ease the pain was to close my eyes and wake up to a new day.

Before you knew it, it was time for college. I'd registered for my classes, been approved for financial aid, and had a meeting scheduled with my guidance counselor. I started working with my guidance counselor when I was in high school. She would be the one to keep me on track and help me write my scholarship applications in order to get a fully paid academic ride to the school of my choice and my choice was Bell University. I'd always heard good things about them and I knew if I kept my grade point average at a 3.5 or above, I would qualify for a full scholarship and my financial aid grants would be money in my pocket and I wouldn't have to get a part-time job to help pay for college. I was excited to embark on this new journey but first I had to meet with my counselor.

I knocked on the door and heard, "Come in." Mrs. Wright was a brown-skinned, medium built woman with brown eyes and locks that went to her shoulders. She always reminded me of Lauryn Hill from the Fugees except she wore glasses. They were always some fun colorful designer type.

"Hi, Mrs. Wright. You wanted to see me."

"Yes, come in Yasmine and close the door behind you."

I walked in her office and there was this sense of calm and peace. She had essential oils radiating in the atmosphere and her room was painted this calming blue color with some tan and white accents. She had a colorful lamp on the corner of her desk and inspirational sayings on the walls, the throw pillows on her sofa, and on her desk. It was the type of place that you would feel welcomed telling all of your problems and secrets. She should have been a psychiatrist, or they should at least use her room for their sessions. She was finishing up an email when she turned and faced me.

"Hi Yasmine. How are things going? Are you ready for college?"

"Yes, I'm ready. I just received my letter from the financial aid office and registered for my classes but one thing that I noticed was that there was a balance on my account so I'm glad that you called me." There was a concerned look in her eyes. She removed her glasses and placed them on her desk.

"Well, that's what I wanted to speak to you about. Remember when I gave you that deadline to complete your scholarship application in order to get a full scholarship at Bell University? Well, I mistakenly gave you the wrong date and your application missed the deadline but no reason to worry, you can still apply for student loans."

"No need to worry! I had a whole plan for my time here. That financial aid money was going to help me get an apartment so that I could move out of my parent's house and now you're telling me that because of your mistake, all my plans are ruined? Can't you call them and tell them you made a mistake?"

"Yes, I tried but unfortunately they have strict rules in submission requirements and there was nothing that I could do. I'm so sorry, Yasmine."

I couldn't believe what I was hearing. This whole plan that I had made for myself was just shattered with one conversation. Her room no longer felt warm and calming. Now it felt cold and dark. The grim reaper had just come and stole my dreams. I wanted to cry but I didn't want to give my tears to a room that had just crushed my plans.

"So, what do I do now?"

"Go back to the financial aid office and tell them that I've already talked to the director about your situation and you need to apply for the loans you declined previously and again, I'm so sorry, Yaz."

Without saying a word, I left the essential-oil-filled room and headed to my car. I would have to deal with the financial aid issue later because at this moment it was too hard to hold back the tears. As I sat in the car sobbing, I couldn't help but to think of what I did to deserve this. I'd been trying to do everything right, but it seemed like right always led me wrong.

"God, what do you want me to do now? I don't want student loans. I don't want to be in debt my whole life. This was not part of the plan."

Growing up, we stayed in church. We were there for Wednesday night Bible study, Friday to sell catfish plates for the building fund fundraiser, Saturday for choir rehearsal, Sunday for service, and another fundraiser after service selling dinner plates for the building fund and still had to go to a second service at someone else's church in which we also helped out in the kitchen. We were always doing some sort of fundraiser for the building fund but that one squeaky step still squeaks. We never understood what the building fund was really for but that didn't stop us from fundraising. I knew who God was. I mean, I heard mention of His name a time or two and heard about the different stories in the Bible and I knew John 3:16 by heart because if you didn't memorize it by the next Bible study, you would be looked at crazy by the other kids because we had to stand up and recite it every week until everybody got it. So, you can say I knew of God but at this point in my life, I had no idea how powerful and instrumental He would be in my life.

I cleaned up my face and headed back into the building. I knew I needed to go speak with someone in the financial aid department as soon as possible because classes were set to start within the next couple of weeks. When I reached the financial aid office, I couldn't believe my eyes. I thought I was just going to walk in, state my case, fill out some forms, and walk right back out but not today. Because the financial aid office was located within a suite in this huge common area, which also housed the cafeteria, the line wrapped all the way around the cafeteria and down the hall. Now because of someone else's mistake, I had to wait in this long line. Count it all joy, they say.

Two hours later, I heard someone say, "Next." I eagerly walked up to the counter.

"Yes, I need to apply for student loans. I've already received my financial aid award letter, but I only wanted grants at the time but now I need the loans as well. Mrs. Wright stated she had spoken with the director here about me."

"Ok. Let me look up your account in the system. What's your name?"

"Yasmine. Yasmine Payton."

"Last four of your social."

"1411."

After about five minutes of clicking on the keyboard, she walked over to the printer, picked up some papers, and came back.

"Please look these over. This is your award amount. This is how much you will receive in a refund if you choose the full loan amount or you can choose enough to just cover your classes."

I grabbed the papers and looked everything over and I saw the word "refund" and next to it, I saw $3,549.54.

"Excuse me. Are you saying that my refund will be $3,549.54 if I accept the full amount?"

"Yes, it will."

I couldn't believe my eyes. Maybe I could still move out if checks like this would be coming in every semester. I guess my luck was finally turning around. I decided to accept the full amount. I signed the papers, gave them back, and she gave me a copy.

"You're all set. Is there anything else that I can help you with?"

"No. That'll be all. Thank you."

"You're welcome. Enjoy the rest of your day."

"You too," I said as I left the office.

To think that I had just wiped tears from my eyes and now you could see all thirty-two of my teeth. Wow, God. I guess this prayer thing really does work. I walked back to my car as if I was walking on air. How could everything change in a matter of hours? One minute I'm looking at my counselor and wondering how she could have made such a colossal mistake and the next I was walking away from the financial aid office with more than $3,000 set to be given to me in a matter of weeks. I didn't know what all this meant but I was happy that I didn't have to pay for my classes out of pocket. I knew that I would have to pay this money back one day but for right now, I took it as being heaven sent.

BRAVO

Classes started and everything seemed to be going as planned. That was until I got to statistics. "What is this mess?" I thought to myself. I was an accounting major and I always thought that statistics was similar to good ole math. Boy was I wrong. It was like I was taking a foreign language and I wasn't scheduled for that until next semester. Man, what was I going to do? I needed to pass this course in order to take the next one, so I had to figure out fast what my game plan would be.

"Ok, everyone, today we are going to be pairing up. Grades have been slipping and rather than failing ½ the class, let's see if pairing up will help make things a little easier." If half the class is failing, maybe it's not just us, professor. Maybe it's you. Oh, if I said the things I was thinking.

"This will be your partner for the duration of the semester. The semester isn't that long so I am sure you can endure working with the person I assigned until then and if you can't, well then just try harder."

Dr. Donelson was one of those "no-nonsense" type of professors. He was 6'1", almost bald but you couldn't tell him that with this comb-over he tried to pull off. Always wore brown pants and this dingy white shirt with a brown tie. His glasses were way too thick, in my opinion, but I guess he needed them to see. Maybe I needed them to better understand what I was looking at.

He decided to pair us up based off his own statistical formula: eeny meeny miny moe. Hey, couldn't go wrong with this system, I guess. As I looked around the room, I wondered who he would pair me up with. All I could do was pray it was someone who understood this language more than I did.

"Mr. Anderson, you'll be paired up with Ms. Payton. Ms. Payton, raise your hand." Three of us raised our hands. We were in the South and half of the population in the whole state of Georgia was Payton.

"Well ok then. Yasmine Payton keep your hand raised, everyone else, put your hand down." All I could do was smile. The process of elimination works every time.

As I gazed over at Mr. Anderson, I noticed his long-braided hair. He seemed to be a mix of black and Indian. His skin was almost flawless but for some reason, it works out that way for guys. Smooth baby bottom skin and women have to put on so much makeup to hide their blemishes that we look like totally different people when we take it off. He wore a black shirt, army green fatigue pants, and Timberland boots. You could tell he wasn't from around here. As he walked over to me, I slowly put my hand down.

"Hi, I'm Jason," he said with a voice so soothing it could put a baby to sleep.

"Hi, I'm Yasmine. It's nice to meet you."

"So, it looks like we're going to be partners for a while."

"Yeah, looks that way," I said with a smirk on my face. Looks like Mr. Donelson's method may have some validity to it after all.

As we settled into the day's lesson, I couldn't help but to think of how handsome Jason was, but I knew I needed to focus on the task at hand. I couldn't afford messing up this partnership, especially if he understood this better than I did. After about an hour and a half of teaching, Mr. Donelson gave out our first assignment and it was due the following week. At least we had a little time to get together and discuss a game plan for how we would get things done.

After class, we both stayed around to discuss how we would move forward with the assignment.

"Do you want to meet up today to go over the assignment?" asked Jason.

"Yeah, that'll work. I have class till 4 pm. Can we meet around 4:30 pm?"

"Sure. Let's meet in the cafeteria. Normally people are either gone or in their next class by then so it shouldn't be too noisy."

"Ok cool, 4:30 pm it is."

"Well, let me get your number just in case something comes up or something," he said as he stumbled for words. It was kind of cute to see a guy fidgeting around. Normally it was me dropping my keys or biting on my pen top but this time, it was someone else.

"Ok, cool." I took out a piece of paper and wrote down my number and gave it to him. "See you later," I said as I brushed my hair from out of my face to behind my left ear.

"Ok, see ya," he said as he walked off down the hall and I turned and went in the opposite direction. I still hadn't figured out if he knew this stuff or not, but in that moment it didn't even matter.

As I was sitting in my last class of the day, it felt like it was taking forever to end. I sat and watched the clock knowing that my teacher somehow tampered with it because it seemed to be going slower than usual. She was talking about what happened to who way back when and I was thinking about what could happen between Jason and I right now. We could start dating and then in about a year, he'd propose. We'd wait till we graduated and then get married, have 2.5 kids, including the dog, and life would be great. Everyone knows that we women plan our whole future with a guy as soon as he says "hi."

As I sat there daydreaming and smiling, the class ended. All of a sudden, I got extra nervous. "What are you nervous for? You were just rushing the clock?" I thought to myself. Maybe because it's easier to think about what could be rather than to actually make it happen. Whatever the case, I was about to find out. I walked over to the meet-up spot, put down my bag, took out our statistics book, and a notebook. I had to at least play like I was ready to study. As I sat there waiting, I saw it. He was walking across the cafeteria with his arm around someone's shoulder. Hold up! How was he so nervous earlier asking me for my number but is walking with his arm around someone's shoulder? Really though? Really?! The conversations I have with myself can be so intense sometimes. They get a little closer and I'm able to see her more clearly. She's cute, about 5'1" with curly brown hair. Jason was only about 5'4" so looks like they were made for each other, height wise.

"Hey, Yasmine, this is Veronica. I thought y'all should meet since we will have a lot of studying to do and now she can see that I'm not lying."

"Hi, Veronica. It's nice to meet you," I said with this big smile on my face. Sometimes you just have to fake the funk.

"Hi Yasmine. It is so nice to meet you. Jason has told me all about class and how y'all got paired up and how no one knew each other and how y'all had this test…"

She was going a mile a minute. I could hardly make out all the words she was saying. It actually made me breathe a sigh of relief. At least she wasn't one of these snobby girls with a stick up her butt looking at me with the death glare that said, "THIS IS MY MAN. TOUCH HIM AND DIE!" This chick was actually pretty cool. I couldn't help but to laugh.

"Veronica, do you ever take a breath?"

We all laughed.

"You know, I get that a lot."

"I bet you do. It's really nice to meet you, though. Are you going to stay while we study?"

"Oh heavens no! I hate statistics with a passion. I took it once and barely got through it then and I refuse to go through it again," she said smiling.

"I definitely understand."

"Besides, I have to get going. I have a shift at Wall of Flowers. It's a little flower shop off Peachtree Street."

"Um, which Peachtree Street?" It seemed like every street in downtown Atlanta was named Peachtree Street. That's why I never went downtown. The last time I drove downtown, I ended up going up a one-way street the wrong way. I always get lost and confused so I stay close to home and school. Whatever I needed was between the two.

"Ha! I know right. It's like Peachtree Street, Avenue, NE, SW, Drive, Court…" And she went on and on. Why did I get her started?

"Veronica! You're going to be late," I said.

"Oh yeah, that's right. Sorry, you know me."

"Yes, I do." It was my first time meeting her but I could tell we were going to be really cool. Jason had already put his bag down, took out his statistics book and notebook, and went to get a snack and drink before heading back over to the table. When he got back, he saw that Veronica was still there.

"Y'all still talking, I see."

"No, babe. I got to go to work. I'll see you later."

"Call me when you get off."

"Ok, love you."

"Love you too." He gave her the sweetest kiss goodbye. I remember kisses like that. I remember when I had a love. "No! Snap out of it! That love crushed you and you will NOT be going back down that road." I had to talk myself out of certain conversations because if I let them play out then I'd be picking up my phone and calling someone that I didn't need to be calling. Eventually, Veronica left and it was just Jason and me.

"So, do you know how to speak this foreign language?"

"What foreign language? This is statistics."

"Exactly! So why does it sound like Greek to me?"

He laughed and shook his head. All my nerves had magically disappeared after I met Veronica so now he would get the real me—real crazy, real goofy, and really in need of help with this statistics class.

"Yes, I know how to speak this language. I'm actually very fluent in it and really enjoy it."

"Enjoy and statistics should not be used in the same sentence. That's blasphemy."

He laughed. "Watch, I'll get you to like it too. You don't like it because you don't understand it but once you do, then you'll be fluent in it too and you'll be able to use those two words in a sentence."

"Yeah, I'll have to see it to believe it."

"Well, put on your glasses because it's going to come quick."

We both shared a good laugh and dove into the assignment.

By the end of our first session, I was starting to see some light but this was a long tunnel. It was going to take some time.

"Ok, that's enough for today," I said. "I don't think my brain can take anymore."

"I'm with you. I like it but we've been in classes all day. Wanna go get some food?"

"Wait a minute. Did he just ask me out on a date?" I thought.

"Don't you have a girlfriend and isn't her name Veronica?"

He laughed. "Yes, I have a girlfriend and yes her name is Veronica, but I said let's go get some food. Men and women can be friends."

"Yet another foreign language to me."

"You've never had a guy friend?"

"Yes, when I was in kindergarten and we were all eating sand. These days guys are not trying to be your friend unless they can be friends with benefits."

"Well looks like I have something else to teach you."

We both laughed.

"Ok, if you say so. Where do you want to go?"

"The Spot?"

"Cool. I'll meet you there."

"Why take two cars. You can just ride with me."

"Mmmhmm. Just friends my butt." We burst into laughter.

"Come on girl and let's go."

We grabbed our things and headed to his car. We got to the parking lot and I had to stop in my tracks.

"Wait a minute! Is that your car?"

"Yes," he said with this smirk on his face. "Is something wrong?"

"This is my favorite car of all time."

He had a red and black Lexus with all black rims. The car was so shiny that I could see my reflection everywhere—the driver side door, windows, and even the rims.

"How do you have a car like this and are going to school? Let me guess, it was a graduation gift from the parents."

He laughed. "No. I own a couple of businesses but figured I needed to come back to school so that I could show my employees that even though I make money with no degree, that I'm smart and am always bettering myself and they can too. Yes, I could have continued to make it without one but I wanted better for myself and my future and I didn't want others to think that they could get what I have without sacrifice and never want to better themselves as well. The good Lord tells us to live by example and I take that very seriously."

"You sound like a PBS special," I said with a serious look on my face trying not to laugh but I couldn't hold it in because I started laughing with him.

"All you had to say was don't worry about it or I bought it but you had to go and break down the keys to success by Jason Anderson. But that's awesome. I definitely understand where you're coming from and I applaud your hard work and sacrifice. You're a pretty cool dude from what I know so far," I said with a smile.

"You're pretty cool too and funny as hell."

"Not as funny as I am about to be when you see me tear into these wings. We're not dating so I don't have to eat all cute."

It was about to go down because I was starving at this point.

"Well, if you're done looking at yourself in my car doors, let's get in and go eat."

He opened my car door and made sure I got in safely before going to his side of the car.

"I opened your door. You couldn't open mine?" he said.

"Have you seen your car? Your door is all the way over there," I said smiling.

"Whatever."

He got in and we headed to The Spot. The Spot was the local hangout for us college kids. We didn't have to worry about crying kids or hand-holding couples. This was a place for us to come and just have fun and let loose after exams or on the weekends or whenever you didn't have anything else to do. They even opened on the holidays for folks who didn't have family in town or those who wanted to avoid their families altogether. I was never there during the holidays because my family rocked and the food was always on point. It was so good that it would make you want to slap yo momma but you didn't and didn't even think about it because if you even thought about slapping a black mother, your casket would be picked out and your clothes ironed and placed neatly on your bed. Black mothers played no games!

We got in and the place was packed, as usual. It was Friday night and no one had anything to do in the morning but sleep. We saw two people paying their checks so we rushed over and just stood there small talking like we were not about to snatch these seats at the time they got up, but we noticed other people were doing the same thing. Hungry stomachs think alike. Jason noticed the others trying to get the seats. He walked over, leaned over the bar, whispered something to the bartender, and shook hands with him. They had a little laugh and he came back and stood by me.

"What was that all about?"

"Oh, nothing. I just had to talk to him about something real quick," Jason said smiling.

"Uh huh."

Eventually, the two left and others tried to rush to the seats.

"Nope!" said Lou, the bartender. "These seats are taken."

Jason pulled back my barstool and made sure I sat down before he did.

Where did this dude come from? Very successful, a gentleman, smart, and knows God. Too bad he's already taken because he'd definitely be mine.

"So, is that what you had to talk to him about?"

"Didn't you say you were hungry? Lou, can we get two menus?" he said looking around.

"Nice way to change the subject but yes, I'm starving."

I decided to get some wings and fries. He ordered a burger with the works and fries. With this wait, it was going to take forever to get our food. So we talked to kill time.

"So, tell me about you and Veronica," I said curiously.

"What do you want to know?" he said with this, "I'm an open book," look on his face.

"I want to know the foundation. How did you two meet, etc.?"

"You're a little nosey thing, aren't you?"

"No. I'm just very curious and besides, we're friends now. Friends ask each other these types of questions."

"This is true. Well, Veronica and I met a long time ago. We went to elementary together and then middle school. Halfway through middle school, her dad won the lottery so they had to move. We lost contact for years and my senior year in high school, this new student was introduced to our class. I looked up and it was Veronica. We were close in middle school when she left and it was like we just picked up where we left off. We were good friends, then one night we decided to become more than just friends and we've been together ever since. We've had our share of ups and downs but she's always been there for me. She's loyal and I need that in my life."

"Here we go again with another public service announcement on loyalty."

He started laughing. "You asked and now you're messing with me. What about you then? Where's your boyfriend?"

"Probably out with a girl somewhere. I had, emphasis on had, a boyfriend but he couldn't be faithful so I ended it. We had our ups and downs too but there were way more downs than ups. I started to feel like I was in this deep, dark hole and our ups were just me jumping up in this hole because soon gravity would be bringing me right back down. It was a cycle that I needed to break. So one day, I climbed out of that hole and walked away. That's my sad little story for your question: 'where is my boyfriend?'"

"You're talking about me. Your story sounded like a high school after school special on the dangers of dating."

"Ha! Well at least she walked away; dirty and all."

"This is true."

"That must be your favorite line: 'This is true.'"

"Why do you say that?"

"Because you've said it like three times now."

"I've never noticed it," he said smiling.

"Ok, since I just brought it to your attention, you'll be noticing it more. Just watch. You'll see."

As soon as I said that, our food arrived. It was very good and well worth the wait. I was so engulfed in the wings that I had forgotten all about what we were talking about. We had a really good time. We played pool, darts, and met some cool people. He eventually tried to hook me up with some random guy whom I later found out was one of his really good friends. The night was great and relaxing but I knew that eventually it would have to end and I'd be back alone with my thoughts.

We got back to the school around midnight and I still had to drive about thirty minutes to get home. I really wished I lived closer to the school.

"Well, that was a lot of fun. We will have to do this again sometime."

"I'm game!" I said as I hopped out of the car. "I guess men and women can be friends after all."

"Of course they can. It's all about the motive. What's the motive behind the intent? If the motive is pure, you'll have nothing to worry about but if it isn't, run away. My motives are pure and I'm a faithful guy. I never cheat because I don't see any point in it. If I'm unhappy, I'll tell you about it and if we can't fix it, I'll leave. That simple. People make relationships more complicated than they need to be. I choose not to."

He always had the most profound things to say. Things that made you go "hmm" and then ponder on it some more. I was glad I got paired with him and I knew it was by no accident. God knew exactly what I needed at this point in my life and what I needed was a friend.

"There you go again. I'm going to start calling you PBS."

"I just have things to say. You better listen. I know you need these specials," he said with a laugh.

"Yeah, I do. You have no idea." I unlocked my car door and got in.

"Drive safe and text me when you get home."

"Ok, I will. Have a good night."

I got home around 12:45 am. It was late and all I wanted to do was take a shower and go to bed, but it wasn't going to be that easy because by the time I opened the door, who was sitting on the sofa waiting for me? My dad.

"Where have you been?"

"School and I went out afterward."

"You missed curfew."

"What curfew? I'm in college."

"I don't care where you are. As long as you live in this house, you will be in this house by 10 pm."

"By 10 pm? Some of my classes don't even end till 10 pm."

"Well, you need to call when you get out and say you're on your way."

"That's crazy! I'm in college."

"Yeah, you already said that but you still live in my house."

"Well, maybe I don't need to live in your house."

I don't know what was in that wing sauce but I was over it. I was tired of being treated like the youngest; tired of curfews. Just tired of it all and tonight, I was going to let him know exactly how I felt.

"What is all this yelling about?" my mom exclaimed as she came out of her room.

"Dad is fussing about me just coming home. I went to school and just hung out with a friend. That's all and now he's giving me the 3rd degree. I'm not a criminal."

Dad treated us like perps that he chased all day and didn't catch. We were always guilty until we were proven innocent. We got out sometimes for good behavior but it never lasted long. But it wasn't always like this. Things started to change once he got back from Desert Storm. He came back different. He was angrier and little things would set him off.

When we had friends come over, he would bring out "the book." The book was a photo album that he kept of pictures he took during the war. There were a lot of dead people with half their bodies blown off or half bodies and the lower half with nothing but bones, no skin at all. At first it was a little disturbing because he was so excited to show people but then it just became the norm. We knew that he would pull out "the book" during family cookouts, when new people would come over, and even during sleepovers. We had to warn everyone about "the book" before they agreed to come over. I really think the war changed him. They say you don't know what people go through when they are in the military. I guess we don't but we have to deal with the residue when they come home.

I remember one day we had a family cookout and everyone was laughing and having fun. A couple of us were sitting at the dining room table. He came up to me and asked me to do something. One second later, he grabbed me by my shirt and threw me onto the table. I looked up at him in total shock and he said that I had rolled my eyes at him. Now that very well could have been true but the intensity of the event was so embarrassing. I wanted to get out of that house as soon as I was old enough and right about now seemed like a good of a time as any.

"Just go to bed. I'll talk to your dad."

I stormed to my room and slammed the door.

"What I tell y'all about slamming my damn doors? Y'all don't pay any bills around here!"

"Carl, cut it out! All this is uncalled for. You need to calm down and go to bed. You have to work tomorrow and you planned on doing some yard work in the morning. Just go to bed."

"I don't want to go to bed! I'm sick and tired of this. No one is going to disrespect me in my own house. No one!"

I heard the front door open and the slam. He cranked up his truck and then he was gone. No one knew where he had gone and frankly, I didn't care. The house was much quieter when he wasn't there. Felt a little normal. As I sat there looking up at the ceiling, all I could think of was trying to find a way out of here. I didn't know how or when but I knew I had to make a plan and stick to it. I had to get out of here before my next suicide attempt turned into a completed one.

When morning arrived, things were semi back to normal. Dad was mowing the grass and Ma was in the kitchen blasting her gospel music and cooking breakfast. We knew what time it was—time to get up and start cleaning. The whole house was to be cleaned before anyone went anywhere. College or not, as long as you lived in this house, you got up, got dressed, and started on your chores but I couldn't shake the feeling of wanting to run away. I know, running away when you're in college. I may as well move out. I'd run away when I was in high school but I'd run over to Eric's and hide out for a couple of days and go back home. I got tired of the fussing and fighting between Mom and Dad and I just needed some moments of peace and solitude.

Eric's house had its share of issues too but they were his issues and not mine, so it wasn't as emotionally taxing for me. Eventually, I always made my way back home but this time was different. This time I just had to get away. "I could use my refund money," I thought, but if I ever left school I'd be stuck and I'd have to pay that money back eventually. "I could stay with someone else." But then if I don't like the way they do something because I know how picky I am, where would I go? It seemed like there was no option. All I knew was that I couldn't stay here too much longer. I just couldn't.

Later on that day, I was sitting in the den watching TV when this navy commercial came on. I'd seen this commercial a hundred times but this time it stuck out to me. I wondered exactly what all it took to join the navy. This could be a way for me to get out of here and have a job. It looks like they also get to travel. Maybe I should go talk to someone about this; yeah, someone other than myself. I decided that I'd go to the navy recruiter's office on Monday because it wasn't that far from our house. I'm sure they could tell me about the process and what all it took to join.

It seemed like it took forever for Monday to come. All I could think about was the option of being able to get away from this house as soon as possible. No one knew I was thinking about joining and I wanted to keep it that way. Besides, I was just looking at this as an option, not the only option.

I arrived at the office around 10 am. When I went inside, there were two guys sitting at two different desks. They reacted like I was the first person to come into the office all year.

"Hello. How can we help you?"

"Yes. I wanted to get some information about joining the navy."

"Great! If you could just sit at my desk, I'll get some papers and then I can answer any questions that you have and tell you all about the process."

"Ok," I said with hesitation because he was a little too eager to get this process started.

"My name is Tony Walker. What's your name?"

"Yasmine Payton."

"Hi, Yasmine. It's nice to meet you. Let me tell you about the navy." He told me all about the history of the navy, the different places you would go, all about the benefits, and the criteria for entrance into the military. It all sounded very intriguing. Why hadn't I thought of this before?

"You mentioned a sign-on bonus. What exactly is that?"

"That's an amount you will get just for joining. Right now, the sign-on bonus is $3,000." That sounded pretty good to me seeing that I didn't have a job at the moment.

"Will I have to pay that money back?"

"No. As long as you stay in through boot camp, you will be able to keep it."

"Oh, ok. So, what would my next step need to be?"

"Well, if this sounds like something you want to do, we will get you tested. You will need to sign some papers and then take the Armed Services Vocational Aptitude Battery (ASVAB) test. It will let us know what types of jobs you can choose from while you are in the military. After you pass the ASVAB, because I know you will, you will need to take a physical. Once you pass your physical, you can be sworn in two days later and be on your way to boot camp. How does that sound?

"Sounds good but I only came to get some information. I wasn't planning on joining right now."

"That's the good thing about it. You don't have to join right now. Because there are different steps that have to take place first, you can get the process started and we can go from there. Right now, just finish your paperwork. I will give you the name of a book you can check out from the library so that you can study for the ASVAB. When you think you are ready to take the test, just come back and see me. Here's my business card. If I'm not here, then just let them know you will come back. I want to make sure that we treat you right and give you everything that you need for your military entrance."

"Ok, that sounds good."

I sat at his desk and completed my paperwork. There were questions in regard to why I wanted to join and if I had completed any schooling and such. Maybe this would be the best option for me. So far, it was sounding like the only option.

I finished my paperwork and Tony looked it over. He had me correct some things and add verbiage to some other things.

"Looks like we are all set. Go get that book and study. Once you are ready to take the test, give me a call and I will set it up."

"Ok, sounds good. I will go get it today and start studying."

"Great! If you have any questions in the meantime, you have my card. Call anytime."

"Ok, I will. Thanks for all your help."

"You're very welcome. It was nice meeting you, Yasmine."

"It was nice meeting you as well, Tony."

I left the office and just sat in my car for a moment. Could I really be joining the navy? It sure sounded like a viable solution to my problem and they gave you a sign-on bonus. I understood what it meant but then again I didn't. It sure sounded good. Guess I will head to the library to check out this book and start studying. This is something I plan on keeping to myself for a while. I haven't made any concrete plans as of today so no need to mention this just yet.

CHARLIE

Time had passed and before I knew it, it was summer break. We had gotten through fall and spring semester and I was definitely not picking up any classes for the summer. I needed a break. I just wanted to get away and go see something new. Jason, Veronica, and I were as tight as thieves. We hung out all the time and they always had one of their friends tagging along to keep me company but I didn't want to get into a serious relationship. I just needed some time to figure some things out. The home front seemed like it was getting worse and worse and whenever I could, I would sleep over one of my friends who had their own apartment off campus. Bell University was a private school so everything was extra expensive—even the off-site dorms. I couldn't afford it and that's the only reason I was still at home and with my school workload, I couldn't get a job. Seemed like all the odds were against me.

"Yaz, what are you going to do for the summer? Are you going out of town? Visiting family? Traveling? I mean, if I were you, I'd travel and..."

"Veronica, girl, what did I tell you? I can only answer one question at a time," I said laughing.

"Yaz, you should know me by now. Learn how to anticipate the questions that are coming from the first one."

"Yeah, I do that and you still go back and ask me the same questions because you forgot something else."

We both laughed.

"My girls, y'all are a trip," Jason said. That's what he called us when we were all together. We all had each other's back. It was like they were family now. I'd met their family and they'd met some of mine. We'd been to family cookouts, birthday parties, and holiday parties. It was like we were the three amigos.

"Honestly, I don't know what I'm doing this summer. I have no plans. What are y'all doing?" I hadn't told them that I was thinking about joining the navy and that I was going to take the ASVAB test in a couple of weeks. I didn't want to ruin their summer by thinking about me possibly not being here when they returned. Besides, I was just taking the test. I hadn't decided if I was actually going in or not. The ASVAB would tell me what kind of job I could get and that would also be a deciding factor on whether I was going or not.

"I'm going to visit some family in Indiana and then I'll be back," said Jason.

"What about you, Veronica?"

"I'm not quite sure yet. I don't really make plans. I let the plans find me." Veronica was definitely a free spirit. She went wherever the wind took her. I loved that about her. I wanted to be more like her. Just pick up and go and not worry so much about tomorrow. Her motto was tomorrow has enough problems of its own. I choose to live for today. That was the way that I wanted to live—free.

"I hear that but I think plans may have lost my address."

We decided to go to the movies one last time before everyone separated for the summer. One last hoorah before summer started, was over, and it was time for school again. I hadn't told them that I was thinking about going into the military yet because I knew they would try to stop me. They were the closest things to me and I was only wavering in my decision because of them. I'd take some more time to think about it before I finalized anything.

I eventually decided to stay in town for the summer and get a job and work some double shifts. I figured summer would be over before you knew it so I may as well try to stack up as much money as possible in hopes that I could get my own one-bedroom apartment a little closer to campus. It would definitely help with the late-night studying, I mean partying. Wait, I was right the first time, studying. I still had many thoughts running through my mind about leaving this place but no concrete opportunity presented itself other than going into the military.

I had already taken the ASVAB and one of the jobs that I was approved for was the equivalent to an accountant. It looks like this option was starting to turn into an actual possibility. I saw what it did to my dad and wondered if the same thing would happen to me. I had talked to Tony and he said that everyone's experience is different but because the navy really doesn't go into any war areas, I shouldn't have anything to worry about. For me, that was a sigh of relief. He told me that the next step was for me to take the physical and I could leave a couple of days afterward. He stated I had a couple of weeks to make my decision. I told him I would get back to him as soon as I knew something.

I still hadn't told anyone that I was thinking about going to the military or that I had even taken the steps to go speak with a recruiter and taken the actual entrance exam. Everything was moving so fast and I knew I would have to tell someone at some point but it wouldn't be until I had actually made a decision.

I hadn't spoken to Jason or Veronica in a while. I guess they were out living the life. I was just living this work life. Oh the joy. I was just getting off work when I got a text.

"What have you been up to? I miss you." It was Jason.

"Hey man. I was just thinking about you. I miss you too. I was just getting off work and heading home. What are you up to?"

"About to go play ball with the boys. I can't wait to start school again so we can hang out. I'll call you later."

"Ok. Make a 3 pointer for me."

It was always good hearing from him. He was my best friend and we could talk about any and everything. I knew he would be in my life forever.

I got home pretty late because as I was leaving, I got a call that someone didn't show up for their shift and they wanted to know if I could cover for them a couple of hours until someone else came in. I should have said no because I was so sleepy but I turned around and went back. The person that was supposed to show up never did and I stayed there until it died down. Some people are really selfish and don't care about anybody but themselves. When I walked in, I was expecting to see my dad sitting on the sofa scouring like always and I'm glad I was expecting it because there he was. For someone who worked the night shift, he sure was always home. He was dressed in uniform so he must have been at work, called to see if I was there, and came home just to fuss at me.

"Where have you been?"

I looked at him like, "Really?" but instead said, "Work."

"Did you call?"

"Yes." I was not about to argue with him. I was too tired. I proceeded to go to my room to get out of these stinky clothes.

"I'm not done talking to you!"

"Well, I am."

All of a sudden, he lunged at me and choked me by my neck as he threw me against the wall. At this point, I could feel that my feet weren't touching the floor and when I looked in his eyes, it was like he wasn't there. He was gone to another place. Not sure where he went but he wasn't in this house anymore. I tried to break free but I couldn't. I couldn't scream. I couldn't breathe. I couldn't think. All I knew is that if someone didn't come and stop him, I'd be dead.

"Carl! What are you doing?! Get your hands off her. Carl! Carl!" I heard my mom speaking but I couldn't see her because my eyes were closed. When I opened my eyes, I could see that she was trying to pry his hands off my neck but since she's 4'11" and he's 6'2" and crazy, no one but God could have snapped him out of it and that's exactly what happened. After my mom hit him a couple of times and threw some water on him, he snapped out of it and let me go. I fell to the ground gasping for air, but I couldn't find any. I was weak and panicking. How could he do this to me? What was he thinking? Could he have killed me? My mom came over to me and tried to get me to breathe and calm down but how could I. The person that tried to kill me was my father.

After realizing what he had done, he quickly bolted out the front door. I stayed on the floor for what seemed like hours trying to catch my breath and after a while, I finally did but then I couldn't stop crying. It was like you see this type of stuff happen in movies or on the news, but you never think it could happen to you.

Lexy ran over to me. "Are you ok?!"

"Can you get up?" my mom cried.

But I couldn't speak. I was still in shock. All I wanted to do was lay there.

"Where did he go?!" shouted Deonte. "I'm going to kill that SOB!"

"No! We don't need any more violence tonight!" shouted Mom.

Eventually, I was able to get up, take a shower, and head to my room to put on my pajamas. I didn't know how I was going to get to sleep in this house tonight. He could come back at any time. I didn't feel safe but I was tired because of all the crying I had just done. My face was puffy and I had another shift in the morning. I needed to get some sleep. I got up out of my bed, walked over to my bedroom door, and locked it. At least I would hear him before he came in. I was a light sleeper so I would hear if he came in the door.

As I laid down to go to sleep, I saw that I had twenty missed calls and some voicemails. I didn't check to see who it was because I just couldn't deal with anything else tonight. I just wanted to sleep and hopefully never wake up.

Unfortunately, I did wake up. I didn't feel any better than when I had gone to sleep and now I had a major headache. There was no way I was going to work today. After about thirty minutes, I reached over to get my phone and forgot that I had missed calls. It had to be serious because now there were like fifty missed calls. Most of them had been from Veronica and some from other classmates of ours. I knew something serious had happened and that I needed to call Veronica back as soon as possible.

"Hey, Veronica." I couldn't get out another word before I heard Veronica crying uncontrollably.

"Veronica, what's wrong?"

"I, I, I," is all she could get out.

"I, what? What happened? Veronica, say something!"

"Yaz, he's gone!"

"Who's gone? You're not making any sense. What happened?"

"Jason. He's gone."

"What do you mean, he's gone? Gone where? When is he coming back? Did y'all have another fight?"

They argued here and there so I figured it was the big one this time and he left to blow off some steam. He's done it before but he always came back. He loved Veronica and he wasn't going anywhere for too long.

"No! No! He's dead. He's never coming back."

It felt like the life had just left my body and all my limbs went numb. The phone dropped to the floor and I was lying right beside it. I couldn't believe this was happening. Was he truly gone? Was this an awful prank? Was I dreaming? Questions kept swarming through my mind and I couldn't stop them. What did she mean, he was dead? How? Why? When? Who did it? So many questions but did I even want to know the answers. As I laid there going through mental anguish, all I could hear was my name being called over and over and over again. Who was calling me? Then I remembered that I dropped the phone but never hung it up. I reached over to grab it and heard Veronica crying out to me.

Charlie

"Yaz! Yaz! Are you ok? Speak to me! Yaz!"

"I'm here. I'm here," I said in a daze. "What do you mean he's dead?" I was in total disbelief and almost angry that I even had to ask.

"He died yesterday on the basketball court. He was playing basketball and went up for a layup and fell back first to the ground. He wasn't moving so they called 911 and tried to revive him before the ambulance got on the scene. Once they arrived, they also tried and couldn't revive him. He died on the court. They said that when they checked his phone, you were the last person that he texted. They tried to get in contact with you last night but you weren't answering your phone so they called his mom and she called me."

It sounded like a dream. I remember going to sleep not wanting to wake up so maybe this was hell. Maybe this was a nightmare. Maybe I didn't wake up and I'd be tortured and tormented for the rest of my life. Whatever it was, it hurt and it hurt badly.

"Veronica, I don't know what to say. I literally have no words right now. I wish I would have answered the phone. Maybe he would still be alive."

"Yaz, don't do that. There wasn't anything you could have done. He was already gone by the time they called you. They were just looking for someone to tell his mom so that she could come identify the body. This was not your fault."

Jason had a heart problem. He had a hole in his heart when he was a baby and the doctors had always warned his mom of the possibilities of a future heart failure. His mom was a praying woman and she took whatever the doctors said and placed the notes in her Bible and prayed over his healing. It had worked all this time but this one time, his heart stopped and never beat again. Why did he have to go? Why couldn't it be someone else? He was a great person. He loved God and people. He did right by everyone and was doing something that he had done a million times before. Why God? Why him? All these thoughts ran through my head and I just needed to get away. Get away from it all.

"Veronica, I have to go."

"Yaz! Where are you going?"

"I don't know. I just gotta go."

"Yaz. Calm down and talk to me."

"I can't right now. I'm sorry. I will call you later."

I hung up the phone, got dressed, got in my car, and just drove. I drove for what seemed like hours and ended up finding myself at the park. I just sat there thinking and playing different scenarios over and over in my head. If I wasn't so tired after work, maybe I would have told him to meet me at The Spot instead of going to play basketball. I should have spoken to him more during the summer instead of working these doubles and it went on and on and on. All of a sudden, it was like something hit me and I just snapped out of my thoughts and burst into tears. I couldn't stop crying and I could hardly catch my breath. I wanted to die because the pain was too much to bear. My best friend was gone. He was one of the only reasons why I was still here and now he was gone. What am I going to do now? I can't stay here. I got to get away from here.

My phone had been ringing none stop and I was scared to answer it. Had someone else died? At this point, I didn't even want to know. I knew I had to get away and I knew exactly how I was going to do it. I started the car and went to the only place I could think of.

"Hi Yaz. How are you today?"

"I'm fine. Is Tony here?"

"Yes. Let me get him for you. Are you sure you're ok?"

"Yes. I'm fine. I just really need to speak with Tony."

I don't know if it was God or just timing but I had a decision to make and Jason had just made it for me.

"Hi Yaz. What's going on?"

"I want to go in."

"Wait. What?"

"I want to go in. What are the next steps?"

"The next step is to tell me what's going on with you."

"It doesn't matter. I just want to go."

"It does matter because once you get in, it's not only your life that you have to worry about but the life of your shipmates and I need to make sure you're in sound mind. Now sit down and tell me what happened."

I didn't want to sit down but I knew if I stood up any longer, I'd probably turn around and walk out. I sat in the chair across from his desk and tried to hold back the tears while I tried to explain.

"Jason died last night."

"What?! Oh My Gosh! I'm so sorry Yaz."

I had told Tony a lot about what was going on with me because he asked me why I wanted to join the military in the first place. He knew all about Jason and Veronica and my home life. He would give me advice here and there. I considered him a friend.

"Yes. So I gotta go. I can't stay here any longer."

"Ok, Yaz. You're making this decision because you're hurt but this isn't something you can take back after you're feeling better. Once you're in, you're in."

"I'm well aware of that and I want to go in."

"How about if you take a couple of days and come back to me with a decision."

"I don't have a couple of days. I want to go as soon as I possibly can. I've already taken the test. All I have to do now is my physical so set up the appointment and get me in with the next group. It's going to take some time to get all this processed anyway, so let's start the process."

Tony looked at me with concern in his eyes. He knew the last time he talked to me I was on the fence with my decision and now I was ready to go. He knew I needed some time to think and calm down. "Ok, Yaz. I'll get the process started. I'll call you when I have the appointment scheduled. Just call me if you need anything and again, I'm so sorry."

"Thank you, Tony," I said as I got up and walked out the door. I had finally made a decision and I wasn't turning back.

Once I got back to my car, I called my job and told them that I had a death in the family and was going to need a couple of days off. My boss tried to say that I was a no call, no show. So what if I was five hours late, I'm calling now. Excuse me, but this job wasn't on the top of my priority list this morning. He decided to suspend me for a week. I told him not to worry about it because I quit. I figured I'd be gone in about a week anyway so I didn't need this job anymore.

After I hung up on him, I called my mom and told her what happened and told her I'd be home later. She told me to take all the time that I needed and that my dad wasn't there so I didn't have to worry about him fussing when I got back. I just couldn't believe how this day turned out. It felt like it was still night; like I hadn't woken up yet. My world felt very dark and I thought I'd never see the light again. I drove around for hours just in a daze. I wasn't sure which way to go and I didn't want to talk to anyone. I just wanted to be alone but without my thoughts. My thoughts kept playing the phone call with Veronica over and over again. All I kept hearing was "he's dead." I still couldn't believe it. My best friend is dead. My best friend is dead. My best friend is dead. Maybe if I say it enough, it'll feel real because right now, it doesn't.

I didn't know what to do with myself. If I went home, then my mom was going to want to talk about it and about what happened last night and if I went anywhere else, all I'm going to do is cry. I wish I had an apartment right now. I just want to get away. I ended up going home because I noticed my gas tank kept dwindling. I just quit my job so money was going to be tight for a while, which really didn't matter because I'd plan on being gone in a week anyway. I could wait till then.

"Hey honey. How are you doing?" my mom said as she came and gave me a hug.

"I'm fine."

"Do you know when the funeral is going to be?"

I looked at her like she had lost her mind. He just died last night and you were already putting him six feet under. Really, Ma? Really?

"No, I don't."

"Well let me know when you find out. I want to send his mom some flowers."

Why did everyone always want to send flowers when someone died? That wasn't going to magically make everything all right.

"Fine," I said as I walked to my room. I didn't feel like going into details and because of my frustration with her question, I opted to be alone.

"Yaz, what happened to Jason?" Lexy and Deonte asked in unison. Although I didn't want to talk about it, I knew they'd ask until I told them something.

"He died last night playing basketball."

"What! Are you serious?" Deonte screamed.

"Why would I lie about something like that?"

"I'm so sorry, sis," Lexy said with her head held down. They both were fond of Jason. He'd been over to the house a lot and always joked around with the both of them.

"Thanks."

"So, what are you going to do about Dad?"

The questions just kept coming. I knew this would happen once I got home.

"What do you mean, what am I gonna do? I'm not doing anything. I'm going to the navy."

"Navy?!" they both screamed.

"Yes, navy. I gotta get out of here. I can't stay here any longer. It's either stay here and kill myself or leave and find myself."

"You can't leave me," Lexy said with tears in her eyes.

"You'll be fine. You can write and I'll visit and you can come visit me."

"No! You can't leave me here with them."

"Well, you better start making a plan to leave too."

Lexy was five years younger than me and Deonte was three. We were all close because we had the same issues with growing up in a dysfunctional home but hey, who didn't? You just learn how to take the dysfunction and make it functional for you to live.

"Man, that's messed up," Deonte said.

"How is that?"

"Because now, he only has two kids to fuss at. I gotta find me somewhere else to go too. This dude is crazy."

"Yeah, I know. Ever since he came back from the war, he's had some screws loose."

"Or missing."

"Yeah, Lexy, that too. I just can't stay here any longer."

"Have you told Ma yet?" said Deonte.

"No, not yet. You know her. She'll just try to talk me out of it. I'll tell her in the next couple of days."

"What do you think Dad is going to say?"

"I don't know, Lexy, and frankly, I don't care. He can't stop me from going so I don't care what he has to say. He's put his hands on me for the last time."

"All I know is he better not ever put his hands on me like that."

Dad and Deonte had an interesting relationship. Dad was always trying to give Deonte the world and Deonte was trying his best to dodge it. If Dad said, bring home all C's and I'll buy you a car, Deonte would bring home all D's. If he said, your curfew is at 10 pm, Deonte would come in at 11:30 pm. It was always this back and forth with them two. Deonte was trying so hard not to be like our father that he was actually turning into him. But that's what happens when you try so hard to run away from something or someone. Eventually they catch up to you.

"Boy please. He's put his hands on you too and y'all just fight and be done with it."

"Yeah, but he hasn't done me the way he did you."

"Ok, whatever. I'm not about to go back and forth with you. I just want to relax for a minute before bed."

Deonte and Lexy went to the den and I was alone again. Sitting and thinking about Jason and how I would no longer be able to see him or laugh with him or talk to him. My best friend was gone and there was nothing I could do about it.

The next couple of days were a blur. I would sit in my room and cry and sleep. I didn't want to do anything or talk to anyone. I still hadn't called Veronica back and I didn't want to talk to anyone from school. I felt like I was in a cocoon and no one could enter but I knew I needed to call her back. Because I had so many missed calls, I decided to check my voicemail first. Message after message were from either people from our school or from Veronica checking to see how I was doing. How did she think I was doing? I just lost my best friend. To be fair, she just lost the love of her life and I hadn't even checked on her to see how she was doing but at that moment, I didn't care. I was down to the last voicemail.

When it started, I immediately began to cry. It was Jason's mom. She called to see how I was doing and to give me the funeral arrangements. Out of all the things she had to do, she was calling and checking in on me. How did she find the strength because I surely didn't have it? I knew I had to call her back. That was the least I could do. When I called her, it was as if she was waiting for my call because she picked up immediately.

"Yaz, my darling. How are you doing? Are you ok?"

"Mrs. Anderson, are you ok? How are you checking on me when I should be checking on you?"

"I've cried as much as I can for right now. I had to get up and get these funeral arrangements in order. How are you doing?"

She knew he was one of the closest people in my life. I was always at their home. His dad had passed away when he was younger so it was just him and his mom. We got along really well and would laugh and joke and make fun of Jason about how insightful he was. It was like every word out of his mouth could have been combined into a Hallmark card. It was so funny. We would laugh for hours. I loved visiting with her and now we were talking about funeral arrangements.

"I'm not good. I'm doing the best that I can. I still can't believe this has happened."

"I know darling. I feel the same way. I wanted to let you know that the funeral is set for this Saturday at 11 am. I didn't want to make it too late in the day because I don't think I can handle it. The nights are always the hardest because he would always call me or come into my room to tell me good night and now I don't have that. I think I'm losing my mind over here."

As she was speaking, all I could do was cry. I've been so consumed with myself these past days that I never even considered how she was doing. My heart hurt so badly for her and there was nothing that I could do to help ease the pain. All I could do was sit and listen.

"I have a couple of people coming over Saturday morning to help out and some of his cousins and two uncles will carry the casket. I think everything is already taken care of."

"Mrs. Anderson, I'm so sorry. I'm so sorry. I miss him so much. Please let me know if there is anything that I can do to help. I'm so sorry." I could no longer hold back my tears from her. I burst out crying and at that point, no one could console me.

"Yaz. Yaz."

"Yes, ma'am."

"It's ok. It's going to be ok. He loved you and wouldn't want you to cry over him. He'd want you to celebrate him. Try to celebrate him and the time you had with him."

"Yes, ma'am."

"Will I see you at the funeral?"

"I can't," I said between tears. "I just can't."

"I understand. It's ok. I know it's going to be hard so do what you feel is best but know that I'll always be here for you. If you ever need anything, just let me know. I'm here for you."

"Thank you, Mrs. Anderson. I love you and I will call you later. Let me know if you need anything because I'll always be here for you too. No matter what."

"I know darling. I know."

After I hung up the phone, I wanted to call Veronica but I just didn't have the energy. I decided to give her a call tomorrow. Maybe I'd be up to it by then.

It seemed like the night came quick but that could have been because I slept and cried all day. I decided to take a shower and get ready for bed. When I went in the hallway, I saw my dad. He just stood there staring.

"Come here and let me talk to you," he said as he headed to the living room. My mom was already sitting on the sofa and he sat next to her. I sat on the love seat across from them.

"I wanted to let you know that I'm sorry for what I did. I should not have grabbed you but I blacked out and didn't realize what I was doing until I came out of it and saw what I was doing. I realize that I have some issues and I know I need to go see someone about it and I will. I just want to say that I'm sorry and I'm sorry about your friend."

"Thank you," I said, not having the energy to debate his apology. "I guess I should tell you guys that I'm going to the navy. I went to my recruiter a couple of days ago and told him to start the process. Hopefully, I can leave out next week."

"What?!" yelled my mom. "Going where?!"

"The navy. I can't stay here. I need to get away."

"Well, you go over your cousin's house or go on vacation. You don't go to the military!"

"Well, I've made my decision and when it's time for me to go, I'm going." There was nothing they could do or say to get me to change my mind.

"Well, at least you're not going in the army or the marines. I think the navy would be good for you."

"Thanks," I said sarcastically as if I cared what he thought. "I'm going to take a shower now. Are we done?"

"Yes, you can go," said my mom with this hurt look in her eyes. I didn't want to hurt her but I knew if I'd stayed, I'd hurt me more.

After I got out of the shower, I put on my pajamas and got into bed. I decided that I needed to send off one text before I laid down for the night. The text read, "Good night," and it was sent to Mrs. Anderson. I knew I wasn't her son but I wanted her to know that she had someone else who was still here that would tell her good night.

It was the morning of the funeral and I had decided to go. I got up, got dressed, and had a little something to eat before I headed out. I got in the car, put the keys in the ignition, and just started to cry. I didn't know where it came from. It was like a wave of sadness had just swept over me. I reached into the glove compartment to get a napkin and this envelope fell out. I picked it up and it had "Jason" written in big letters on the front of it. I had forgotten that I had put that card in there. His birthday was over the summer and I had gotten him a card and was going to give it to him once we got back to school but I never got the chance to. That letter opened up the flood gate of tears that I was saving for the funeral. I just sat there and cried and cried and cried. I couldn't go to the funeral because I couldn't drive. I just stayed in the car, looking at the envelope.

It was going to take some time to go on in this life without him. I didn't know how much time but it didn't feel like it was going to be any time soon. I was just going to have to take it one day at a time. I texted his mom to let her know that I wasn't going to be able to make it and I knew she had a lot to do and would probably get back to me the next day but surprisingly, she texted right back and said, "I know darling. Jason came to me last night in a dream and said you wouldn't be able to make it because he wanted to spend some time with you." I immediately dropped the card and started shaking. I couldn't believe it. Even with him being gone, I could still feel his presence. Maybe God allows our loved ones to stick around for a while to help us with our grief. Whatever it was, I welcomed it to stay as long as it wanted. I needed a sense of peace and that's exactly what it gave me.

The next day, I decided to call Veronica. We had been friends for quite some time and although I was closer to Jason, I still considered her like my other best friend. I was acting like they both died. Veronica was still very much alive and I needed to start acting like it.

"Hello Yaz."

"Hi Veronica. How are you doing?"

"I'm ok. I know it'll get easier."

"Yeah, it will. I'm sorry that I didn't call you back. I just really didn't feel like talking to anyone or even talking about Jason. It's still so surreal to me."

"Yeah, I understand. I can't believe he's gone either. The funeral was very hard. To know that I would never see him again was hard to take."

"Yeah, I knew it would be and that's why I couldn't go. I was all dressed and in my car but just couldn't find it in myself to start the ignition. I didn't want my last image of him to be him lying in a box. I don't think I could have handled that."

"I understand. It was a nice turnout, though. A lot of people from school were there and some people spoke about the good times. I can take you to the grave site if you want to go."

"No, that won't be necessary. I don't plan on being here too much longer anyway. What I didn't tell you both is that I'd been speaking with a navy recruiter and I decided to go in. I should be leaving at the end of next week after I take my physical."

"The navy? But why?"

"I can't stay here anymore. I had been thinking about it for a while but just didn't know how to break the news to you two. I have a lot of things going on at home and just need to get away. I know it may sound a little extreme but it's just something I need to do for me."

"I get it but I'm going to miss you so much."

"I'm going to miss you too, Veronica."

"I'm actually going to take a couple of semesters off myself. I don't know how to be me without him. We'd been together for so long that I just don't know what to do and I definitely can't walk down those halls without him."

"It's funny how one person can affect your life so much that you don't even realize how much they are affecting your life until something like this happens."

"I know right. It's going to take some time to feel normal again so I'll just exist until then. Well, I have to go, Yaz. You take care of yourself in the navy and if I don't talk to you before you leave, you've always been a great friend to me and I'll cherish all the times the three of us had together. Make sure you do the same."

"I sure will, Veronica. I sure will. Bye."

Somehow, she knew that this would be the last time that we would talk to each other. It felt so weird talking to her without making plans for the three of us to hang out. Maybe Jason was the glue that held us together and without him, we were destined to fall apart. I kept our friendship in the sea of my heart and revisited them from time to time. I was finally ready to be on my way. It was time to journey into uncharted territory and the navy would be the catalyst to get me there.

COURAGE

Have the courage to step out into the unknown.

DELTA

We were all standing in this cold, gray hallway. It felt lifeless and sterile. If the lights hadn't been on, you would have sworn you were in a tunnel. We were standing shoulder to shoulder and I could hear people shouting, crying, and yelling. I looked over to my left and saw that one girl had sat on the floor with her knees to her chest and she was rocking back and forth and crying while this guy in military attire was standing over her yelling for her to get up. We had just gotten there not too long ago and we were already being screamed at and called names. Why didn't my recruiter warn me about this? I'm sure he figured if he had told me, I would have changed my mind and he would have been right. They didn't show this part on the commercials nor tell you about it while we were at MEPS learning about what would happen after we were sworn in. We were told that after we were sworn into the United States Navy, our military career would begin. Is this what our military career was going to look like because if so, I quit. Oh right, like my recruiter said, once you're in, you're in.

As I looked over to my right, I could see that I was getting closer and closer to this door that was radiating brighter light than the dull one in the hallway. "What was in that room?" I thought to myself. You could tell that we were being funneled in and out of this room and then taken back down to another hallway. I saw people going in terrified and coming out sad. Some were crying and some were so emotional that their faces had turned red. "What was in this room?" No need to ask any longer. I would soon find out.

The closer and closer I got, my heart started to beat faster and faster. Soon, it was my turn. What should I expect? Should I make a run for it? Probably not a good idea at this point. These guys didn't look like they'd like the idea of chasing someone through these halls so I decided to stay where I was. I peeked into the room and it appeared to have phone booths in the center. Each person was on the phone and a second later, they were off and the next group was up. There were about four to six phone booths for use. The officer in control called me in.

"Hey you! Get over here!" I rushed to the phone booth where he was standing.

"You have five seconds to call your mom and tell her you're safe and that's it. Now hurry up!"

As I tried to dial our house number, my hands were shaking so bad that I couldn't press the button. All of a sudden, I forgot our phone number. We had this same number for the past fourteen years and somehow I couldn't remember what it was. If he would stop yelling at me and allow me to think, I could remember. He went over to scream at someone else who was on the phone for more than five seconds. I'm sure some were saying how scared they were or that they'd made a big mistake but it was too late now. We were in the military and were now property of the United States government.

Eventually, I remembered the number and dialed it quickly. I was surprised that my mom answered since it was so early in the morning.

"Hello," my mom said sounding like I had woken her up out of her sleep.

"Mom, I'm here and I'm safe. I'll call you later."

"Hang up the phone now!" he said as he started walking toward me.

"I love you," I said crying as I hung up the phone. He didn't even allow her to respond. I did what he said because I didn't think I had any other choice in that moment.

"Keep it moving!"

He motioned for us to leave the room and go down to this other hallway. This hallway was crowded. You could tell that everyone was confused as to where to go next but there were a lot of military personnel directing us. As I got closer to the chaos, I could see this room ahead of me where people were getting their haircut. The haircuts seemed to be as quick as our phone calls. At that moment, I was glad that my recruiter told me to make sure I got my hair cut prior to leaving for boot camp. He told me to get it cut mid-neck length because my hair couldn't touch the collar of my shirt and that if I didn't get my hair cut prior to leaving then the military would do it for me and I wouldn't like the results. So a week before I was sworn in, I got my hair cut. Those that waited till they got here were now mad because they weren't asked how they wanted their hair cut. Everyone was getting the same thing and you didn't have any input in the matter.

I was ushered down this other hallway where they had different bins of clothing and other supplies. There were T-shirts, shorts, socks, hygiene products, towels, rags, and anything else we would need on a day to day basis. Everything was travel size. At the beginning of the line were white meshed bags. We were to go down the line and place the items into this bag. The yelling continued.

"Grab a bag, read the labels on the bins, do what it says, and keep it moving! If you can't read, get out of my line."

I would hope everyone could read because we all had to take the ASVAB to get into this place. We all did as we were told. We were all in a line, one behind another. We went to each bin, read the label, and did exactly as the label instructed. One bin was labeled: "T-shirts. Pick 5." I picked up five, placed them in my bag, and went down to the next bin. "Socks. Pick 3." I picked up three pairs of socks and placed them in my bag. There was another bin that said, "Take one." It looked to be an army green belt of sorts with a canister attached to it. I wasn't absolutely sure what this was for but it said take one so that's what I did. We continued the process all the way down the line. When we got to the end, there was a bin that had the word "Recruit" on it. When I looked inside the bin, there were black baseball caps with the word "RECRUIT" written across the front in gold lettering. I got one, placed it in my bag, and waited for more instructions.

We were ushered into rooms that were divided between girls and boys. Inside of the room were long tables one behind the other. We were told to stand in front of the tables and empty out the items we had just placed in our meshed bags. Once we had all of our items placed on the table space in front of us, we had to form a line and come to the front of the room. There was a table in the front of the room with blue jogging suits, T-shirts, and some army green bags laid out on them. There were three women standing behind the table who were to issue the supplies to us. Since it was all women, maybe now we wouldn't be yelled at so much.

"Listen up! You are to tell us your size quickly as you move down this line. We will hand you your gear and then you are to grab a seabag at the end of the table and go back to your place. You will remove your clothing and place it inside of the white mesh bag. This bag is not to be opened for the duration of your time at boot camp. You are to place everything that you've gathered today inside of your seabag and put on your navy jogging pants, your navy T-shirt, and your navy hoodie. This will be your attire for the rest of the week. You are now recruits! You have to earn the right to be called sailors and you haven't begun to earn that right yet. Do you understand?"

"Yes," we all said with a murmur.

"I said, DO YOU UNDERSTAND?"

"Yes!" we all yelled.

"That's not good enough! When I ask you a question, you say, Yes, Petty Officer."

"Yes, Petty Officer!"

So much for not being yelled at. The women were scarier than the men. God, what have I gotten myself into and why didn't You stop me?

As we walked down the line, the women asked us our sizes. We picked up all the items on the table then headed back to our places with the things we had just picked up from the bins. I was looking around to see where the bathroom was so that I could change my clothes but there wasn't one in sight and from the looks of things,

I wasn't the only one looking. We all just stood there waiting for someone to inform us where the bathrooms were located.

"What are you waiting for? Change!"

Oh, are we taking off our clothes in front of everyone? What type of place is this? I have home training and this is not how I was raised to change my clothes but it didn't look like they cared one bit about my home training. We all got undressed and put on our jogging pants, which had "Navy" going down the side leg, our navy T-shirts that had the navy seal on the front, and our navy hoodies, which also had the navy seal on the front. We looked like smurfs and apparently, that's what they called us during this week.

"The belt with the water bottle attached, put it on. You are to wear these at all times. When it's time to hydrate, you will be drinking water from this water bottle only, so make sure that it's filled at all times. When we say hydrate, that means stop what you are doing and hydrate. Understood?"

"Yes, Petty Officer!"

Once we were all dressed and our seabags tied up, we were ready to go to the next destination.

"Put your seabags on your back and let's move!"

I picked up my seabag and tried to put it on. We didn't collect any bricks in any of those bins so how did this bag get so heavy so quickly? I attempted to put on my bag again. Failed! There had to be a method to this. One doesn't simply just put on a seabag. I decided to bend down a little and put my arms through the straps and stand up slowly. I had to catch my balance on the way up but it worked. I was able to stand. I was still trying to wrap my mind around how heavy this bag was.

We followed the petty officer down the hall and then outside. By this time, it was light out. What time was it? We hadn't been to sleep all night and now it was morning and we were starving. There were some other groups already sitting on the cold concrete devouring these bag lunches they had received. As we walked over to our spot, there was this guy in navy fatigues with a box in his hand. Inside were all these brown paper bags. Maybe the hard part was over. We all sat there scared out of our minds when the guy started handing us these brown paper bags. We started to go through them to see exactly what was inside: a sandwich, a bag of chips, a banana, and a bite-size bottle of water. When I opened the plastic wrap to take out my sandwich, I noticed the meat was bologna. Ew! I hated bologna. We grew up on this stuff and if I had my choice, I definitely would have chosen turkey but I didn't have a choice. Everything here was apparently already decided for us and besides, I was starving. At this moment, I would have eaten anything and today, anything was bologna. When we finished our bag lunch, we were told to stay seated until our Recruit Division Commander (RDC) came to get us.

As I sat on the cold concrete feeling like I was freezing to death, I couldn't help but to think of how I wished Tony had put me in with the group that was going to boot camp that summer but he hadn't. He put me in with the group that wouldn't leave out until November. He knew that I needed time to clear my head and deal with these emotions prior to coming into the military. I ended up completing another semester of college and staying at home. Things didn't get better but I was able to keep my distance by going to school early and staying late to study. It started to remind me of my days in high school. When Tony did finally call me to give me the date I was set to leave, I was ecstatic. I was finally getting ready to leave this place and start a new adventure. The day that I left, my parents took me to the MEPS and watched me swear in. I was able to hug them goodbye before they put us on a bus and took us to the airport. We were off to Great Lakes, IL. I'd never been there before but I knew it was somewhere up north and it was November. It was going to be cold and because I was 100 lbs soak and wet, I didn't know how I was going to handle it. In the winter, I always had on a lot of layers and had a heater somewhere near me so to be this far from home with no control over my layers was going to be a challenge.

When we got to the airport with our brown folders in our hands from MEPS, the people at the airport were applauding and saying, "Thank you for your service." It made you feel good, as if you were about to embark on a journey that really meant something not only to you but to others as well. It was a great feeling but now I was freezing on this concrete looking like a smurf. Oh the choices that we make.

"Get up!" yelled this guy with different pins on his shoulder. He had to be someone of importance because he looked a little different from the rest. He didn't have on navy fatigues but was dressed like the men in black, navy edition. He definitely snapped me out of going down memory lane.

"I don't want no crap out of none of you! We are not your baby sitters and you're far from home. Don't make us do anything that you will regret!"

Doesn't he mean, anything that he would regret? He looked at me like he had read my thoughts and answered them with, "No! I said what I meant!" I didn't know who this guy was but I knew I didn't want to be on his bad side. I wasn't even sure he had any other side but I was determined to stay clear of him.

"Your RDCs will be Petty Officer Smith and Petty Officer Savage. If I hear anything negative about any one of you, then I'll be coming for you! Petty Officers Smith and Savage, they're all yours."

He walked away and went to another group to give them the same spill. Petty Officer Smith was a very muscular white guy with a thick mustache as if it was mature enough to speak on its own. You couldn't tell that he had the same haircut as everyone else because he had on a hat that was different from ours. Petty Officer Savage was a black female. She wore glasses and was short, but you knew not to mess with her because the look on her face dared you to try her and trying her, I would not be doing.

"We have a full day planned, so let's go! When you march, you start with your left foot, then right but you won't have to worry about marching for a while. Everywhere we go today, you will be jogging. You got that?!"

"Yes!" we all yelled.

"Yes, what?!"

We had no idea what to say. The other petty officer dressed different and told us to call her petty officer but he didn't say what he wanted to be called. So, we all said what came naturally.

"Yes, sir!"

"Sir? Don't call me sir! I work for a living! It's Petty Officer!"

"Yes, Petty Officer!" we all screamed.

"Good! Now keep up and stay in line."

He took off running. Now, how were we supposed to keep up and stay in line? Where were we going and how far was it? I could tell this was going to be a long day.

We jogged down to this building that said "Medical" on the outside. I had already completed my physical before I came and I was guessing everyone else had too, so why were we here? It took a minute for everyone to catch up to the group. For some of us, this was probably the first time we had ran since high school.

"What took y'all so long? Yeah, it's time to get y'all lazy sack of bones into shape! Whose war are you going to fight running like that?"

Um, I didn't come here to fight no one's war. I came to get away from home and to get college money. My recruiter told me that they would pay for my college and pay off any student loans that I had incurred prior to joining but obviously he had other reasons as to why we were here.

"Each of you will go to medical. You'll fill out paperwork, have a real physical, and meet back here lined up when you're done. You got that?!"

"Yes, Petty Officer!"

We walked inside the building in one single line and there was more activity going on here than in the other building but this place had the same sterile feeling. It was a medical processing unit—processing you in and sending you on your way. We were all pretty freaked out from having to run all the way here and now had to endure only God knows what.

"Next!" shouted a lady from this room on the right. When I entered the room, I saw two long tables and a pathway between the tables. On the tables were a lot of different medical supplies and equipment. This was way different from any doctor's appointment I ever had. What were they about to do to us?

As I stood there, one of the ladies motioned for me to come forward.

"Where's your paperwork?"

"Here it is, Petty Officer." I handed her my paperwork that I held in my right hand.

"I'm not a Petty Officer. I'm a nurse."

"Sorry." I thought everyone was a petty officer at this point. If I didn't know what to call you, you would be called petty officer first.

"What's your name?"

"Yasmine Payton"

"Social?"

"1411."

"Your full social?"

I whispered my social to her because I was always taught that you didn't say your social aloud for everyone to hear. She accepted my response.

"Take off your hoodie."

I took off my hoodie and hoped she didn't want me to take off anything else. I was already weirded out from getting undressed in front of women that I didn't know and I didn't want to do the same thing in front of the guys too.

"You'll be receiving a set of shots. Afterward, if you feel any discomfort, the spot gets swollen, or red, let someone know."

"Ok."

She proceeded to pinch my upper left arm, grab a needle off the table, and stuck me. She got another needle and stuck me again. She then sent me to the next nurse who repeated the steps in my other arm. I only saw them take one valve of blood so what were they putting inside of me. I was already caught up on all my shots but apparently that's not good enough here. After they were done, I walked out of the room with two sore arms. I could barely carry my hoodie, let alone this heavy seabag. We were then ushered down another hallway and were told to stand in this line that had already formed ahead of us. I started to cringe every time I saw a door because I had no clue as to what was going to happen on the other side of it.

About thirty minutes later, it was my turn to enter yet another door. It was the same type of room as before but we would be sitting in chairs so they could check our hearing and then our eyesight. If you didn't pass the eye test, they would give you these huge glasses that you had to wear. The lens was as big as a birth control pack and the frames were super thick. I'm glad I never had any problems with my eyesight. After we left that room, we had to go back toward the front door and wait for everyone else to get done. I was so sleepy by the time I got to the front door. They allowed us to sit on the floor as we waited for our other group members. I didn't know what would happen if I dozed off and I tried my best not to but eventually, the sleep came over me. I don't know how long I was out but I woke up to someone yelling.

"Get up, recruit! Who told you to fall asleep?"

No one told me to but no one told me I couldn't either but I knew I better not actually say what I was thinking.

"Since you like being on the floor, stay there and give me twenty!"

Twenty what? Dollars? My recruiter told me I couldn't bring any money and if he did mean twenty dollars that would have been one of the most expensive naps I'd ever taken. I looked at him bewildered. I'm guessing he was reading my mind.

"Twenty push-ups recruit! I need my twenty!"

Push-ups? Twenty? Who did he think I was? I could probably give him about five but twenty was definitely a reach. I proceeded to get into girl push-up mode.

"Oh no! Not here! We don't do push-ups the wimpy way! We all do them the same way!"

He proceeded to get down on the floor with me to show me what a proper push-up was supposed to look like. It seemed to take him only 2.5 seconds to do ten push-ups. I knew mine would take much longer. I got in the same push-up position that he was in, kind of, and began my attempt at a push-up. I went down and came back up. Then went down and struggled to get back up.

"If I can't hear you counting, that means you haven't done any! Start over!"

Was this dude serious? I just struggled trying to get back up from the second one and you want me to start over. I don't think you're getting twenty from me today. I attempted to go down again and as I came back up, I counted "One" then I went back down again.

"What's my name?! You're not doing push-ups for you! You're doing push-ups for me! Start over!"

"Ahhh!" I said not even realizing it was coming out of my mouth.

"What did you say? If you have something to say, I need to hear the words!"

"Nothing, Petty Officer. I don't have anything to say."

I struggled back up and attempted yet another push-up.

"One, Petty Officer."

"Finally! That's one! You have nineteen more to go!"

But for my body, I had no more. If I went back down, I wasn't coming back up. I went down and like I suspected, I couldn't come back up.

"What are you waiting on, recruit? I need my nineteen!"

How do you tell someone who is yelling at you that you can't do anymore? I didn't know what to do but my body obviously did and that's when the tears began to flow. I didn't want to cry but I had nothing else.

"You're crying?! I don't care about your tears! I want my nineteen! Oh, y'all are in for a rude awakening around here! I want all y'all to hear this. Tears don't mean nothing around here so you may as well cut those tear ducts out now because when you're in a war, no one is going to care about your tears and I don't want to see any more! Get up, recruit!"

I got up feeling embarrassed and sore. I had just had four shots, hadn't slept in almost two days, and had to run to this clinic. I didn't know how much more of this I could take. Everyone was looking at me like, "I'm glad it ain't me," but I looked back at them as to say, "But your time will come."

We finished our rounds at the clinic and headed to the lunch building. We had to jog there too. Everything seemed to be a million miles away and all this jogging alerted us to how out of shape we all were. When we got to the building, there was a yellow half circle that said, "Welcome To Galley 939: Navy's dining facility." There was a group coming out as we prepared to go in. As we approached the doors, we got another lecture.

"Listen up, recruits! Only get what you're going to eat. We are not in the business of wasting food. This is not social hour and you don't have much time to eat so I suggest you get your tray, get your food, sit down, shut up, and eat! When you get inside, get nut to butt. Close up those lines and move it along! Understood?"

"Yes, Petty Officer!" we all screamed with as much force as we could muster. The concept of nut to butt didn't really register at the moment because we were so tired but it definitely was a discussion for another time.

We walked in and immediately smelled food. Maybe we would learn differently but it smelled so good compared to the bologna sandwich that we had devoured earlier. Anything at this point was going to be better. We all filed in line one behind the other, grabbed a tray, and headed down the line. I chose mashed potatoes, chicken fried steak, green beans, and fruit. At the end of the line, we were able to grab silverware and follow a galley worker's motion to where we would be sitting. I let out a sigh of relief when my butt hit that chair. It never felt so good to sit and enjoy a meal and I ate like my life depended on it. He said we weren't going to have long to eat and I wanted to make sure that I ate everything that I had chosen. It reminded me of being in elementary for the first time—a new school, new faces, and new food. Soon we would get used to the routine of things but this first day was becoming more and more eventful.

As I was eating, I was able to look up and see others in my group. Some were eating just as fast as I was, while others looked dazed. They were probably pondering the decision they had just made and wondered if it was the right one. I know I was, but I was also taking this opportunity to eat something other than what was in a brown paper bag. Besides, I didn't know if this would be our last meal of the day.

Not too long after the last person took their seat, our petty officers came over and announced we had ten minutes left to eat. Ten minutes? We literally just sat down. That just showed me that I never wanted to be last in line. We all seemingly swallowed our food and then it was time to get up, hydrate, and head to the next processing unit for today. This time, we went to an administration building. You would think they'd just let us rest for the remainder of the day. I mean, we were going to be here for eight weeks. We had time to get all this stuff done later but nope. They had other things in mind. We just went from one thing to the next.

In the administration building, we all were led to a room with long tables and chairs. It reminded me of a college classroom only darker. The tables were brown wood and so were the chairs. I guess they didn't want anything to be comfortable around here. We were told to find the brown folder with our name on it and sit in that seat. The brown folder was similar to the one we received from MEPS. You would think they could spring for different colors as to not confuse the folders. I guess I had a lot to learn about the navy way.

They discussed what we could expect over the next eight weeks—the good, the bad, and the ugly. As I listened to her, it seemed my recruiter left out a lot of details. He told me about being in the navy itself but just so happened to leave out everything that would happen in boot camp. All I knew was that I asked to get away from home and now I was very far from it. I could sit here and complain or learn something and make the best out of it.

She got to the part where she started talking about battle stations. The word battle stations sounded scary all by itself and now you tell us if we didn't pass it, then we would have to stay in boot camp an extra week. Nope! I knew that staying back was not an option for me. I didn't want to stay here any longer than what was required.

After she gave us the rundown, she asked if anyone had any questions. One brave soul raised his hand and asked, "Has anyone ever tried to run away from this place?" Everyone turned and looked at him. His face was beet red and you could tell that question came from a place of sincere pondering. "Yes, we have had a couple of cases but I would highly discourage you from doing that. Besides, after a couple of weeks, you'll realize it's not so bad."

Not so bad? We jog everywhere, y'all made me eat bologna. Granted, I didn't have to eat it. I could have just starved or passed out from all the jogging. Y'all gave me more shots that I've had in my entire life and you say it's not so bad? I don't know who she thought she was talking to but with this group, if looks could kill, she'd be gone.

After she was done talking, she guided us through each page of this thick packet and explained everything and had us sign as we went through it together. After a while, I stopped listening and only recognized the words, "Ok, now sign." We had just eaten and y'all bring us in this room and have us hear a speech and sign papers. I'm literally falling asleep as I'm signing these documents. If they don't allow us to get some sleep soon, they are going to have to kick me out because I'm going to find a way to get some sleep and not get caught this time.

By this time, it was almost 3:30 pm and as I looked around the room, I could tell we were all in this ship together—the USS Tired. Eventually, we got to the last page and everyone let out a sigh of relief.

We were finally done. We were told to leave our packet where they were and get back into line. We left the administration building and did a mixture of marching and jogging all the way to the building we would be staying in. Just our luck, our building was next to the last building on this whole base. When we arrived, there was already another group lined up outside. We were told to line up next to them. After the two sets of petty officers spoke to each other, the group that was there before us, went in.

On the outside of the building, it read "Ship 972." It was a three-story-high brown brick building with a lot of windows. It was cold outside and I was ready to get in and take a nap.

"Looks like we have some quiet time, recruits!" yelled Petty Officer Savage.

Quiet time? That's all we've been doing since we got here. Y'all are the ones that have been screaming this whole time. After about fifteen minutes of standing in the cold, in silence, we were ushered into the building. Once inside, we were separated. The boys went to the second floor and the girls went to the third. Outside of yet another door, there was the word "barracks." Interesting choice of words. When we entered the room, there were about sixty racks and thirty lockers. There were four tables about 8 feet away from each other down the center of the room with four chairs to each table. In the front of the room, there was a flag that had 028 on it and in the back of the room, there was a flag that had 027.

"This will be your home over the next eight weeks. See how clean and organized everything is? It better stay that way! We are division 027 and this is division 028," Petty Officer Savage said as she pointed at the ones who came up fifteen minutes before we did. "This will be your sister division since you both are sharing this space. Both divisions will have chores and will make sure this place stays clean. You all better learn to get along because if you don't, there will be consequences. Your racks are down that way. Find your name and stand by your rack." Petty Officer Savage pointed to the back of the room to signal that 028 were in the front of the room and we would be located in the back; figures. Our building is in the back, why not put us in the back of the room, I mean barracks.

We all located our racks and stood in front of them and waited for further instructions. "Now that you have found your racks, this will be yours to take care of for the duration of your time in boot camp. Look to your left and now look to your right. Just like the outside of this building states, you now live on a ship and these ladies are now called your shipmates. You will be working with each other every day. If one of you falls, you all fall. If you are running late, you're all running late. If one of you is lost, guess what? You're all lost. Your shipmates are now the only family you have. Got it?"

"Yes, Petty Officer."

"We still have a lot to do but all in due time. Place your seabags behind your racks and get in line. It's time to go to the mess hall for dinner."

Mess hall? Another interesting choice of words. I could tell that our normal way of thinking was about to be replaced with the navy way. We all did as we were told and lined up. I felt like I had just eaten but I dared not say what I was thinking. We got back to the mess hall and followed the same routine as earlier—got nut to butt, grabbed a tray, and went down the line. This time I chose a turkey sandwich, soup, and a cup of mixed fruit. I didn't want to waste anything and since I wasn't that hungry, I decided to get the least amount of food possible. I must say, even the soup was kind of good; especially on a cold and foggy day like this. Of course, it wasn't like Momma used to make but it passed the stomach test. We all swallowed our food because we knew what happened last time we were in this place and no one wanted to leave hungry or with food left on their plate.

Just like clockwork, we got the ten-minute warning. This time I didn't mind because I had finished my meal. I was just thinking about going back to this bark place to go to sleep. I had forgotten the name already. We reached our ship around 6:30 pm and were told to fold our smurf suits up and place them at the end of our racks. None of us knew what a rack was but since she was motioning to our beds as she was talking, we figured it meant bed. We could sleep in our shorts and the T-shirt we had on if we wanted. One brave soul raised their hand.

"Yes, recruit."

"Aren't we going to take a shower?"

"What's your name recruit?"

"Ayana, Petty Officer."

"I don't care what your first name is. In here, you only have one name and that's the last one."

"Davis, Petty Officer."

"Well, Davis. I'm guessing, all of your shipmates have the same question. Let me explain something to all of y'all. Y'all haven't worked hard enough yet for a shower. A shower is a privilege and it's not something that any of you have earned so there will be no showers tonight. Now fold your smurf suits and get in your rack. Lights off in fifteen minutes."

Everyone looked at each other like that was the most disgusting thing we'd ever heard. We'd been jogging, running, and doing push-ups all day, and we didn't deserve a shower? Again, what kind of place is this? I didn't give it much thought though because I was too sleepy. I was happy to be in bed in fifteen minutes. Shoot, I'd be in there in five minutes and I didn't care who saw me undress. We could have all been butt naked and I would have still gotten into bed.

When fifteen minutes had passed, the lights went out; whether you were done and in your rack or not. "Lights out! No one better get up for nothing!" I had stopped listening after my head hit the pillow. I was just happy that I survived the first day and I could finally get some sleep. I was too tired to think about the next day. Like Veronica said, the next day had enough problems of its own that I cared nothing about at the moment. It was time to sleep and I was happy to oblige.

It seemed like I had just closed my eyes when I heard banging and felt the light hit my face. What time is it? Why are they waking us up in the middle of the night?

"Reveille! Reveille! The day has begun. It's 0400 and we got a lot to do!"

Who was Reveille and why she got us getting up so early in the morning and what is 0400? It was too early for all this military jargon that no one knew anything about. They had just said lights out and now lights are back on? But why? I struggled to open my eyes and noticed it was still dark out. Are they serious? Is this going to be the norm? Oh God, help me please! They are messing up my sleep.

The banging continued until everyone was out of their racks and standing next to them.

"Ok, recruits. Today is your lucky day. You will be inside for most of the day so that you can learn how to take care of your ship. Right now, get on your smurf suits, get into bathroom rotation, and let's go. You have thirty minutes."

Thirty minutes? It's like eighty girls in here. How were we supposed to get ready in thirty minutes? I didn't think Petty Officer Savage cared. She said we had thirty minutes so we had better be in line in thirty minutes. We all rushed to brush our teeth and use the bathroom. We weren't taking showers so I guess that cut out the majority of our time.

We headed to the galley for breakfast and after we finished, headed back to our ship and upstairs to the barracks. We would soon learn that the same thing could have several different names. Like galley meant the same as mess hall and the ship meant the same thing as the barracks. We knew that there would be plenty more to come but for right now, we just concentrated on what we needed for today.

"Get to your rack. Today you will be learning cleanliness and how to keep your area neat, wrinkle-free, and clear of contraband."

We all hurried to our racks and stood still. This was starting to be a routine for the barracks. Come in, rush to your rack, and stand there.

"First thing, when I walk in or if any other petty officers walk in, whoever sees the petty officer first is to yell, 'Attention on deck,' and you are to get in front of your rack and stand at attention as quickly as possible. That means back straight, eyes looking straight ahead, arms to your side, and feet at a forty-five-degree angle."

"How are we supposed to put our feet at a forty-five-degree angle?" asked Rudy who was a brown-skinned, short girl from South Carolina. She looked like she could be your little sister.

"This is how," Petty Officer Savage said as she walked toward Rudy. Rudy stood still with her back straight, eyes looking straight ahead, and her arms to her side because she thought she was about to get in trouble. Petty Officer Savage came closer to her and as Rudy's feet were side by side, Petty Officer Savage put her foot forward and ran it between Rudy's as to separate her feet from being together.

"Keep your heels touching but open the space between your feet."

When Petty Officer Savage was done, Rudy's feet were in a V shape.

"Everyone look at her feet. This is how they should be."

We all walked over to Rudy and stared down at her feet before attempting the task on our own. Pretty simple. Now let's see if I can remember to actually do it.

"Your hands are to be on the side of your leg right where the crease is. If there is no crease there, pretend like there is. Close your fist so that your fingertips are touching the lower part of your palm and your thumb is facing straight down."

She showed us exactly how we were to hold our hands on the side of our legs. Some people got it, while others were still a little confused. All I needed to do was see it and I could do it. I was a visual learner. I needed to see it rather than you telling me how to do it. It only took one time and I had it down. She took us through some other motions like standing at parade rest and how to salute. I used to see these types of motions on the TV or in movies and had no idea how technical they were.

As we all stood there watching and learning the commands, we were able to start to get to know each other. I got a feel of who were going to be the ship clowns and those that were so terrified that they would probably try to run away. We were only on day two. We had time to change their minds.

Throughout the day, we learned how to make our beds with ninety-degree angles, fold our blankets with ninety-degree angles, fold our socks, shirts, and shorts. We emptied out our seabags and put all of our items away—the navy way—and kept the bag that had the clothes that we came in within our seabags. Day two was over and the barracks started to feel like a permanent place.

The rest of the week would involve getting our chore assignments for the barracks. We had different shifts since there were two divisions living in one area. Our shifts included bathroom duty, sweeping the floors, keeping the common area clean and free of debris, and shoveling snow. I never wanted to be on shoveling duty. I grew up in the South and we didn't have much snow and when we did, it melted the time it hit the ground but not here. The snow fell, stayed, and had babies. I knew eventually, I would be in that rotation but I was definitely not looking forward to it.

We had our chore schedule posted on a board in the front of the barracks where division 028 was so that both divisions could see it. Every time we would walk in their area, they looked at us like, "Why are you in our area?" Um, we are all sharing this whole space. Your division just so happens to be in the front of it.

We learned quickly that the 028 girls were our competition although they were supposed to be our "sister" unit. Outside of the barracks, we had to win different competitions against other divisions in order to get to carry flags that showed our accomplishments for our division and we had to compete against 028 as well. We were told that at the end of boot camp, certain divisions would get awards based off their performance during their time here and we had to be the best. Our goal was to get every award. So that's what we committed to do.

It seemed as if the week went by pretty fast. With going to bed by 1900 and waking up at 0400, it would make any week go by fast.

We couldn't believe that we had made it to Friday. Did we get weekends off? Was this going to be some sort of celebration that we made it? Nope! The day started off like any other day.

"Reveille, reveille. We have a lot planned." We all jumped out of bed and got to attention. We were learning the navy way and how prompt we had to be once that light came on. If you weren't prompt, your wake-up routine would involve push-ups and I was tired of doing push-ups at 0400.

"Today we will be picking up your dog tags. Once you receive them, you are never to take them off. They are to be worn around your neck and inside of your clothing. We will also be picking up your uniforms. You will be trying them on and making sure they fit before we come back and learn how to fold them."

The navy was serious about space management. They informed us that once we were on an actual ship, we would have less space than what we had here. How was that even possible? We were supposed to live on a ship with no space for our clothes and other necessities. Great!

We knew we had thirty minutes to be ready to go and we had come up with a system where half of us would go into the bathroom immediately while the others would get dressed and then we would switch. We had our time down to twenty minutes. Although it was a lot of girls, we got along well because we considered the 028 girls enemies. It made us bond together quickly and made our bond even stronger. We had to carry our seabags with us so that we could carry our uniforms back to the barracks. It was definitely a lot lighter than before but I had a strange feeling that it would dramatically change after we got our uniforms.

We all got lined up and headed to the building to pick up our dog tags and uniforms. We were starting to get used to the fact that our building was practically the last building on the base and all the buildings we had to go to in order to pick up anything were all the way in the front of the base. I guess this was how they were getting us in shape for battle stations. On Wednesday, we had to go get measured for our uniforms. They even measured our head size. We were guessing that there were hats that went along with the uniforms because all we had were baseball caps and they didn't warrant any measuring.

We went to the galley first because it was on our way there and we always started off the day with breakfast. We got three meals a day and because of the schedule of these meals, it felt like we were always eating. We marched and ate, marched and ate, threw in a couple of appointments, and ate some more. It was exhausting at times but we weren't in the complaining business because if they took away one meal, it would probably feel like we were starving to death. We just learned how to control the amount of food we ate at lunch.

We arrived at building J, separated into two groups (guys and girls), and filed into separate rooms with bins. Petty Officer Smith went with the boys while Petty Officer Savage stayed with us. Inside each bin was a set of clothing and paperwork with our name on it. There was also an envelope placed on the top.

"Find your bin and stand in front of it. Don't touch anything until you're told, understand?"

"Yes, Petty Officer!"

We all found our bins and were excited to finally get out of these smurf suits. Maybe now she'll let us take a shower. We were all women and at this point, we were all funky. I couldn't imagine staying in the barracks with the boys.

"First order of business is the paperwork. Take out your inventory sheet and lay it face down to the right of the bin."

We all did as we were told.

"Now take everything out of the bin and place it to the left of the bin."

We had enough room as to not be in anyone else's way. We were just excited with anticipation of putting on something new.

"Now flip your inventory sheet over and check off each item you just removed from your bin."

We all picked up our pens and began our inventory. Inside of the envelope was our dog tag. It had our social security number on it and also a different tag if you were allergic to anything or had any other medical issues that someone would need to know in case of an emergency. There were daily uniforms, which consisted of dark blue pants and a light blue button-down long sleeve shirt and black socks, a uniform called dress blues that in actuality looked black to me but they were pants and a long sleeve top with a V-neck. There was a ribbon that went along with the uniform and some more black socks. We also had another black uniform that looked like dress blacks but instead of the V-neck, there was a long sleeve button-down shirt. We also had dress whites, which were similar to the dress blues only a different color as the name mentions. We also had black dress jackets, white long sleeve button-downs, black shoes, black boots, and other accessories that went along with the uniforms. We were informed to put the inventory sheet face down on the table and stand at parade rest when we were done. This would alert Petty Officer Savage to give us the next set of instructions. After about thirty minutes of ruffling through pieces of paper and asking a ton of questions, everyone was in parade rest.

"Now it's time for you to try on your uniforms." There were three people that weren't part of our division who were dressed in each uniform in our stack. They were models if you will, to show us what the uniforms were supposed to look like and how they were supposed to fit when we put them on. Oh, to get ready to take off this smurf suit and never have to put it back on again. "Calm down Yaz. You don't get to wear them today." "I know. Just let me enjoy the moment." I'm glad no one else could hear me having a conversation with myself.

"Someone will be coming around to check on you. Do not change into the next uniform until you have been given the green light."

"Yes, Petty Officer," we all said with stronger voices since Monday. We were a little more relaxed since our arrival. I think we had come to the conclusion that, for right now, this was home and these ladies were our family. It was starting to feel like normal life.

The whole processes took about two hours or so because there were some sizing issues with some of the uniforms and some of the girls were a little large in the bust area and that had to be corrected pronto. Overall, it was a good appointment. Most of us had no issues with the uniforms and we were good to go. We were told that we could begin to put the uniforms in our seabag and place our dog tags around our necks. There was a picture in front of the room on how to pack your uniforms into the seabag. They gave us a white bag to put our dress whites in because it was winter here and we were informed that our dress whites were only for the summer. Yeah, it would be a while before we had to take those out. Hopefully, we could still wear them by that time or they would issue us new ones.

It was looking like this place wasn't that bad after all. Besides all the yelling, I could get used to this. And even with the yelling, my dad did that most of our entire childhood so I could get used to that too. Eventually, it would be time to head to lunch. I didn't know it would take this long for the uniforms' process but I guess when you have over forty women and sizing issues, it could take a while. I decided to go to use a bathroom that is called the "head" here. I knew soon we would start back on our marching quest to the galley and even that would take a while.

On my way there, I noticed a guy that was in our division coming from the head. We didn't get to talk to the guys much but I had noticed him from lunch and lining up.

"Hey."

"Hey," I said back with a smile on my face.

"How are y'all doing in there?"

"We're doing good. It's taking forever but I think we are almost done."

"Good, because we're waiting on you all to get done. We've been done for a while," he said jokingly.

"Whatever. We women just like to take our time."

"I don't think that's allowed here." We both laughed.

"Well, I'm Sanchez. Hopefully, we'll get to talk more."

"Yeah, hopefully."

He walked back to where the guys were and I went on to use the head. When the door shut behind me, I remembered that I didn't give him my name. Oh well. We still had seven weeks together. I'm sure the opportunity would present itself.

When I got back to the room, it looked like we were all finished and it was time to head to lunch. Some of the girls had to come back to pick up their uniforms after they had been adjusted. They said they should have them back by Monday or Tuesday at the latest and they could come back individually to pick them up. Sounded like a plan to me because this building was far from our building and it was cold outside. I'd rather be in the barracks making sure my bed was in a ninety-degree angle. At least it was warm in the barracks.

We put our seabags on our backs, which now felt like we had two tons of bricks in them and headed out the door. It's funny how you don't think clothes could possibly weight this much until you put them in a seabag.

We went to the galley and then back to our barracks to fold our uniforms and put them away. I didn't think we had any more room to put anything but I was wrong. You would have thought that we were folding our uniforms so we could put them in our back pockets because of how small they were but somehow folding them this way would ensure they would fit into our lockers. Genius! I have to continue this folding method forever. It may take a little more time to fold but it saves so much room. After we were done, Petty Officer Savage had us line back up in front of our racks.

"I have a little announcement, recruits." We thought someone was in trouble. Anytime we did or said something wrong, we had to drop and do at least ten push-ups. By the time these eight weeks were over, I knew we would all be some toned women. We were all anxious to hear what she had to say. She never declared that she had an announcement. She just said what she had to say and that was it, but this time it felt different. What could she possibly have to say? Who got in trouble this time? And how many push-ups would she add on since this was an announcement? I was already in the lead for most push-ups and it had only been five days.

"You all have done a good job this week and have been staying on track. You all have earned bathroom privileges. You may now take a shower."

You would have thought the Braves won the World Series or better yet, the Falcons won the Super Bowl. We cheered and screamed and were high fiving each other. Petty Officer Savage just stood there and cracked a smile. Were we actually getting through to her?

"Ok, ok. Quiet!" she yelled.

"You can go eight at a time. You have five minutes per group. If you're not done in five minutes too bad. The water will be shut off whether you have soap on or not. Those of you that are not taking a shower, get ready to do laundry because y'all stink."

I didn't know laundry duty was part of our chores. You mean we don't have janitors or someone to come and take these clothes? Man, we learn something new about our jobs every day. The first eight went in and the rest of us stayed and separated the clothes. Because we were all wearing the same thing, we had to put our initials on the inside tag of all of our clothes with a black sharpie. Those of us that were separating the clothes had to take off our smurf suits too and put on our T-shirts and physical training (PT) shorts until our clothes were clean. We got a load of clothes for the wash and followed Petty Officer Savage to the laundry room. It was like she was taking us to a dungeon or something and if we went missing then, oh well, because no one would even know. That was until it was time for them to do laundry.

"This is where the laundry goes. You all will have shifts and you will wash whatever is dirty. You may want to use some gloves because soon all of your menstrual cycles will be synced together and you will all come on at the same time." We all laughed because we thought she was joking but the look on her face said she was serious. I didn't want to be responsible for washing no one's bloody underwear. We could already tell some of these females were nasty. Not flushing the toilet or washing their hands. I was not looking forward to this chore.

We put a load in and headed back upstairs. When we got back, the second group was coming out of the shower and it was our turn. Glory! Shower time! Yeah, we only got five minutes but that was more time than what we had all week. We reached the shower and our time had started. There were eight shower heads in the open space. Eight naked women all trying to hurry and take a shower.

"Payton, you sure are skinny."

"Robertson, you better pay attention to those sagging boobs of yours and leave me alone," I said laughing.

Robertson was one of the funny ones in the bunch. She was always making us laugh with jokes under her breath and would blame it on me. That's why I've had to do so many push-ups. She was from New York and you could tell by her strong accent.

"Both of y'all better stop that laughing before Petty Officer Savage comes in here with those glasses way down her nose like she's mad that they slid down there," said Brooks.

"I know right. One day those glasses are going to fall off her face and she's gonna make them drop and give her fifty," said Rudy.

We all busted out laughing. We didn't care that we were all in there naked. Upon first glance, it was kind of weird but once the jokes started, it eased the weirdness.

"If y'all have time to laugh, y'all must not need five minutes," yelled Petty Officer Savage.

"No, Petty Officer. We need the whole five," we said trying not to laugh.

At the four-and-a-half-minutes mark, the water stopped.

"The water stopped!" said Franklin.

"Oh, really. I didn't notice," said Brooks.

"Let's go ladies. Y'all didn't need the whole five minutes since y'all were laughing and carrying on."

We were all pretty much finished anyway. A little soap wasn't going to hurt anyone. Franklin went to the sink to try to rinse off some of the soap from her arms and legs. We all snickered. Petty Officer Savage came in and caught her in the act.

"Since you're putting water all over my floors, you have bathroom duty once you're done."

"Yes, Petty Officer," said Franklin terrified that she got caught.

"And since none of your shipmates tried to stop you, they will all be helping."

"Aww man, Franklin," yelled Robertson.

"You should have stopped me then."

"Oh, I'm going to stop you all right."

"Y'all both stop and give me ten," yelled Petty Officer Savage.

She didn't care where you were. If she was irritated with you for any reason, you were going to drop and give her ten. Brooks and I looked at each other trying our hardest not to laugh as we saw two naked women doing push-ups. Only in the navy.

After they were done with their push-ups and we got dressed in our T-shirts and PT shorts, we headed back in for bathroom duty.

"I can't believe we all have to clean the head," Robertson said as she started wiping down the sinks. "I get this one for all motto but nobody told yo crazy ass to try to rinse off in the damn sink."

"I didn't want extra soap on me. It would have made me itchy."

"So use a towel," I said.

"Right, Payton."

We were really pissed that we just got out of the shower and now had to come back in here and clean it up. Franklin had ruined our whole mood. Well she and Petty Officer Savage. We cleaned the head and still found time to get back to laughing and joking about the 028 girls in our barracks. They were a weird bunch. It was as if they took all the weird girls in the world and put them all in one division. They probably thought the same thing about us but we didn't care. All we cared about was killing them in the navy competitions.

When we were done, we headed back to our racks and found our clothes lying on top of our rack. The rest of the division had completed the laundry and separated the clothes. Petty Officer Savage made us put back on our smurf suits until everyone had their uniforms. This wasn't ideal but at least they were clean this time.

It seemed like "lights out" came around quick tonight. We were all in our racks and Petty Officer Savage was nowhere to be found.

"Payton, what are you doing?"

"Trying to sleep. I'm not messing with you, Brooks." Brooks was my partner in crime from Houston, TX. I knew that whatever was going down, she would have my back. She always wanted to talk after the lights went out but I was trying to get some sleep.

"Payton, you're not going to sleep tonight. You're going to stay up with us," said Robertson.

"No, I'm not. I'm tired of doing push-ups for y'all. Now good night."

"Now good night," Robertson said trying to mock me.

We all had a good laugh and managed to fall asleep without anyone getting into trouble.

ECHO

Before we knew it, it was Tuesday and we all had on our day to day uniforms with our dog tags around our neck. It felt so good to finally be out of our smurf suits. We were told that we still had to wear them to PT seeing that the weather kept dropping and today it was like ten degrees. Why in the world would my recruiter send me here during the winter? I'm a southern girl. My body can't handle these temperatures and of course, our petty officers didn't care. To them, it was just another day in Great Lakes, IL. I guess I needed to imagine that I was in Florida on the beach somewhere. Maybe that would take away how cold it was here.

Since we were now into our second week, it seemed like a light switch had turned on. Petty Officers Savage and Smith were now a little nicer than last week and it felt like we had been here for months. We were laughing and joking a lot but were still getting in trouble as well. It was going to take some time to turn us into these sailors they kept talking about.

We were told that today would start the process of training us to become United States sailors and also to prepare us for battle stations. There was that word again—battle stations. It literally scared me to think that I would have to stay here longer if I didn't pass. Yeah, it's a cool place for right now but I knew there was something more that awaited me and I wanted to be a part of that world. One day at a time, Yasmine. One day at a time.

Today we would be going to class. Each class was to teach us something about the navy and how to do things the navy way. We were already learning how to fold clothes and bed sheets at ninety-degree angles, what more could there be? We had come back to the barracks from breakfast to pick up notebooks for class and headed right back out. The training center was, of course, in the front of the base. I don't know whose genius idea it was to put us all the way in the back but they should be fired immediately.

One good thing about being in the back of the base was going through the tunnel. There was this tunnel on our way to everything and every time we entered, we had to sing the second verse of Anchors Aweigh. The first couple of times we did it, no one could remember any of the words to the song, but by Thursday we were about fifty percent there. It was always a treat when we knew we were going in the direction of the tunnel because it was one of the highlights of all this marching.

We all smiled as we neared the tunnel. We had to march in place for a little while as this other group was coming out of the tunnel. We both couldn't fit at the same time so whoever was in the tunnel had to sing loudly to alert whoever was on the other end that a division was coming through. Once they passed us, we headed in. "Anchors Aweigh, my boys, Anchors Aweigh. Farewell to foreign shores, we sail at break of day-ay-ay-ay. Through our last night ashore, drink to the foam. Until we meet once more, here's wishing you a happy voyage home." We normally got to the part of the song, "drink to the foam," before we were all the way out of the tunnel. That was our favorite part.

We got to class and it was the first time that they allowed the girls and guys to be together. Finally, we get to interact with the guys in our division. I wanted to get to know Sanchez a little more. We all took our seats and our instructor walked into the room. He wore a brown uniform and had a gold pin on his collar. We saw people with brown uniforms around the base and they carried themselves like they had power and people acted differently around them. Maybe this wasn't going to be the place to get to know Sanchez after all.

After our petty officers left, the instructor closed the door behind them. "Hello class. I'm Lieutenant Commander McGrady and you will have several classes with me. I am not like your RDCs. I'm not going to fuss or yell at you unless it's warranted and I will follow-up with your RDCs when they return to pick you all up. You will be spending four and a half hours of instruction with me and we will be going over navy history, navy life, and how to become successful once you get into the fleet, meaning once you graduate boot camp and transition into navy life."

Wait a minute? Is this not navy life? Is navy life going to be worse or better than it is right now? Oh, I had plenty of questions but I had to feel him out first.

"This is a place where you can let go of the stress of day-to-day life and relax a little. You'll be able to interact with each other and ask questions. I'm here to help you succeed. You get enough of that other stuff when you leave my classroom. You will have other teachers that may not operate as I do so take full advantage of these classes. Ask whatever questions you have about navy life—the dos and the don'ts. There's much knowledge to be learned here."

We all looked at each other with these weird smiles on our faces. We were waiting to see if he said this was really a joke or if our RDCs came busting in the class with a "gotcha" expression but it seemed to be legit. Finally, some free time while we learn. This was going to be a good class.

"Ok, open your books to page 5. We are going to go over the military alphabets. There will be weekly tests but you have the books with you so there's no reason for any of you to fail."

Military alphabet? Was there a difference from the ones we had known our entire lives? Ok, navy, I think you guys are doing way too much here.

"They are also known as phonetic alphabets. We use them to communicate effectively and to ensure that there are no mishaps in translations. Please see the document in your training manual."

Oh, ok. This is starting to make sense now. So, it's the same alphabets but with meanings behind them like A for Alpha, B for Bravo. I'm already learning that the navy loves acronyms. Now all we have to do is learn all the new jargon.

The class went by fairly quickly. We went over things like how to record the time, when to salute and when not to, and the different levels to achieve in your military career. I even learned that the officer uniforms here are khaki and not brown. Who knew? We got to converse with each other and I got to talk to Sanchez and actually let him know who I was. It wasn't hard though because with our new uniforms, our last names were sewed right above our shirt pocket. Sanchez was a pretty cool dude and very attractive I might add. We were told that our petty officers were actually called RDCs in boot camp but their titles were petty officer. So when we called them by their name we were to use petty officer then their last name but that they were actually considered RDCs for boot camp job purposes. Things were starting to come together and we were only in week two. Guess since we only had a total of eight weeks here, things had to be accelerated. We were beginning to learn why we did things instead of just doing them.

Since we were so used to eating around the clock and now we had classes that could last four to five hours, it felt like we were off our schedule and we were starving. After a while, we started looking at the door to see if our RDCs were coming.

"Ok, recruits. It's time to pack up your things. Your RDCs should be here any moment." With the navy, there was this motto that we were to live by: if you're early, you're on time; if you're on time, then you're late; and if you're late, you may as well don't show up meaning you're in trouble. So we knew that they would be, at least, fifteen minutes early and they were right on time. Lieutenant Commander McGrady walked over to the door to let them in.

"Girls, let's go!" yelled Petty Officer Savage. And off we went. We didn't know why we were being separated because we normally marched with the guys on our way out so we had to be going somewhere else. We marched to this other building and once inside, we were all handed these bags and then we were off to the barracks. What was in these bags? They were medium size bags and not too heavy. I figured that it could only be one thing. I mean all the girls and a private little bag; yeah, had to be feminine products.

We got back to the barracks and were told to put the bags in our lockers and line back up so that we could meet the guys at the galley. Thank God because I was starving. We got to the galley, got out trays, and sat down to eat. By week two, we were able to converse with our shipmates but quietly. We also sat close to division 028. It was nice to get to socialize with the guys every so often. As I was eating, Jones, one of the girls from 028 handed me a piece of paper and said it was from Campbell, who was a guy in division 028. I had seen him staring at me a couple of times but he never had the opportunity to say anything because we never had the opportunity to interact with the guys from 028. I took the note and it read: "Hi Payton. It's Campbell. I just wanted to let you know that I think you're beautiful and I would really like to get to know you. If you want to get to know me, write me back and give it to Jones." I looked around the galley to see if I could locate him and once I did, he just looked at me and smiled. I smiled back. I decided that I would write him a letter. Sanchez and I weren't dating. All we could do was flirt and get to know each other and that is what I was doing.

After a while, it was time to go to another class. On the way there, we had to go back through the tunnel. When we got to the entrance, we all smiled and started yelling, "Anchors Aweigh, my boys, Anchors Aweigh." We loved that tunnel. Besides, it was week two and we didn't have many highlights in our world. The tunnel was it and we took full advantage of it whenever we could.

When we got to class, we thought we would have another cool teacher like Lieutenant Commander McGrady but nope. We got Lieutenant Lewis and boy was he boring. I didn't know how we were going to get through his class. We had just eaten lunch and now we had to listen to someone who dragged out every word. This was the equivalent to torture. He should be used by the enemy forces. He could bore us into submission. Halfway through his class, a couple of people fell asleep and were snoring so he walked over to their desk and said, "Excuse me. Excuse me! But you are sleeping in my class." As if they weren't already aware. "I need you to stand up in the back of the classroom with your training material in your hand until it's time for you to leave." He had three people standing up in the back of the classroom and they were still trying to fight against closing their eyes. This guy should have been first and Lieutenant Commander McGrady after lunch. He would have probably let us sleep in shifts. We only had one hour to go but it felt like five.

As I was sitting there dosing off, Wright passed me a letter. I looked over at him as to say, "Who is this from?" He motioned over to Sanchez. I smiled and read the letter which read, "I heard that Campbell wrote you a letter and he's trying to talk to you. That guy is trash and you want to stay away from him. I know how he is since he is in our barracks and he is no good. You're too good for him." I was perplexed. How did he know I got a letter from Campbell? What I didn't want was to be in the middle of any mess between these guys. All we were doing was talking to each other. We couldn't hold hands or go out on a date or anything. He just needed to calm down. I took a piece of blank paper from my training manual and decided to write him back. "Hi Sanchez. Thank you for the warning. But there's nothing going on between us." And I left it at that. I didn't feel the need to explain myself any further because I wasn't tied down to either of them. I was single, away from home, and didn't have my parents breathing down my neck telling me what I could and could not do. I was free and I was going to enjoy every minute of it. I passed the note back over to Wright and he passed it to Sanchez. He read the note, looked at me, and smiled.

Before you knew it, our RDCs were back to pick us up. They didn't have to tell us to grab our things because we all hurried to grab them, rushed to the door, and lined up. Our RDCs looked at each other and then us and smiled. When we got outside, we were told we had to go back to the barracks because the galley was full at the moment and we had to wait until it cleared out a bit.

Petty Officer Smith looked at us and said, "How was the class, Robertson?"

"It was great, Petty Officer Smith."

"Honestly?"

"No. That was the most boring class I've ever taken."

We all busted out in laughter.

"All of our classes should be taught by Lieutenant Commander McGrady," said Wright.

"Yeah," we all said in unison.

"Well too bad. You can't pick your instructor just like you can't pick when you wake up," said Petty Officer Smith with a chuckle.

"All right. Let's go home. Rogers, lead us in cadence."

Rogers was one of the RDCs kiss-ups. Everywhere they went, he was right by their side. If someone did something they weren't supposed to do, you could guarantee that Rogers was going to tell. He was a suck-up and a snitch and no one liked him but he was our shipmate and if anyone outside of our division messed with him, they would have to deal with all of us. We were family now, whether we liked it or not.

Rogers started the cadence and we repeated after him.

"Everywhere we go-o."

"Everywhere we go-o."

"People wanna know-o."

"People wanna know-o."

"Who we are."

"Who we are."

"So we tell them."

"So we tell them."

"We're not the Army."

"We're not the Army."

"The backpackin' Army."

"The backpackin' Army."

"We're not the Air Force."

"We're not the Air Force."

"The low flyin' Air Force."

"The low flyin' Air Force."

"We're not the Mo-rines."

"We're not the Mo-rines."

"They don't even look mean."

"They don't even look mean."

"We're not the Coast Guard."

"We're not the Coast Guard."

"They don't even work hard."

"They don't even work hard."

"We are the Navy."

"We are the Navy."

"The world's greatest Navy."

"The world's greatest Navy."

"The mighty-mighty Navy."

"The mighty-mighty Navy."

"The mighty-mighty Navy." We repeated this all the way to our barracks except, of course, when we got to the tunnel. It was really starting to feel like we were actually a part of the navy.

We got back to our barracks and had some time to kill. The girls went upstairs, while the boys stayed downstairs. Once we got to our racks, we stood at attention. "Recruits, take the items out of your bags that you received today and put them in the second drawer of your lockers." We opened the bag and I smiled. It was feminine products and just like Petty Officer Savage had said last week, it seemed like all of our cycles were beginning to sync up because some girls were supposed to have started theirs last week and didn't and mine was set to start next week. It's funny how the same daily routine can sync a group of women together. I thought it was so crazy when she mentioned it but here we were. As we were putting our things away, we got to talking.

"Payton, what are you doing with those two boys?"

"I'm not doing anything with them, Brooks. All I'm doing is talking."

"Mmhmm."

"We all are together every moment of every day. How can I possibly do anything with either of them?"

"There is always the laundry room," said Robertson.

"Y'all ain't getting me kicked out of here."

"Yeah. Try the laundry room and see what happens," said Young.

We all looked at each other and busted out laughing. Young was the quiet one from Chattanooga, TN. She never said anything and kept her head down. She had this strong southern accent like she lived in Alabama but had moved to Chattanooga.

"Ooh, you little freak," Brooks shouted. Young just smiled.

"All y'all can leave me alone and go get some business of your own."

"I have some business of my own," said Rudy.

"Who have you been over there talking to, Rudy?" Robertson asked.

"Adams."

"Adams?" we all said.

"Yes, Adams," she said laughing.

None of us could picture it. Rudy was short and Adams was tall like a giant. He would crush this little girl if he tried to hug her but she didn't have to worry about that for a while because we couldn't touch each other anyway.

"Yeah. He's sweet and handsome and really likes me."

"How can he really like you? We've only been here for a week and a couple of days," said Brooks.

"Well, when you know, you just know."

"What I know is that you better slow down with your fast tail. There's plenty of guys that are sweet and handsome. Don't be trying to get married now," I said as I sat on my rack waiting for dinner.

"I'm not trying to get married. I just really like him."

"Hey, we have six more weeks. Like him as much as you can because you don't know where they are sending you from here," Robertson said as she threw the menstrual pad box at Rudy.

"Yeah, that's true. At least we can write each other."

"Yeah, like Payton over here with her two lovers."

"Lovers?" I laughed. "Not even close. They are just attractive and cool to talk to. That's it. We will all be going our separate ways in six weeks. I'm sure going to miss you crazy ladies."

"Don't start that mess. It's too early," yelled Brooks.

"I know that's right," said Robertson. "We just got here."

"Attention on deck," yelled Brooks when she saw Petty Officer Savage walk in. We all jumped up and stood at attention.

It was finally time to go eat again. The overflow in the galley was going to throw off our sleep schedule. I hope they were planning on taking that into account when it was time for us to wake up but knowing Petty Officer Savage, we will still be waking up at 0400.

We got to the galley and took out seats. Everyone was talking about how boring Lieutenant Lewis was and how we hoped to have Lieutenant Commander McGrady on Thursday. As we were talking, Jones handed me another note. I knew I needed to read it now because I didn't want to get caught with any contraband in my locker. I opened the letter and it read, "Hey Payton. Your boy Sanchez has been giving me dirty looks. I'm not sure what's going on with you and him but he better keep his distance. I like you a lot and I'd fight for you." What's going on with these dudes? How did something so simple escalate so quickly? All we were doing was talking here and there and passing notes but they were taking things way too far. I knew right then that I needed to end things with both of them. I didn't want anyone to get into any trouble, most of all, me. I decided to write them both a letter tomorrow and just leave it at that. I had no plans on leaving boot camp with a boyfriend anyway. Sounded like a win-win situation. Before long, we headed back to the barracks and it was lights out.

Wednesday came and went and today we were getting ready for class. We had Lieutenant Commander McGrady today and we were all excited. What would he be teaching us today? I still hadn't written those letters. Wednesday was a busy day and I didn't find time to get it done. We had to get back into our smurf suits and go to the PT building. We learned that we would need to be able to do fifty push-ups and sixty-six sit-ups to pass the PT portion, run all night, go through extreme activities, and swim for battle stations. This was not going to be an easy task because I couldn't even do twenty push-ups. I was able to get to ten because of all the push-ups I've had to do because of getting into trouble. Maybe I needed to get in trouble a little more often.

We spent pretty much all Wednesday doing exercises and it was exhausting. We also learned that at four weeks, we would be getting jobs on the base. Not paying jobs but like extracurricular activities. Assignments would include working in the galley, the PT building, and even the archery building. I didn't know which one I wanted to choose just yet but they all sounded interesting. I was just excited that we got to do something different than marching and class and PT.

Petty Officer Savage arrived to make sure that we were ready to go.

"Attention on deck!" I screamed as we all got in front of our racks and stood at attention.

"At ease ladies," she said as she looked around the room. "Payton, front and center." Everyone's eyes got real big and hoped they weren't next. I walked to the front of the room and stood at attention.

"Yes, Petty Officer."

"Is there something you want to tell me?"

"No, Petty Officer. Why? What have you heard?" I was surely not about to incriminate myself when I had no idea what was going on.

"Don't get smart, Payton. There have been some arguments in the guy's barracks and guess what they have been about? You!"

"Really?" I said acting as if I was shocked, which I actually was because I thought things would have died down by now. Two days had passed since I spoke to either one of them so why were they still arguing.

"Yes, really. If anything is going on, you better end it now."

"There's nothing going on Petty Officer Savage."

"Ok. I'm just issuing you a fair warning. You are dismissed."

I walked back to my rack in disbelief. Why are they arguing about me? They both need to let it go and move on. We had Lieutenant Commander McGrady today, so I planned to talk to Sanchez during class.

We got to class and everyone took their seats. I decided to sit next to Sanchez so we could talk. He started the lesson with an outline of a ship and proceeded to tell us about the different aspects of it—port side, starboard side, the bow, and he went on and on. We had to know this stuff for our major test that we had to take the week of battle stations. I was always good at school work so I knew I had nothing to worry about there so I decided to clear some things up with Sanchez.

"What's going on in the barracks between you and Campbell?"

"What's going on between you and Campbell?"

"Nothing. I just talk to him from time to time as a friend. Nothing more."

"Well, he's telling everybody that you're his girl."

"No, I'm not. I never told him that."

"Well, he's saying you are and I told him you weren't and it started from there."

"You need to end this feud between you two. You both are friends of mine and I'm nobody's girl. Y'all need to learn how to co-exist and just leave this alone."

"But I want you to be my girl."

"What does that even mean right now? We can't go out, can't hold hands, or anything. We are here to do a job and that is to pass boot camp and get on with our navy careers. We all need to focus on what's going on right now and maybe after we graduate, we can keep in touch or end up with the same orders. I don't know but what I do know is this needs to end and it needs to end now"

"Yeah, you're right. I'll try not to argue with him anymore. Will you still write me though? I like getting your letters. It makes me feel like someone cares."

Against my better judgment, I decided to keep writing him. After all, he was still my friend but I just didn't want to be in the middle of any mess between them.

"Yes, I'll still write you with your crazy self."

Sanchez smiled and we went back to paying attention to the lesson.

"Ok, class. One thing I do want to mention is since you guys are closing in on week two, your RDCs will let you know tomorrow or Saturday that you can attend church service. I highly recommend that you go. That's another place where you will be free from getting yelled at and will be able to socialize. RDCs can't even go inside. It's seen as a safe place for recruits. If you have any issues with anyone or just want to talk to someone about your experience, you are free to speak to a chaplain there."

Church sounded like another place to get away from a ton of rules and push-ups for a moment. Yeah, I'm definitely going.

We were all chatting and interacting with Lieutenant Commander McGrady when we saw our RDCs outside the door. Time sure goes by fast in his class and we learn so much about the navy. He was really preparing us for the big test. We made our way to the galley and back to the barracks. We couldn't believe that week two was close to an end. Everyone tried not to think too much about it because we all knew that we would be split up in different parts of the world soon and that was too much to bare right now.

We changed into our PT shorts and T-shirts and commenced the barrack duties. Some had the common areas, while others had the laundry. My group had the head and it seemed like we always had the head. We hated cleaning it because we lived with some nasty females. I would hate to see what their houses looked like. There were dirty panties left behind the toilets, blood in the sink from flossing, I'm hoping, and tampons floating in the toilet. Don't they know you don't flush tampons? I thought only boys were nasty because in our house it was, but even he had to clean up because Dad didn't play that; but here it was a whole other ball game. I wish we could put cameras in there to see who the nasty culprits were, and Petty Officer Savage would make them drop and give them ten but if it was the other girls, then Petty Officer Rodriguez would make them do it. She had the girls in division 028 and she was mean to us. She treated her girls like they were princesses or something and we were mere peasants. So rude because Petty Officer Savage treated everyone the same. She may have been a badass, but she was a fair badass. She carried herself the way we all should carry ourselves: respectfully in a male-dominated career. This was a place where they barked upon the idea that we were all equal, but you could tell that the guys were treated differently than the girls. When we got to talk to the guys, they made it sound like they got to do whatever they wanted. The term nut to butt alone alerted us that this was a man's navy. They got to watch TV for goodness sake. The guys gossiped more than the girls, so it was easy to get information from them, but it was ok. If we did our job and stayed out of trouble, everything would be fine.

After we did our chores, it was time to get dressed and head to the galley for dinner.

"Attention on deck!"

"At ease. It's time to get ready for dinner."

"Petty Officer Savage," I said. "Can we shower first? We just got done with our chores and these nasty females don't know how to take care of themselves."

"You don't have time for that. Besides, taking a shower and going out in twenty-degree weather is not the smartest thing to do but you can put on your smurf suits."

"No, thank you. I'll change."

I didn't mind putting on the smurf suits, but we had just a new set of recruits that were going through their processing days (P-days) and we didn't want to be mistaken for them.

As we were sitting and conversing with our division, we saw the new recruits lining up to gather their trays. They looked terrified. They had just gotten their haircuts and some were rubbing their arms, while others looked like they had just finished crying. Although we were only a week ahead of them, it felt like a lifetime. It's crazy how you feel so advanced within a week. Boot camp was only eight weeks so everything had to be accelerated, which meant that your maturity level would also be accelerated. Boot camp was shaping us into some awesome sailors.

We got up to put our trays away and head back to the barracks. When we passed the newbies, I leaned over to one of the girls and whispered, "It gets better," and gave her a smile. She looked at me with a sigh of relief. Hey, we were all shipmates at this point. I wish someone had said the same thing to me my first time in the galley.

Before we knew it, it was Saturday. We noticed that the weekends had begun to actually feel like the weekend. We were able to socialize more, and we didn't have a long list of things to do except for our chores. We didn't have class, but we did have PT.

"Brooks, you better get those push-ups done this time," said Robertson.

"Man, I'll do as many as I can. You're in the same boat as me."

"Same ship. It's called a ship." We all laughed.

They told us that if we weren't at a certain level by the time we got to week five, we would have to stay back a week because we wouldn't be ready for battle stations. Two of the girls, Brooks and Robertson, were having problems with push-ups, sit-ups, and the run. We had three more weeks to work on it and we went to PT three times a week as well as exercise in our barracks so I was sure they would be good by the time week five rolled around.

"All I know is that we are all graduating together so if y'all need help, just let me know," said Young.

We got her out of her shell and she talked more than ever now. Maybe we should have left her alone after all.

"Right. We are shipmates. One for all and all for one. Hoorah!" I said.

"Hoorah!" everyone repeated.

As we were doing chores and talking, Petty Officer Savage walked in.

"Attention on deck!"

"At ease." She had this look on her face like she needed to tell us some good news but you really couldn't tell because she always had this one mean look on her face. But we noticed that if she had something good to say, she coupled the mean look with a side smile. "You ladies have been doing a good job this week besides Payton," she said smiling.

"Yeah, Payton. She's a trouble starter," said Brooks as the other ladies joined in.

"Oh get out of here. No, I'm not."

"All right. All right. Because y'all have done a good job, y'all have earned a few more privileges. Tomorrow is Sunday and there are a couple of services that you can attend. They will all be in the chapel and start at 0900. There are different services depending on your religion and they will take place in breakout sessions within the chapel. You are free to go."

We all looked at each other and smiled because of what Lieutenant Commander McGrady said earlier in class. He was right and we were all going. Well some of us, that is. There were a couple of girls in our division that never really took to us. Maybe they didn't want to get in trouble with us or maybe it was because they were friends with the enemy camp: division 028. Traitors! But we didn't care. We were loud and obnoxious just to get on their nerves.

"Also, Sundays will be your relax days. You will be able to write letters home and read the letters you receive. Some of you have already begun to get letters and care packages. You may want to tell your family that you cannot receive care packages. The only things you can receive are letters and I must say that the chips and other food that y'all have been receiving are delicious."

They had the right to open up all of our packages to ensure nothing dangerous or hazardous was being sent to us. Some of the girls were mad about it but I didn't care. I just wanted the mail. To get letters from the outside world was going to be great. I wanted to see who wrote me and what the family was up to.

"Petty Officer Savage," said Young. "How will we write back with no paper or stamps?"

"Good question. We will be going to the navy store today. The NEX is where you can purchase some items. You are being paid while you're in boot camp but you are limited in what you can purchase. Once you get to week four, you will have more liberties in what you can buy, like a perm, because some of y'all look busted." We all laughed because we all knew it was true but neither us nor the guys cared what we looked like at this point because we were the only women they could get close to.

"So, once y'all are done with your chores and putting up these clothes, we will go to lunch and then go pick up some items. You can only get pens, papers, and stamps. Nothing more."

"Yes, Petty Officer." She left, and we went back to work.

"I'm so excited to write to my boyfriend," Torres stated. She was an island girl. I believe she was from Puerto Rico. She and her boyfriend had been together since the seventh grade. How cute. Let's see how this distance would tempt this relationship.

"Girl, you know he has gotten another girlfriend by now," Simpson said.

"No, he hasn't. We're soul mates."

"You know the soul changes what it wants every seven years. It's almost time for a change," Simpson said as she folded her clothes.

"No, it doesn't. Where did you hear that?"

"Ask Jeeves. Jeeves knows everything."

We all laughed knowing that Simpson was crazy and always quoting things she found on the Internet.

"I can't stand you, Simpson."

Those two were hilarious. Torres was so in love and always talked about her boyfriend, Javier. And Simpson was always playing devil's advocate. We definitely had some characters in our division. Nothing like the navy to bring us all together.

Not too long after cleaning up, we headed to the galley where we had lunch then headed to the NEX to pick up our stationery. We had dinner and were in our barracks with the lights out by 1900. For some reason, I wasn't sleepy so I just laid in my rack and stared at the ceiling while the other girls laughed and joked.

"Will y'all hush down there?" someone said from division 028.

"No, but you can," said Brooks.

"Some of us gotta get up in the morning."

"Honey, all of us gotta get up in the morning."

"Even more reason to shut up and go to sleep."

"Come make me shut up."

I guess Petty Officer Rodriguez heard the racket and came in to see what was going on. She was in the office that was in front of the barracks. That's where the petty officers stayed when it was their shift to watch us but I do remember the scary guy when we first got here that said we wouldn't have babysitters. Well, I'm not sure what they call them in boot camp but they sure did feel like the equivalent to a babysitter.

"What's the problem in here, Parker?"

"They won't be quiet down there."

"Is there a problem down there, ladies?"

"No, Petty Officer."

"I didn't think so. Now go to sleep."

"Yes, Petty Officer," we all said snickering.

Petty Officer Rodriquez left and went back in her office.

"Snitches get stitches," Brooks said and we all laughed. Not too long after, we were all asleep.

The next morning came and we all jumped up out of our racks. It was time for church and we were all excited. We got ready in record time and when Petty Officer Savage came in, we were all dressed and in front of our racks standing in attention.

"Attention on deck!"

Petty Officer Savage smiled and walked in between us looking us up and down. We had periodic inspections to make sure that the seams of our shirts were in line with the seam of the zipper of our pants, boots were shined so well you could see your face in them, and our hair was short enough not to touch the collar of our shirts or it was time for the barber.

"Oh, looks like somebody is ready for church. Now if only y'all would get up like this every day." We all smiled still looking straight ahead. "Ok, let's get downstairs so we can head to breakfast."

Just like clockwork, we were in line, gathered our trays, and went down the line grabbing whatever we had for the day and took our seats. We were all talking about going to the chapel and getting to socialize even more. It seemed like the guys were more excited than we were. They heard that we would be there with different divisions and that's how a lot of people were able to meet others and since we could now write each other, all we needed was a last name and division number. Pen pals were now created. Seemed like things were changing for the great.

We nearly swallowed our food so that we could get there as soon as possible. When we saw our RDCs coming, we all jumped up, emptied our trays, and lined up. They just laughed at each other because they already knew why we were so prompt.

We got to the chapel and had to wait on the sidewalk because there were a lot of other divisions waiting to enter. You had the RDCs alerting them of the consequences if they got in there and acted as fools and ours would be no different. In our heads, we were thinking, "Yeah, yeah, yeah. We know. Just let us go!"

Eventually, we were in and seated. We got to sit wherever we wanted. The girls and I sat near the back. Rudy, of course, sat with Adams. I didn't see Sanchez or Campbell, so I stayed in the back. Behind us was another division but we had no idea who they were. The service got underway and we were told that we could talk but quietly. They gave us pocket Bibles and a little notepad and a pencil in case we wanted to take notes. The message was on forgiveness and how forgiveness was more for you than it was for the other person. I had never heard it put that way before and I knew I needed to jot it down. As I was writing, someone tapped me on the shoulder. I turned around and it was this brown-skinned handsome guy with gorgeous teeth. I loved a man with nice teeth. I had braces in high school, so I had straight teeth as well. I looked on his shirt and it said, "Simmons."

"Hey, did you get what he said last? I saw you taking notes, so I figured you did."

"Yes. He said forgiveness is more for you than the other person."

"Ok, thanks."

He leaned back and continued to listen to the service. I turned around and did the same.

An hour had almost passed and soon it would be time for our RDCs to come back and pick us up. I really enjoyed the service and wished it had been longer. Oh well, an hour of time was better than no time at all. I heard someone say, "Division 058" and when I looked around I saw Simmons's row start to get up. Simmons-058. Noted. I looked over at Rudy and Adams and they were just as happy as they could be. Then, I felt another tap on my shoulder. It was Simmons. He handed me a piece of paper, smiled, and left with his division. I opened the piece of paper and it read, "I enjoyed sitting behind you. Hopefully, I get to see you again next week. In the same seat. Simmons-058." I smiled and knew that I would be back next Sunday.

After about fifteen minutes, our division was called and we headed back to our barracks. When we got back, we were told to put on our PT gear. We didn't have PT but we wore our PT gear to lounge around in. We were all happy about having gone to church.

"Rudy, I saw you and Adams," I said changing into my shorts.

"Mmhmm," snickered Robertson as she did the same. Rudy just smiled and put her head down.

"They say ninety percent of relationships that start in boot camp don't last," said Simpson.

"Says who?" said Brooks.

"I'm sure, Jeeves," Robertson said sarcastically.

We all laughed and motioned to Simpson to leave Rudy alone.

"Rudy, this is your life. Do what you feel is right."

"Thanks Payton. I will and this really does feel right."

"Well there you have it."

I didn't tell anyone about Simmons because they were already messing with me about Sanchez and Campbell.

"Attention on deck!"

"At ease. It's mail call ladies. Torres and Young, front and center."

Torres and Young got up and rushed to the front of the aisle. "You two will be handing out the mail and just to let you all know, if your mail is open, it's because it was thick and we had to check it for contraband."

"Yes, Petty Officer," we all said.

Petty Officer Savage left and went back to the office because it was her shift today.

Torres started to hand out her stack and Young followed with hers. Family members must have been writing all along but we couldn't receive them until the second week. Young finally got to me and handed me my pack. Yes! Mail. I had a couple from Lexy, one from Deonte, one from Mom and Dad, and one from Shonice. It felt good to get mail because some girls didn't get any. You didn't know everyone's story or how they decided to come into the navy in the first place. Maybe they came and didn't tell anyone they were coming. Whatever the reason, you could tell they felt left out.

For a while, we were all quiet as we read our letters and responded back. It felt good to have some time to connect to the outside world. I wrote my family back and let them know that I was all right and how navy life, well boot camp life, was so far and how I missed them. I told them to keep writing and to give my address to others in the family. Instead of the tunnel, now church and mail were our highlights.

Tuesday came quick and we were ready for class. We knew on Tuesdays we had Lieutenant Commander McGrady so this was another social hour with work attached. It made learning much easier because we weren't on edge thinking about what we were about to get yelled at for next. We had left the galley for breakfast and headed on to class but we noticed that we turned instead of going straight like our normal route to Lieutenant Commander McGrady's class. We were making a detour, but why? Did the class change location? We would soon find out.

We went to a similar building that was like Lieutenant Commander McGrady's but when we walked into the class, there were ropes all around the room—on the floor, on the walls, and drawings of ropes on the board. There were even ropes on the ceilings. I wonder what we would be learning about today. Oh yeah, ropes. This wasn't Lieutenant Commander McGrady's class so, who would be teaching us today?

"Ok, recruits," said Petty Officer Smith. "We are in week three and in two more weeks, you will be having battle stations. If you want to pass, you will pay attention. If you don't, you will still pay attention. You are not here to distract those that want to pass. So, listen carefully and make us proud." Petty Officers Smith and Savage walked out and then this lieutenant walked in. He was a bit older than the other two lieutenants that we had but he looked like he worked out more. He was full of energy and seemed to enjoy his job. We all stood in the room wherever we could find some space.

"I want you all to line up around the wall, shoulder to shoulder." We did as we were told, trying to figure out what was about to happen. "Turn to page sixty-three in your training manuals. Today we will be going over the different types of ropes and knots. There are many out there but I will be teaching you the ones that you will need to know for your test and battle stations. By the way, I'm Lieutenant Baker. I'm your lieutenant, not your buddy. You will have several classes with me. If you have a question, I can help. If you're late for my class, I cannot. I don't want to hear your sob stories. If you're late, don't bother knocking on the door. Pull out your book and take a seat outside the door and study."

"Yes, Lieutenant!" we all yelled.

"Good. Looks like y'all have been learning something. Ok, let's get to it. First, we will learn about the different ropes. You see the ropes all around the class? Well, all these ropes serve a different purpose and we will go over each one."

While he was a little scary, his class was a hands-on class and I learned better that way. It seemed that this was going to be a good class. After about an hour, we all took a break and used the head and got water. Sanchez walked up to me with this weird look on his face.

"Hey, how are you?" I asked.

"I'm ok."

"You don't look like it. What's wrong?"

"It's that damn Campbell. He's been running his mouth about you and I don't like it."

"Sanchez, just let it go. He doesn't know anything about me other than what I've told him and I haven't told him anything I wouldn't tell anyone else."

"I just don't like him talking about you at all. He's not a good dude. Any information he gets, he turns it into something else."

"Like what?"

"He said that y'all were going to get together for liberty weekend." Now I knew that wasn't true. I wasn't even thinking about liberty weekend. They informed us that after graduation, we would have a weekend all to ourselves. We would get to go wherever we wanted from 1700 that Friday to 1900 that Sunday. We could go off base or stay on base, but we just had to be back at our barracks by 1900. I still had questions about liberty weekend so I know I hadn't told anyone that I'd be spending it with them.

"I never told him that."

"I know but this is what he does. He lies and spins things and has everyone thinking the wrong things."

"Just forget about him. He can talk all he wants but the truth will prevail. You know that."

"Yeah, I know but I still don't like it."

I didn't know what else to say. Nothing that I said would change his mind. All I could do was reassure him that nothing was happening between Campbell and me on liberty weekend, but it looked like he was still in his thoughts and he was pondering something. I just didn't know what.

Fifteen minutes had passed, and Lieutenant Baker called us all back in to continue with the lesson.

"Now we are going to learn about the different knots that we tie on the ship. All of you will be stationed on a ship so you will need to know what knots are used at what time point. The first two we will learn how to tie are called the noose and the Duncan knot. They look similar but are tied differently. These knots are used for..."

He was talking but I blacked out after I heard the word noose. Why are they teaching us how to tie a noose knot? And what in the world would we need to use one for in the navy? Growing up we learned that the noose knot was used to hang ancestors and it related to death and torture for our community, but we are here learning how to tie one. I couldn't believe my eyes or ears. He continued to describe how the knots were used on the ship and their purposes but if they are hundreds of knots out there, why hasn't this one been eliminated?

I came out of my trance as he was handing us our ropes so that we could practice tying the knot ourselves. We had to learn how to tie the knot to pass boot camp, so I didn't feel like I had a choice. I had to tie it and I had to do it right. It felt like a piece of me had died when I told Lieutenant Baker that I was done, and he said good job. Although we were tying these knots to use on the ship, it felt like I had just tied one for one of my ancestors that was next in line.

The rest of the class was a blur. I couldn't get my mind around their choice of knots and I dared not ask about it in fear of getting kicked out. It was something that I had to mentally and emotionally get through, but I wouldn't get through it today.

Our RDCs showed up and I was relieved that it was time to go. Some shipmates felt the same, I could tell, while others did as they were told not thinking twice. I wonder what would have happened if we had a discussion about the noose. Who was for it and who was against it? At that moment, it didn't matter. We all had one goal in mind and that was to pass and graduate boot camp.

We got to the galley and were able to finally talk about what had just happened.

"A noose, really?" said Brooks.

"Exactly! What were they thinking?" I said.

"I wanted to say something, but I knew I was going to get in trouble," Young said.

"My eyes got so big when I saw that knot. I couldn't believe they were teaching us this," said Robertson.

"Yeah, they were trying to educate us all right but there's always a way to introduce a topic like that. Don't just introduce it like you have no idea what we are all thinking. Take it all into consideration and speak on it. Yes, you don't want to make us feel divided, but you chose the knot. The division was already set. I understand that the military may have started off one color but now we are a very colorful bunch and their training needs to be adjusted as such."

"That's so true, Payton," said Young.

"I heard that over eighty-five percent."

"Oh, be quiet Simpson," we all yelled and laughed because we knew she was about to give us some sort of statistics from Ask Jeeves.

As we were laughing and talking, someone passed me a letter. It was from Campbell. I didn't want to be involved in any more drama and today certainly wasn't the day, so I bawled up the letter and put it on my half-finished tray.

After about five more minutes, it was time to head to PT but first we had to go back to the barracks and change. PT was a little harder this time because they were adding running into the equation. I was fine with the push-ups and sit-ups, but the running was kicking my butt. Where I'm from, the only time you took off running was if a group of people all took off running at the same time. You ran and asked questions later but other than that, there was no need for running. Today's PT consisted of relay races, pull-ups, sit-ups, push-ups, eight-count bodybuilders, and rope climbs. They were preparing us for war and by the time boot camp was over, we'd clearly be ready. Every so often, I'd look over at Brooks and Robertson to see how they were doing. They were still struggling a little, but it looked like they were improving. I hope they got their levels up and were able to graduate with us. Only time would tell.

Afterward, we headed to the galley for dinner and back to the barracks for showers and lights out. This had been a long day and I was tired. I was ready to hit the rack and start all over tomorrow.

Lights went out and as I was drifting off to sleep, I heard someone call my name.

"Payton, front and center and put on your smurf suit." What? What did I do now? I was asleep. I couldn't have done much. I started playing the day out in my head trying to figure out what I could have possibly done to be woken up and told to put on clothes. I couldn't figure it out, but someone would soon tell me.

Petty Officer Savage led me down to the boy's barracks. I had never been down there before, but you could tell it was where the boys stayed because it had this distinct order of funk. Why was I down here and this late at night?

"I'll be right back," Petty Officer Savage said. Where was she going and why was she leaving me down here with them?

I looked straight ahead and was looking into the office that the male RDCs stayed in when they had watch.

"Come in, Payton," Petty Officer Collins said. Petty Officer Collins was the male RDC for division 028. He was on watch tonight while Petty Officer Smith was out. I walked into the office and stood at attention.

"At ease, recruit. I'm not sure if you've heard but there was an incident that happened tonight, and your name was in the center of it."

Incident? My name! What was going on? I told them to let things go but from the sounds of it, they didn't.

"Sanchez and Campbell got into a fight in the laundry room and they are both in the brig until we get to the bottom of this. Obviously, they had been at odds with each other over you. Did you know anything about this?"

I didn't know how to answer that question. I knew they didn't like each other but I had no idea how much.

"No, Petty Officer." I figured I'd answer the question about the fight instead.

"They said that you were talking to them both."

"They are both my friends, yes, but that's it."

"So, who is to blame here?"

"I don't know, Petty Officer. I told them both that we were just friends and nothing more."

"Did either of them tell you they didn't like the other."

"Yes, Sanchez stated he didn't like Campbell because he was spreading lies about me."

"So, it was Sanchez's fault."

"I wouldn't say that. You asked me a question and I answered it."

From the tone of his questions, it seemed like he was trying to save his own. After all, I never read Campbell's last letter, so I couldn't speculate on what it had said.

"Campbell did say that he would fight for me."

"And why is that?"

"Because he said that Sanchez was giving him dirty looks."

"Oh, really? Ok, that's all I needed to know. You are dismissed."

Shoot! I should have never said anything. I should have just said I didn't know anything and kept it like that. I feared that I said too much and that Sanchez would be the one to get in trouble.

I turned around and went with Petty Officer Savage who had come back downstairs. Once we started up the stairs, Petty Officer Savage stopped me.

"I told you to deal with this and now one of them is about to be disciplined."

"What's going to happen to them?"

"Well once they identify blame, that person will be sent back a week."

"Oh, no! I told them to leave this alone, but they wouldn't listen." I started to tear up.

"You better not cry. Just learn from your mistakes. You have no control over their actions. You can only control your own. Now go get some rest."

We headed back to our section of the barracks. I laid down in my rack and looked up at the ceiling. I couldn't believe that I was in the center of this. I shed a couple of tears and then Petty Officer Smith's voice rung inside my head, "No one cares about your tears, so you better stop that now!" I dried my face and turned over onto my side. I didn't know what was going to happen but I knew I played a part and for that, I was sorry.

The next morning, we got up like it was a normal day. We got into our normal routine and headed to the galley. When we lined up with the guys, I noticed Sanchez wasn't there. What had happened to him? When we got to the galley, I told Rudy to ask Adams what happened to Sanchez. He said, "Sanchez is in the barracks packing up his stuff. They said he was found to be at fault, even though he wasn't because we all saw what happened but Petty Officer Collins said that he received some information that Sanchez was the initiator." I couldn't believe my ears. Petty Officer Collins twisted my words to put all the blame on Sanchez. How could this be happening? I told them both to leave it alone but here we were.

On our way back to the barracks, we saw Sanchez dressed with his seabag on his back and looking mad and sad. I couldn't believe what I was seeing. I wish I could have taken back every word that was said to Petty Officer Collins but it was too late. The damage had already been done.

As we were entering the barracks, we locked eyes. His said, "How could you do this to me?" while mine said, "I'm sorry." They sent him to another division, I heard, the same one that we saw the other day looking terrified. I never wanted to do that to anyone else and I vowed not to talk to anyone else in our division or division 028. Of course, I found out later that Campbell was a jerk and was spreading other lies about me but it was too late now. Sanchez was gone and there was nothing I could do about it.

FOXTROT

By Thursday, we were allowing the situation to die down and continued with our training. Today we would be going to the swimming training building. I wasn't worried about the swimming part because I could swim…a little. If you threw me in the water, I could get out of it, by any means necessary. I figured this would be a breeze.

We arrived at the building and when we entered, the place was dark and cold and there were no windows. There was just this huge pool in the center of the room and a diving board type structure in the back. It looked to be a concrete platform so you wouldn't be bouncing off of it to get into the water, so what were we about to do with that? We were told to go to the head and change into our swimming gear, which we received with our uniforms, and come back and line up shoulder to shoulder near the platform. There were four petty officers in the area to assist in today's training. I assumed they were petty officers because they didn't have on a uniform and in my mind, if I had to guess, they were going to be petty officers.

"Ok, recruits. This is the swimming part of the battle stations. This is where you will learn to tread water, swim a short distance, float, and jump off the platform into the water. In order to pass this level today, you must complete all four exercises. We will be here to help you and check you off. When you get to the top of the platform, you'll go to the edge, two by two. Once at the edge, you'll cross your arms across your chest and step one foot off the edge. Once you're in the water, swim to the buoy then around it before heading to the side of the pool so that you are out of the way of others. You can cheer for your shipmates because they are going to need the extra encouragement during battle stations."

You could tell those that couldn't swim because they looked absolutely terrified. I didn't know what treading water was but I was sure someone would show me how it was done. They told us all to climb up the ladder and wait at the top of the platform. It didn't look that high from the ground but once we climbed up all those stairs it felt like we were twenty feet in the air. "I don't think I can do this," I thought to myself. I was afraid of heights and my biggest fear was falling. In one day, they managed to put them both in the same task. They paired us together so that we jumped in two by two. There were two petty officers in the water to assist us when we jumped in. I was the fifth person to get to the edge of the platform. My partner appeared to be scared too.

"You can go first, Payton."

"No, Robertson. You go on ahead."

"Nah, after you."

"No, no. After you."

"You both better jump soon or I'll get your shipmates to push you in." We heard from below.

I felt someone's hand on my back and flinched. I looked back and it was Young.

"Young, stop playing."

"Then jump. It's really not that high. By the time you step foot off the platform you'll be in the water." Easy for her to say, she wasn't standing on the edge.

I decided to just go for it. My motivation was always to pass boot camp and I wasn't going to let nothing and no one stop me from doing it. I took a deep breath, crossed my arms, and stepped one foot forward. As I was in the air, it felt like my stomach was in my throat. I was so scared but then I felt wet. I was in the water and started swimming toward the buoy. Once around it, I made my way to the side of the pool. I couldn't believe it. I did it! Everyone was cheering. It felt good to conquer my fear. Felt even better that there were people pulling for me to make it—my shipmates.

The majority of us were able to jump in and swim to the buoys, while the others needed assistance because they didn't know how to swim. We still had to tread water and float on our backs. Once I was taught how to do it, it was easy. It turned out to be a fun class and a good thing because I needed something to take my mind off the past couple of days.

When our RDCs arrived, most of us were signed off, while the others had to come back for extra classes before they could get signed off. We all headed to the galley for lunch before going back to the barracks for showers.

While we were in the galley, sitting down minding our business, 028 walked in and sat at the tables behind us. I saw Campbell while he was in line and he had this smirk on his face. As he walked by me he said, "Where's your boy, Sanchez?" Martin jumped up and said, "Don't you talk to her or any other female in our division."

The guys in our division were very protective over us and from the looks of things, they didn't like Campbell either.

"What are you going to do about it, Martin?"

The other guys in our division stood up. "You mess with one of us, you mess with all of us," said Adams.

"Same here," said Wilson from 028.

The petty officers that monitored the galley while the RDCs were away, came over to diffuse the situation but tensions were already really high. Everyone eventually sat down and continued with lunch. When our RDCs got there, the petty officers on duty told them what happened and their faces turned from happy to pure anger. They came over to us and said, "Get up! Let's go!" We all knew we were in trouble but at least we stood up for ourselves as a division.

We got back to the ship thinking the girls would go to their barracks and the boys to theirs but today, there would be a change of plans.

"Ladies, follow the guys," Petty Officer Smith said. We did as we were told.

"Everyone stand in front of a rack and push it to the wall."

Petty Officer Savage stood there while Petty Officer Smith gave the orders. Once the racks were pushed back, we all stood in the front of them at attention.

"So, y'all want to fight, huh?" Wait a minute. No one fought anyone. If we were going to get in trouble for fighting then we should have actually fought them. Petty Officer Smith continued. "This is not what y'all are here to do! Y'all are here to become United States Navy sailors and you can't do that by fighting each other. We fight the enemy, foreign and domestic. No one here is your enemy no matter what division they are in. Understand?!"

"Yes, Petty Officer," we all yelled.

"Since y'all have so much energy, let's see if we can work some of that energy off with some suicides." We all looked at each other perplexed. We didn't know what suicides were but we knew it didn't sound good.

"We are going to start with some eight-count bodybuilders until I tell you to stop. Now get in position and begin. And if you don't count off so that I can hear you, you'll start over!"

We started doing eight-count bodybuilders. We kept doing them and wondered when he was going to tell us to stop. We were on fifteen and hadn't had a break yet. When we got to twenty, he told us to stop.

"Now push-ups until I tell you to stop." Push-ups? Can we get a water break or rest or something? The guys were up to fifty, while the girls were right around twenty or so.

"Now turn around, lock your feet to the bottom of the rack, and start on sit-ups."

Geesh! I see now why this was called suicides. We felt like we were going to die. After the sit-ups, we had to do mountain climbers and then start all over again. We were all tired and moaning. They were literally trying to kill us with exercise. Eventually, I just stopped and laid on the ground.

"Payton, get up!" said Young.

"I can't. I can only do what my body will allow me to do and my body said no more."

Petty Officer Savage was walking up and down the aisle making sure we were doing what we were told. She got to me and had this scowl on her face.

"Payton, what are you doing? No one told you to rest!"

"My body did. I can't do anymore."

Petty Officer Savage looked at me, smiled, and then focused her attention on the entire division. "Ok, recruits. We will be doing eight-count bodybuilders until Payton's body tells her to get up and join you."

Why did she say that? Now everyone was fussing at me, telling me to get up, and threatening me. I didn't want to let my team down but I was beat. Eventually, I found some more strength from my resting and began doing eight-count bodybuilders with the team. I was going slower than everyone else but I was doing them. After about an hour and a half, they let us stop and hydrate.

"Now, if I hear of this happening again, it's going to be even worse. Now pull the racks back up to the tape and ladies head back to your barracks."

There was tape on the floors so that we knew where the racks went during chore days. It allowed all the racks to be aligned with each other. On the way back to our barracks, they were still fussing at me.

"Thanks a lot, Payton," said Young.

"You're welcome."

"We would have been done a long time ago," said Torres.

"How do you know? She just said that because I was resting. We were going to be there all night anyway. Don't fool yourself, Torres."

We got back to our part of the barracks and were told to start shower rotations but this time it would be car wash showers. Car wash? They were always coming up with something new.

We were to get in two lines. Since there were eight shower heads with four on each side, we had a minute at each shower head. The first one was to get wet. The second was to lather and start to wash. The third was to finish washing and the fourth was the rinse off. When Petty Officer Savage said go, we went. A minute sure does go by fast when it's intentional. I hated car wash showers. So many people left with soap all over them. It felt like we only had thirty seconds instead of sixty. We did not like getting in trouble but this wouldn't be the last time.

We finished our shower rotations and made our way back from the galley. We could barely hold our spoons let alone try to eat anything. We wanted lights out to come earlier tonight but it didn't. It was 1900 on the dot just like every other day. We quickly got into our racks and didn't say a word. "It better not happen again," said Petty Officer Savage. We hadn't planned on it happening this time and as long as division 028 left us alone, it wouldn't.

Sunday came quick and it was time for chapel. We were surprised that they allowed us to even go after getting in trouble a couple of days ago. Once inside the chapel, everyone pretty much sat in their same seats from last week, everyone except one person—Simmons. With all the stuff that went on this past week, I had forgotten all about him. This Sunday, instead of sitting behind me, he decided to sit beside me. That was a pleasant surprise. The good thing was that he wasn't in our division or in 028 so I couldn't get him or myself in trouble. For the first time in a while, I felt no pressure.

"Hi." He looked over to view my name on my shirt. "Payton."

I smiled. "Hi, Simmons."

"How has your week been?"

"Long."

"I know the feeling. So where are you from?"

"Atlanta and you?"

"A little city in South Carolina that no one knows about."

"So, you're a country boy, huh?"

"Yes, I am. Is something wrong with that?"

"No, not at all. I like men that work well with their hands."

"That's good to know," he said with a smirk.

"What's that about?" I said smiling.

"What?"

"That smirk."

"Oh nothing. You'll find out in due time."

"Oh, really?"

"Really."

We both smiled and tried to concentrate on this week's topic but my attention was not on the word today.

"So, will you write me?"

"Yeah, if you want me to."

"I wouldn't have asked if I didn't want you to."

"Technically, you didn't ask. The word 'would' signifies an invitation not 'will.'"

"Oh, you wanna be smart?"

I laughed. "I'm just stating facts."

"Well, Ms. Smarty pants. Would you write me?"

"Yes, I would."

"When you write me, I'll have your division number and I'll write you back."

"Ok, sounds good."

We went back to trying to catch up on what we had missed but we were smiling too hard to care.

I looked over at Rudy and there she was, sitting next to Adams. Adams was talking to another guy and then they looked over at me and smiled. What were they up to and what were they talking about? I didn't know but I was going to find out.

After service was over, we went back to the barracks and put on our lounge gear. Thank God they didn't take away our writing privileges because of the galley incident but they did take away this week's long shower that we got to take on Sundays. We could stay in for fifteen minutes if we wanted. I loved long-shower Sundays.

I decided to write Simmons and get more information about him and this little town in South Carolina. "Payton," Rudy said as she walked over to me with paper in her hand. "Adams told me to give this to you. It's from his friend. He said you'd know who it was from."

"Yeah, him and this dude that was sitting next to him during service kept looking at me and smiling. What were they saying?"

"I don't know but I do know that he was asking Adams about the girls in our division and Adams told him about you. He's cute, isn't he?"

"Yes, very."

"Well, here you go."

Rudy walked back over to her pile of letters that she had received from Young. I opened the letter and it read, "Hey cutie. I'm Carter. Adams mentioned you and I wanted to get to know you better. If that's ok, write me back and tell me a little about you and I'll do the same. Thanks love, Carter. Division 054." The first thing that came to mind was, here we go again with these two guys. Why couldn't I meet one at a time? One thing I knew was that I was going to learn from my past mistakes and make sure they both knew that we were

ONLY friends and nothing more. They were in two different divisions so I didn't have to worry about anyone linking them up to me, so I thought. I wrote them both and wrote some letters back home. It felt like things were finally getting back to normal.

After we came back from dinner, Petty Officer Savage said she had some news to share. "As you all are aware, next week is Thanksgiving. Every year, there are families that adopt recruits for Thanksgiving Day. They take as many as they can, feed you, give you time to relax by watching TV, or whatever you want before bringing you back. If you are not on your best behavior this week, you will not go and you'll be here with me eating galley food. Understood?"

"Yes, Petty Officer."

"You have thirty minutes till lights out."

Petty Officer Savage left and we erupted in excitement.

"Did y'all hear that? We get to leave base. Who's running away?" said Brooks with this huge smile on her face.

We all laughed. "Not me because Petty Officer Savage is like a bloodhound. She'll sniff me out," said Robertson as she was acting like she was sniffing on the ground.

"Ain't that the truth," I said.

"I wonder if they allow boys and girls to group up," said Rudy.

"Now you know that ain't about to happen. They are not going to risk anyone getting too relaxed," I said.

"Yeah, you're probably right. Besides, they probably did it before and someone ended up pregnant during graduation."

"I could see that happening. We are in here for eight weeks. That's a long time," said Young as she was preparing to get in her rack.

"See. Freak," said Brooks messing with Young.

We all laughed and prepared for bed. We had something great to look forward to and no one was going to mess up this opportunity.

When Wednesday came, everyone was still on their best behavior. We had class on Tuesday with Lieutenant Commander McGrady to prepare us more for our test and Lieutenant Lewis that afternoon to prepare us for how not to fall asleep during watch. It was a struggle to stay awake in his class and nothing had changed. Instead of him telling us to stand in the back of the class, when we felt ourselves falling to sleep, we just got up and stood in the back ourselves.

We were on our way to another training facility when it started snowing. It snowed off and on the whole time that we were there but this time seemed different. Maybe it was because we were all happy that Thanksgiving was the next day or we were half the way through boot camp. Whatever it was, we were all smiles and radiating good vibes.

All of a sudden, there was a scream.

"Ahhh!"

"Everybody stop!" yelled Petty Officer Savage.

We all stopped in our tracks.

"Who was that?!" yelled Petty Officer Savage.

"Sorry Petty Officer but there's a snowflake." I had never seen an actual snowflake before. I was from the South so the closest thing I ever got to a snowflake was cutting them out of white construction paper but there it was; so beautiful and right in front of my face. Everyone laughed as they looked back at me.

"Since you are so fascinated with what's coming out of the sky, how about you become fascinated with where it lands. Drop and give me twenty."

That scream caught me off guard but the consequences did not. Today, giving her twenty was well worth it.

We arrived at the new facility and when we entered, we were all amazed. It was like an actual ship but inside of a building. What a wonderful way to start our Thanksgiving festivities.

"Ok, recruits. Pay attention because everything you learn here will be done once you get to your permanent duty stations," said Petty Officer Smith. We were definitely going to pay attention because this was the coolest thing we had seen since we had been here.

"We'll be back. Y'all better stay on your best behavior. Thanksgiving is tomorrow and we can still make you stay here," Petty Officer Savage said as she walked out the door.

"Ok, recruits. I'm Lieutenant Clark and today you will be learning how to board a ship, leave a ship, how to operate during watch hours, how to tie the ship up when you get into port, and how to get underway. Make sure you pay attention to every detail because all of these will be needed during battle stations." They were serious about these battle stations. We heard that word almost five times per week. The closer we got to it, the more excited we became. We were almost ready and we were all going to pass.

We learned so much during the training and it was more like exercising because those ropes were heavy. I hope they didn't expect us to lift them by ourselves when we were in port. This would need to be a team effort except, of course, for Petty Officers Smith and Savage. They were freakishly strong and the exception to the rule. We worked up a pretty big appetite and when our RDCs got there, there was another division coming in with them but we still had to exit the ship the correct way or he wouldn't clear us to exit.

We got to the galley and they had Thanksgiving food mixed in with other types of food. They had dressing, collard greens, ham, turkey, cranberry sauce, pizza, fries, and hot dogs. I guess it was for those that didn't enjoy the traditional holiday meal. I enjoyed Thanksgiving food but this was nothing like what my family made. Everything here was bland and dry. At least we had tomorrow to look forward to and it couldn't come soon enough.

After we were done, we headed back to the barracks. We had an hour and thirty minutes before lights out so everyone got their showers and prepared to get in their racks. About five minutes after lights out, Brooks screamed, "Turkey on deck!" We all busted out into laughter.

"Brooks, don't be getting us into trouble. We got a big day tomorrow," I said.

"I know but I had to do it." We were all still laughing until we heard one of the girls in 028 clear her throat.

"You should get some water for that," Brooks said and we laughed some more.

Once we quieted down and started to drift off to sleep, we heard a big crunch.

"Who was that?" said Robertson. "Somebody is eating an apple."

"Sorry, I was hungry." It was Simpson.

"How did you get an apple out of the galley and into the barracks without anyone knowing it?" I said. We weren't allowed to take any food out of the galley and if we did, we would be in major trouble. And seeing that we were always in trouble, no one dared to take food from the galley.

"No one really pays attention to me. Y'all are the ones who are always getting in trouble. I take food all the time but it's normally something quieter."

"Thief on deck!" screamed Brooks and we all laughed. I was going to miss these girls. We were halfway through and I had a feeling that the next couple of weeks were going to fly by.

When morning came, we were all excited and ready to go. We got to wear our dress blues to meet up with the families that would be adopting us for the day. Earlier in the week, we were able to go to the NEX and get some things for our hair. Everyone made sure they were really cute for their adopted family. We weren't set to head out until 1400 but we were getting ready ahead of time.

When 1400 arrived, we were informed that we had to march all the way to the front of the base to get on the bus that would take us to this high school auditorium where our adopted families would come pick us up. When they announced what divisions would be riding together, I just smiled. We were riding with Carter's division. Looks like I get to see him before Sunday. We marched to the front of the base and loaded onto the buses.

"Girls to one seat and boys to another," yelled Petty Officer Walker. He was one of the chaperones for the Thanksgiving ride since our RDCs had to stay on the base with the troublemakers. Rudy and I sat together and Adams and Carter sat behind us. Carter smiled when he saw us.

"Hey beautiful."

"Hey Carter. How have you been?"

"I've been good but better now that I get to see you."

"Oh, really," I said smiling.

"Yes, really. You don't believe me?"

"Yeah, I believe you."

"You two are going to get on my nerves."

"Um, this is your doing, Adams. You are the one that set this up."

"Yeah, don't remind me, Payton."

It was good to be able to get off the base for a while and interact with society again.

We got to the auditorium and they broke us out into groups of four and five. As we suspected, it was girls in one group and guys in another. Our adopted families came and picked us up. Carter smiled and waved as I got in the car to leave. I smiled and waved back.

We stayed with our adopted families for four and a half hours before it was time to return back to the auditorium. We had a lot of fun. Rudy, Torres, Robertson, and I were adopted together. The food was good and they allowed us to use their phones to call our families. That was so nice of them. They told us that this was their third year volunteering and they loved it. They wished us well and headed back home.

Everyone started to arrive at the same time and we all got on the bus and back into our same seat. Only this time, Adam and Carter had changed their seating arrangement. Adam was now near the window and Carter near the aisle. Rudy also sat near the aisle. Once everyone was accounted for we headed back to the base, which would take us thirty minutes to get there. All of a sudden, the bus driver turned the lights off. It was almost pitch black on the bus. I figured I'd take a nap since I was full and it was an hour past lights out. As I was sitting there with my eyes closed, I heard Carter whispering to Rudy, then they secretly switched seats. To my delight, Carter was now sitting next to me. If we got caught, we would be in a world of trouble.

"I just wanted to be near you."

"You're going to get us in trouble."

"If you be quiet, I won't. We will switch back before we get too close to the base. Now sink into your seat a little so no one sees us."

We both sunk down so only the top of our heads were visible. We couldn't stop smiling. Well, I couldn't because I could barely see him. He came a little closer and turned his body toward mine. He put his left hand on my cheek and gave me this nice soft kiss. I couldn't believe he had just kissed me. I immediately looked around to see if anyone had seen what just happened but everyone was either sleeping or doing their own thing. I smiled and kissed him back. It seemed like we were kissing for hours until Rudy tapped him on the shoulder.

"Come on. We're almost back. We have to switch."

"Ok"

He kissed me once more and went back to his seat. I couldn't believe what had just happened but I was sure glad it did.

When we arrived back, the bus driver turned on the lights. It was so bright that it woke up everyone that was sleeping.

"Ok, everybody file out."

We all got up and walked toward the front of the bus. Carter walked behind me and grabbed my hand and he held it until we got off the bus. I had really enjoyed my time with him, as short as it was.

When we got off the bus, Carter winked at me and motioned to write him later. I nodded and we went back to the barracks.

Sunday came around and we were heading to chapel. I was still thinking about Carter and that amazing kiss that we shared. I wrote him a letter and was going to give it to him once I saw him but then I thought about Simmons. I sat in the same spot every service, so was I supposed to change seats now? I decided to take my normal seat and when I sat down, this guy behind me tapped me on the shoulder and handed me a letter. I didn't know this guy but I had seen him with Simmons last Sunday. When I read the letter, I realized it was from Simmons. He said that he had gotten in trouble and that he wasn't going to make it to service but he'd try to come next Sunday. They only had two more weeks left in boot camp and next weekend was liberty weekend for them. He hoped I'd understand if he didn't make it because some of the guys were planning on getting a hotel off the base just to get away for the weekend. He ended the letter saying that he was sorry. I turned around and thanked his friend for the letter and moved over and sat with Rudy. Carter came not too long after and sat next to me and smiled. I gave him the letter that I had written and to my surprise, he had written a letter also. I decided to read mine when we got back to the barracks. I wanted to enjoy the time that I had with him. He kept brushing my hand with his and then would look over at me. I kept my eyes straight ahead because he was not about to get me into any trouble. After being in boot camp for four weeks, it felt good to have physical interaction with a guy without anyone getting into a fight. Carter definitely had my attention.

After service, we gave each other a smile and headed our separate ways. We got back to the barracks and I read his letter: "Hey my love. I know it's only been a couple of days but I've missed you so much. I can't get you out of my head. I know you said that you only wanted to be friends and I respect that but I want to be more than that. I want you to be my shorty. Write me back and let me know how you feel about that. I'll be waiting." All I could do was smile. No matter how much you make your intentions known, after a while it goes in one ear and out the other. What was I going to do with him? He had three more weeks left, Simmons had two, and we had four.

Time was definitely not waiting for anyone but I knew it wasn't time for me to be in a relationship. I sat there and wrote him another letter and told him that I wasn't going anywhere but I also didn't want to be in a relationship right now. I didn't know where the navy was about to send me and I didn't know how long distance would factor in. I hoped he understood.

Letters that were from division to division were delivered two times a week, once on Wednesdays and then on Sundays. I knew he would get it before Sunday and we could talk about it during service. Simmons wasn't going to be at service so we'd have plenty of time to talk.

GOLF

Monday was our first competition with division 028. It was an obstacle course and we had to work together as a team to get through the whole course. We couldn't leave anyone behind and when the last person finished, the clock would stop. We were so amped to beat them because of the bad blood that started pretty much since week two.

We got to the facility and got into position. We would all start at the same time with different people in different places all around the obstacle course. There was a tag team part, a tug of war against division part, and the last part was an entire team effort part. It sounded like mini battle stations.

We were all ready to go and were told that when we heard the gun go off, we were to begin. It got really quiet, then POW! We were off. We were running here, there, and everywhere—climbing, jumping, running, and falling. We worked our butts off. All of the push-ups, sit-ups, and everything else we had done up to this point were helping us with this competition. I guess there was a method to their madness. When we were down to the wire, Brooks and Robertson were lagging behind. We knew that we were now shipmates and the clock wouldn't stop until everyone crossed the finish line. We cheered and screamed. You could see that they were really trying but that they were also very tired. They tried their best but 028 all crossed the finish line ahead of us. We felt defeated because we did our best to beat them but we still knew that we did a good job and we helped Brooks and Robertson across the finish line.

"Next time, tell your fat friends to do more push-ups," Jackson from 028 said as he walked by us.

We were already mad that we lost and here they come with the insults.

"Keep focus, guys. We don't want to do any more suicides, do we?" Adams said.

"I know that's right," said Young.

"Y'all look like a bunch of losers," they taunted as the rest of them walked by. Their RDCs just stood there smiling. Not saying a word.

"Oh, I got something for them," Allen said as he stood up. As more of them were running by, Allen put his foot out and one person fell and two more people fell on top of him. We all started laughing.

"Oh, you think that's funny. How about this?" And Reyes pushed Allen. That's when the brawl broke out. We may not have won the battle but we were winning this war. It took all the petty officers in there and our RDCs to break up the fight.

"Have y'all lost y'all damn minds?" shouted Petty Officer Smith.

"I don't think they've learned anything from those suicides the other day or the speech you gave today," said Petty Officer Savage. "Now line up! I can't even look at y'all right now!" And she walked out.

We knew we were in big trouble this time but it was both divisions and not just two people. What were they going to do with us? Kick us all out? We left and went back to the barracks. Once we got upstairs, we were told to shower and get ready for lunch and so we did.

"What do you think they are going to do to us this time?"

"Suicides times ten. That's what, Young."

"I'm not ready for all of that."

"We don't have a choice in the matter," I said.

Torres joined in, "But we were defending our own and their RDCs just stood there and laughed. They didn't tell them to stop or anything."

"Right and now we get in trouble. We were just protecting our shipmates," said Rudy

"Right," we echoed in agreement.

"I think we should tell them that."

"I agree, Payton," said Rudy and everyone followed. I don't know where this newfound confidence came from but we were not going to take this lying down or shall I say on the ground doing push-ups forever. We were a team and we were going to defend ourselves like one.

We got to the galley and before we walked in, with 028 behind us, we were scolded again.

"Y'all don't deserve to speak today. You go in, get your food, and shut up. Use all that energy to chew!" Petty Officer Savage yelled.

"But…"

Petty Officer Savage ran up to me with her nose almost touching mine. "Payton, now is not the time!"

"Yes, Petty Officer."

We went in and did as we were told. It was so quiet you could hear a cotton drop. Once we got back to the barracks, they made us stand outside for fifteen minutes. When 028 walked up, Petty Officer Smith told their petty officers that he wanted to punish us so the whole division would be in the guy's division until after dinner. Petty Officer Collins and Rodriquez smiled and nodded in agreement. Petty Officer Smith informed Petty Officer Savage of the decision.

"Ladies, go to your racks and get your training manual, a pen and paper, and get back down these stairs ASAP!" We heard Petty Officer Savage loud and clear. We didn't run but we walked swiftly back to our barracks, grabbed what was requested, and headed back downstairs. Once we got downstairs, the guys had already pushed the racks back. Aww man, not again. We were determined to tell her how we felt before they made us do a night of suicides.

After the guys from 028 grabbed their stuff, they headed upstairs. Before they closed the door, Petty Officer Smith and Savage went in on us.

"How dare y'all fight another division? Did we not have this conversation before? Y'all are not kindergartners fighting over no damn toy!" We were all standing at attention listening to them go back and forth. "I can't believe what I just witnessed! This is ridiculous!" All of a sudden, as Petty Officer Savage was walking down the aisle scolding us, she started making funny faces. What was going on with her? I think she has literally lost her mind. Petty Officer Smith was standing in the front of the barracks smiling.

"If I ever see this type of behavior again, I'll send the whole damn division back to week one!" Then she started moving her shoulders like she was dancing to some music. We were all a little perplexed and couldn't help but smile. She motioned for us to sit on the floor. We were all confused at this point. She ended her speech with the same as any other speech, "Do y'all understand?" She put her hands on her ears as to say, "Y'all better shout it out." "Yes, Petty Officer!" we yelled and Petty Officer Smith slammed the door shut.

"Ok, I had to make it sound like y'all were being fussed at. Y'all can't go around fighting people because of what they say. Yeah, that group is a bunch of idiots but you can't sink to their level. Next time just ignore them and walk away because you'd get in big trouble if you did that in the fleet. I actually wanted to join in but I'm sure that would not have gone over well."

What! We weren't in trouble. Thank you Jesus!

"They need their butts beat!" yelled Brooks.

"Right. We were trying to do the right thing but they just kept at it," Young exclaimed.

"I know but we have to show that we are better than they are. No matter what they do to you, you continue to be who you were trained to be and that is United States sailors," said Petty Officer Smith.

"Now, y'all have some downtime. I had y'all go get your training material so that y'all can study as a group and when y'all join back in with 028, y'all better act like y'all just got y'all asses handed to you."

We all smiled and yelled, "Yes, Petty Officer!"

"Starting tomorrow, you will begin working on the base. Battle stations are next Thursday and we will be making sure y'all are ready. Remember, if you don't make it to the end, you will be sent back a week."

I hated hearing that. It just made us more on edge than normal.

"What jobs will we have, Petty Officer?" I asked.

"You'll find out tomorrow," Petty Officer Smith said. "But you still have more training during the week so you'll be working during the day and training during the evening. You won't have much time to study this week so you better get it done in the best way that you can."

"Yes, Petty Officer!" we all screamed as we got back into our training manual.

Before you knew it, it was time for dinner. We all knew we had to look defeated and torn down because we just got "fussed at" for the fight. As we passed by 028, we tried our best not to burst out into laughter but it was so hard. They had these smug looks on their faces and we wanted to finish what we started but we had one goal in mind—to complete battle stations next week.

Tuesday morning came and we had just returned to the barracks from breakfast. The girls had to go down to the boy's barracks in order to receive our work assignments for the rest of the week. Some of us would receive assignments to the galley, gun range, the archery facility, and PT room, while others got the loading dock, medical and dental buildings. We were all interested in where we would end up.

"Ok, listen up. When I call your name, come forward to receive your assignments. Don't ask to switch or go somewhere else because your request will be denied."

We went up one by one and received our assignments. Then it was my turn. "Payton." I walked to the front and took this piece of paper. When I looked at it, it said loading dock. Um, ok. Not sure what I was going to do there but it sounded interesting enough.

As everyone received their assignments, we noticed there were a couple of people that didn't get assignments and Brooks and Robertson were in that group. What did that mean? Did they not have to work this week so that they could catch up on their PT skills? I wanted to know but I would have to wait to ask because it was time to load up and head to our working stations.

"You all will be working up until lunch every day and will be dropped off right after breakfast. After lunch, you will go to training and then dinner, then it will be time for lights out. This week is going to feel extremely accelerated so get ready."

"Yes, Petty Officer."

They grouped us together by working assignment locations. They wanted to make sure everyone got to their assignments on time and since the base was so spread out, it only made sense to group us to make the drop off more effective.

For our group, we got dropped off fifth. Young and I received loading dock duties.

"I wonder what they are going to have us doing this week."

"Me too. I guess we are about to find out, Young."

They took us to the galley but around the back to the loading dock. Next to the loading dock was this little room. There were already two people in the room when we arrived—one recruit and one petty officer. The petty officer came out of the room to greet us and Petty Officer Savage handed us off.

"Here are your new recruits for the week. You won't have any trouble out of them."

"I better not," he said. "Now let me show you what you'll be doing."

As Petty Officer Savage walked away, Young and I looked at her with these puppy dog eyes as to say, "Don't leave us. Take us with you," because this petty officer seemed a bit aggressive. I know they said we couldn't switch assignments but maybe they would reconsider this one time. Soon, Petty Officer Savage was out of sight and we knew it was too late. This was going to be our fate for the rest of the week.

Golf

We turned to the direction of the petty officer and stood at attention. "I'm Petty Officer Hill and y'all can relax. I just do that so they can leave us alone and I can pretend like we have a lot to do. We never have anything to do unless we get a truck that comes in. That's when you will have something to do. When we do get a truck to come in, I'll show you what to do. Until then, chill out and have a seat. There's a heater inside that room and a radio. You can touch the heater but not the radio."

Young and I looked at each other, smiled, and ran into the little room while saying, "Thanks Petty Officer Hill," along the way.

We introduced ourselves to the other recruit that was sitting inside the room.

"Hey, I'm Payton and this is Young. We are in division 027. Are you on work duty as well?"

"Yeah, but I work in the galley. Sometimes, if we have too many people in the galley, I come in here since he has a radio and a heater. They don't mind in the galley. It's pretty laid back around here. I've heard some of the other working assignments are brutal. I guess we got lucky. Oh, by the way, I'm Moore; division 054."

"Division 054? Do you know Carter?" I asked thinking this world is way too small.

"Yes. He's in my division. He's always talking about this girl of his in another division. He said he met her through one of his friends here and they talk at church but he won't tell anyone what her name is."

Oh great. Here we go again. Well at least this time, he's keeping his mouth shut about who I am but I wonder how long that was going to last. I decided not to let her know that I was the mystery girl. Besides, I'm sure I'll hear about it later somehow.

Eventually, Moore went back inside to see if there was anything for her to do and Young and I had the place all to ourselves. It looked like we were going to have an easy job this week. Well except for when a truck came in. Because we were in the back of the galley, Petty Officer Hill would get us food and hot chocolate that was left over from the breakfast rush. It was the greatest job that we could have received for the next four days.

The time seemed to fly by and before you knew it, Petty Officer Savage had arrived to pick us up for lunch. "Now tomorrow, y'all are going to really work. Now get out my face," Petty Officer Hill said trying not to smile.

"Yes, Petty Officer," Young and I said.

As we followed Petty Officer Savage back to the division, she said, "I know y'all didn't do anything today."

"What do you mean, Petty Officer? We worked hard," said Young.

"Y'all must have forgotten. I know everyone around here." We all laughed and joined the division.

After lunch, we were told we had firefighting training. I wasn't sure why if we were living on a ship but we had other trainings that I didn't understand so why not have firefighting training.

When we entered the facility, it was as big on the inside as the training with the interior ship and this training looked like it was going to be even more fun.

"Ok, we will see y'all later. Good luck," Petty Officer Savage said as she and Petty Officer Smith smiled and walked away.

Good luck? What did that mean? We had no idea what was about to happen.

"Ok, recruits. Grab a net and noise cancellation headphones and have a seat on the bleachers." We all did as we were told. "I am Lieutenant Miller and this is Damage Control and Firefighting training. In this two-day course, you will learn the basic skills on how to handle a fire onboard the ship. Many things could happen while you are out to sea and you need to know what to do in case different scenarios were to take place—even enemy fire. This is a two-day training course because there is a lot to cover in a very short amount of time. If you have questions, raise your hand."

No one raised their hands although I'm sure someone had a question.

"Since there are no questions, I will continue. You will all be putting on firefighting gear and will have to work with your shipmates to carry a body through smoke and to safety all while battling a fire. These are tasks that will be a part of your final battle station. As we are going through this training exercise, you better ask questions because you won't be able to ask questions during battle stations. Understood?"

"Yes, Petty Officer."

"Good. Now let's get started. We will break out into groups. There is a petty officer that is in charge of each station. They will tell you about your particular station, help you get on your gear, and help you with the task at hand. A fair warning: I know you all have seen firefighters in your life but you have no idea how hard their jobs are. Today you will get a little taste of it."

Those that were there to assist with the training broke us out into groups and took us to different parts of this makeshift ship. We would all eventually rotate so that we could battle fires and complete other activities at each station.

With our group, our first station was to check and see if a door was hot, open it, and maneuver within the area, which was pitch black. We had to put on air masks and make sure they were sealed properly prior to entering the area. It was very hot inside of the mask. I wondered how firefighters fought actual fires. We didn't even have on all the gear at this point and I was about to pass out. I could tell this was going to be a long day and the words "good luck" kept ringing in my head. I kept looking for what was to come next. Eventually, I would be in total firefighting gear and boy was it heavy. I couldn't even move without someone helping me.

"Let her do it on her own!" yelled Lieutenant Miller. I thought this was a team effort. Why all of a sudden could they not help me? I tried to walk forward but the suit was too heavy and I felt like I was really about to pass out. Maybe I could drag my feet. Nope! Failed! How did they expect little people to move in this suit?

Lieutenant Miller came over and looked me in my face and said, "I don't know how you're going to pass battle stations if you can't move now. You may as well prepare to get sent back a week." Then he walked away. I couldn't believe he walked all the way over to me to discourage me and then walked off. Oh, I was going to move in that suit if it killed me. Even if it was just to walk over and tell him that he was wrong. All of a sudden, strength came from somewhere and I started moving in the suit. I was sweating and straining but I was moving. How dare he tell me what I should do. I pass at everything and battle stations would be no different. When I made it to the other side of our station, our shipmates were cheering. I took off the mask and looked over at Lieutenant Miller. He turned around, looked at me, and smiled. He knew exactly what to do to get us moving and it worked.

We spent the next couple of hours working with the water hose: dragging it upstairs, turning the water on and off, and maneuvering around the ship with all this gear on and other tasks. It was exhausting. Eventually, it was time to take off all the gear, sanitize it, and put it away. As soon as we placed the last water hose in its place, our RDCs were walking through the door. We were glad to see them.

"Did y'all do anything exciting today?" said Petty Officer Savage.

"Yes, lots," we said as we all tried to talk at the same time.

"Ok settle down. Settle down. We can talk about it later. I'm sure tomorrow will be even better. Now we need to go so that y'all can eat, shower, and study. Fall in line." The day was tough but wasn't as tough as Petty Officer Savage made it seem with her "good luck" comment. I was still wondering what she meant by that.

We made our way to the galley, managed to find some energy to eat, and headed back to the barracks. When we got back to the barracks, we saw Robertson and Brooks talking and their lockers were empty.

"Hey, where are y'all going?" said Torres.

"Yeah, what's going on?" followed Young.

"We're getting asmoed," said Robertson as she continued to pack up her things.

"Asmoed for what?" I exclaimed. We had been here together for five weeks. We only had three more to go.

"For our PT results," said Brooks. "They are sending us back a week so that we can pass the PT test."

"No! We started together. We're supposed to finish together!"

"Well, we weren't going to finish together if we didn't pass battle stations anyway. This way, we're not too embarrassed when we don't cross the finish line with y'all."

"But I'm not ready to say goodbye," I yelled almost to tears.

"This isn't goodbye. It's see you later, shipmate. We'll see you in the fleet."

I didn't want to hear that. I wanted them to stay. Yes, I was being selfish but so what. We had created strong bonds and Brooks was my ace-boon-coon. It was going to feel so weird without them being there. Who was going to talk to us all night long and not let us sleep or holler, "turkey on deck," although Thanksgiving was now over? It just didn't feel right and I didn't want them to leave.

Petty Officer Savage came to get them and told them to say their goodbyes. We were taught not to cry so we threatened that if they didn't write us, we would hunt them down. We all had a final laugh before they walked toward Petty Officer Savage, turned around one last time, and waved goodbye. That would be the last time we would see them in boot camp. This was definitely not how I thought this day would end.

Wednesday approached and we found ourselves back on the loading dock, sipping hot chocolate. We were told we should be getting a truck in today. All we could do was sit and wait on it.

"I can't believe they're gone."

"I can't either, Young. It still doesn't feel real. This is crazy."

"I wonder what division they went to."

"Who knows? Hopefully, they'll write and let us know where they are. We still have Sunday service, so maybe we will see them there."

"Yeah, maybe."

As soon as Young said that, we saw this big truck pull up. Petty Officer Hill went to help the driver back up into this small space without hitting anything—most importantly us. Once they had the trucked parked, Petty Officer Hill motioned for us to come out of the room and head toward the back of the truck.

"Ok, recruits. Come see how it's done."

Petty Officer Hill took a forklift and began taking a pallet off the truck. It seemed like the inside of this truck went on for miles. It was full of pallets. How were all these pallets supposed to fit in this galley? After he took about five pallets off the truck, he told the truck driver that he was all done, closed up the back of the truck, and the truck driver took off.

"This truck makes its way throughout the entire base. All pallets are by building. Whenever the truck comes in, you grab your pallets, which will all be loaded together, and unload them into the storage area and that's it. Once they are off the truck and the truck has left, you can begin removing the items from the pallet and putting them up. Follow me so that I can show you where everything goes."

We followed Petty Officer Hill to this storage room. Everything was so neat. All items were stacked according to the group—i.e., food, drinks, supplies, etc.—and within each group, they were organized alphabetically and arranged by height. All items were faced forward so you could see exactly what it was and the first item in each section was perfectly aligned with the edge of the shelf. This was absolutely the most amazing storage room I'd ever seen. I was taking mental pictures because I wanted to do my cabinets this same way when I got to the fleet.

Golf

"Ok, you see how everything is stocked and where everything goes. You can start putting everything away. Work on one pallet at a time together then start on the next. If you have questions, come get me, but you shouldn't have any. See you later." When he left, we looked at each other, looked at these five pallets in front of us, and then looked at each other again.

"I guess we better get started, Young."

"I guess so."

The good thing about working on the pallets was that it made the time fly by. Before we knew it, we had unloaded two and a half pallets. When we went to grab the next item, we saw Petty Officer Savage coming around the corner.

"Let's go, recruits."

"Ok, I'll go tell Petty Officer Hill we're leaving."

I walked out the back door to the little shack off the dock. We started calling the little room a shack because that's what it basically was; a little room with a lot of crap in it where people hung out occasionally. Petty Officer Hill always kept the door open when he was in there. Guess he liked to be cold and warm at the same time. If this was back home, my dad would be fusing at him saying, "Close that damn door! Are you trying to heat the entire neighborhood?" Maybe he was or at least just the loading dock.

"Petty Officer Hill, Petty Officer Savage is here. We will see you tomorrow."

"How many pallets did y'all get completed?"

"Two and a half."

"Well, the other two and a half will see y'all tomorrow."

I smiled and walked away. I guess he figured we were there to work and he didn't want to take that away from us.

We had our lunch and then made our way back to the firefighting station. It was time for round two. When we walked in, we were greeted by Lieutenant Miller.

"Get in your groups from yesterday. For the first half of the day, we are going to be rotating. Whatever you didn't do yesterday, you will do today and the second half well I have a little surprise for you."

We didn't know if that was a good surprise or a bad one. Our RDCs had these weird smiles on their faces so I was guessing it was going to be a bad one. We donned on our firefighting gear and got started. Today we were battling a fire. Each of us got to stand in the front of the hose while everyone else was in the back holding the hose and keeping it steady when the water was released. When it was my turn to stand in front, I was excited; to be able to turn the water on by flipping this metal piece up just looked so exciting when I saw others doing it. So I grabbed the front of the hose and yelled, "Ready!" and flipped it up. The pressure that came from the water itself was so powerful that it took me by surprise. It's one thing when you are holding the hose in the back but it's another when you're in the front. I was about 100 lbs soaking wet with weights on my ankles so there was no way I could have done this by myself. I struggled to flip the switch to the off position when it was time but I got it. It was fun overall and after my turn it was time to go to our next station.

We completed three more stations before it was time for a break and this "surprise" Lieutenant Miller had for us.

"Everyone, put up all the gear, go to the head, and hydrate. You have thirty minutes. When you are done, sit on the bleachers." I didn't know what was up with the navy and these thirty-minute increments. There were other minute intervals that they could have given us but everything had to be done in thirty minutes. I guess this was the navy way.

We all did as we were told and sat down on the bleachers.

"I wonder what we're about to do," said Rudy.

"I don't know but it doesn't sound good."

"That's the same thing I said, Torres." I knew something was up but I didn't have any inclinations as to what it was.

"Ok, looks like we have everyone back. This next part of the training involves terrorist attacks. You never know what will happen or how but we are here to prepare you in case anything does happen. Follow me."

We all looked at each other a little bewildered at where he was about to take us. We ended up going upstairs to this room. On the outside of the room were baskets. Inside these baskets were masks.

"Everyone take a mask and head inside the room."

As we took a mask and headed inside the room, we noticed a trash can on the left side of the door that was outside of the room. Once we all got in, we were lined up in two lines—shoulder to shoulder. When we looked straight ahead, we could see this big glass window that looked into the hallway that we just came from. There were already two people in there when we entered. Once Lieutenant Miller came into the room, one of the guys shut the door and then they both put on their masks.

"Recruits, welcome to the gas chamber."

Gas chamber? What in the world? I didn't quite know what was about to happen because no one told us about this part of boot camp but I was suddenly terrified.

"When you are in a terrorist situation, you have to act fast but also carefully. As you can see, Seaman Jones and Seaman Wilks have on their gas masks. This is how they should look. They are about to come around and help you with yours. After your masks are on, tear gas will fill this room. You will then all remove your masks at the same time. We will go around the room starting at the end closest to my right and you will say your last name and division number, and then you may exit the room. When you exit, you will drop your mask inside the trash can on the outside of the door. It is up to all of you how long you stay in this room, understand?"

"Yes, Lieutenant."

Now, I did my count. I was the ninth person in so those before me better make it quick. One by one, the seamen helped us put on our mask and made sure they were secured. They also informed us how to take off the mask. Once they had been around to everyone in the room, one of them exited the room and placed his mask inside the trash can to show us what we needed to do when we exited. We were all standing there nervously thinking about the next step.

Then it happened. Lieutenant Miller motioned to someone we couldn't see to turn on the tear gas. The gas quickly filled the room and we all just stood there waiting for him to tell us to remove our mask. Will he say it already so we can get this over with? I had never been in a situation where I was introduced to tear gas but I was about to find out just how painful it was. Then he said it. "Remove your masks." We all removed our masks and the tear gas immediately took effect. Everyone started coughing and groaning. Lieutenant Miller with his mask still on, was standing next to Adams and nodded his head for him to start.

"Adams-027." And he ran out and put his mask in the trash can. One by one, they said their last name and division number and ran out. That was until they got to Young. She just kept coughing and moaning. By this time, all of our eyes were shut tight and we were all screaming at her.

"Say it!"

"Hurry up!"

"Say your name!"

Eventually, she was able to get out her name and division number. She ran out and fell on the ground. No one knew she had fallen until they ran out and tripped over her. Lieutenant Miller got to me.

"Pay-Pay-Payton. 027." I ran out like my life depended on it, threw my mask in the trash can, and ran up against the wall. There was a water fountain in the hallway and we were all pushing each other trying to get to the water to put on our faces. Our eyes and noses were burning and we couldn't stop coughing. Snot was running down our faces and people were spitting anywhere they could. They should have changed the name of that room to the torture chamber.

The last person exited the room and those that had been out for a while were handed cold damp towels to rest on their faces. They had us sit in a room down the hall from the gas chamber so that we could rest and continue to catch our breath. Faces were red, eyes puffy, and Young was a little sore from being tripped over. Now I see why Petty Officer Savage said "good luck" yesterday. We all surely needed it.

As we calmed down, Lieutenant Miller came in and stood in front of the class. "Now you all see the effects of tear gas and what you will need to do if you are ever in the presence of it. This stuff is real and is not to be taken lightly. Good job, everyone. You've passed firefighting training."

We were all happy that we passed but couldn't do much celebrating since our eyes were still burning and we were all traumatized over the whole event. I just wanted to lie down and go to sleep. Good thing our RDCs had just shown up.

"So, recruits. How was class?" Petty Officer Savage said with this, "I told ya," look on her face.

Oh, if looks could kill. "Why didn't you warn us?" said Torres.

"Because this was something that you had to experience first-hand. Even if I would have warned you, you wouldn't have been any more prepared than you were today."

Maybe she had a point because if anyone would have told me any of this was going to happen but I'd never actually experienced it, I would have probably thought I could handle it. Like I was superwoman or something but this definitely showed me that I wasn't.

We headed to the galley and then back to our barracks. Lights off came quickly and we all welcomed it. It still felt weird not to have Robertson and Brooks there. I hope they were doing well wherever they were.

I woke up the next morning not feeling that great. I didn't know if it was the gas chamber or being out in the cold but it felt like my body was breaking down. Nevertheless, I got up, got dressed, and headed to breakfast. The good thing about working on the dock was that right after breakfast we could just go to the back and rest in the shack. Once in the back, I was happy to find that we didn't have a truck today and some other recruits put up the other two and a half pallets that we left yesterday. We could rest for four hours and I needed every bit of it.

"Payton, you don't look so good."

"Yeah, I don't feel so good either."

"You think you need to tell someone?"

"Nah, hopefully it'll go away soon."

I tried to tough it out because next week was battle stations and I didn't want to miss anything and have to be held back. Nope! Not going to happen. I was going to work through whatever this was and rest on Sunday. Oh, how I loved Sundays; getting to sleep as long as you want or till 0800, whichever came sooner, take long showers, write letters, and go to service. Sundays were like paradise around here and I was looking forward to it.

After work, we headed to the gun range. This was our final training before our major test and then battle stations. I couldn't believe we were this close to leaving this place. It felt like we had just gotten here. Inside the range, there were individual stalls and we all had to take turns firing. We thought we were going to use real rounds but it was a simulation. Guess they didn't trust us with the real stuff. We had to practice shooting standing up, laying down, and sitting with our legs crossed. We were told that this would also be a part of battle stations and we had to be able to shoot with accuracy in order to pass this round. I found that I was pretty good at shooting—sick and all.

After we all had our turns and passed, we headed back to the barracks and rested until it was time for dinner. By this time, I was sweating and burning up. I felt like I wanted to vomit. I decided to tell Petty Officer Savage since she had duty tonight.

"Petty Officer Savage. I'm not feeling very well. I tried to fight it all day but it feels like its winning."

"You do look like crap, Payton. Here, take this."

She filled out this form, signed her name, and handed it to me.

"Take this to sick call and they'll check you out. You know how to get there?"

"Yes, Petty Officer."

"Can you make it by yourself?"

"I believe I can," I said as I stumbled a little because I got really dizzy all of a sudden.

"I'm going to have Young go with you, just in case."

"Ok, Petty Officer."

She called Young into her office and informed her that I was going to sick call and she was to go with me to make sure I got there ok and to come right back.

"Yes, Petty Officer," she said and we headed out.

It seemed like it took forever to get there. This was not a good day to have our barracks at the end of the base. We finally arrived at sick call and Young headed back to the barracks. I signed in and had my vitals taken. Obviously, they weren't good because they rushed me to the back and sat me in one of the exam rooms. They made me take off my outer shirt and lay on the exam table. Another nurse came in and took my temperature. It read 104. Geesh. I guess I was burning up.

When she left, another one came in with some bags of IV fluids. What in the world was going on? No one said a word. They just kept moving and coming in and out of my room quickly. Once the IVs got started, I got really cold. A nurse came in and saw that I was shivering and brought me a blanket. She told me to rest and I happily obliged. I laid there and next thing you knew, I was fast asleep. I woke up to someone taking my temperature again. It read 102. Sounded like I was getting better and it felt that way too. Maybe I was sleep deprived and just needed to rest.

After the nurse read my temperature, she looked at me. "Payton, I'm nurse Clark. How are you feeling?"

"I'm ok," I said with the little energy I had left.

"Well, you had a 104 temperature and were extremely dehydrated." How was that possible? We were always hydrating. Anytime we marched, we were stopped to hydrate. We ate, we had to hydrate. We exercised, we had to hydrate. I didn't understand how I got dehydrated. She continued, "You also have walking pneumonia. I'm glad you came in when you did. I'm going to give you some more medicine and give you some to take with you. Get some rest. Once your temperature has gone down a little more and you feel up to it, I'm going to release you."

"Ok, thank you."

She left, turned off the light, and I went back to sleep. I woke up to her turning on the light and taking my temperature again. It read, 99. It didn't go back down to 98 but I guess it was ok because she then handed me a piece of paper.

"Payton. It's time to wake up. Your temperature is 99. You are free to go. Make sure you give this to your RDC and take all your medicine. Take your time getting up and I hope you feel better."

She walked out of the room and I laid there for a moment. I tried to get up but I was extremely dizzy so I laid down a bit longer. I started to feel a little bit better so I got up, put on my shirt and coat, and went and sat in the lobby. I figured someone would be coming to take me back to the barracks in a golf cart that I saw people riding around in or something. After about twenty minutes, the nurse walked passed the lobby.

"Payton, are you waiting on something?"

"No. I thought someone was going to come and take me back to the barracks."

"Oh, no. You will have to walk back on your own."

"Oh, ok." I thought it strange to be diagnosed with walking pneumonia and you're making me walk back to the barracks. Yeah, sounds logical to me.

When I got back to the barracks, I read the doctor's note. It stated the same thing the nurse told me and stated I was on bed rest till Monday. That meant that I got to stay in bed all weekend. Yes!

I walked upstairs and handed the note to Petty Officer Savage.

"How do you feel?"

"I feel a little better. She gave me these pills and told me to take them twice a day till Sunday."

She read the note.

"104? I guess you were sick. Ok, go to bed and get some rest."

"Ok, Petty Officer Savage. Thank you."

It was 0200 by the time I got in my rack. I was tired and sleepy and was happy that I got to stay in for the next couple of days.

The next morning, I heard the girls saying, "Get well, Payton," on their way to breakfast. I wanted to respond but I was too weak and couldn't even open my eyes. When they left, I drifted back off to sleep. I woke up to a lot of noise but I was still too weak to move my head quickly toward the sounds that I was hearing. As I opened my eyes with my head still firmly pressed against the pillow, I saw the RDCs tearing up our barracks. They were throwing clothes out of lockers, throwing the mattresses on the floor, putting some mattresses in the bathroom, and were pushing the racks all over the place. I was too tired to care. Petty Officer Smith walked over to me and said, "Don't worry. Your shipmates will clean your stuff up for you. Get some rest." After he said that, they continued to tear the place apart. I didn't know what the divisions did but they were getting in huge trouble for it. I ended up drifting back off to sleep.

"What?!"

"Who did this?"

"Why is everything in the middle of the floor?"

"Why are there mattresses in the shower?"

I woke up to yelling and disbelief. Both 027 and 028 had just come back from their last day at work and found that a tornado came through our barracks.

"Payton, who did this?"

I looked up and barely saw Rudy's face. "It was the RDCs. What did y'all do?"

"We didn't do anything. We just went to work and that's it."

As soon as she said that, all the RDCs from 027 and 028 came into our unit—male and female.

"Attention on deck!" Everyone tried to stand next to their racks the best way that they could.

"Surprise recruits. Yes, there was a tornado that came through your barracks this morning. You didn't really think that the fight that you all had the other day had no repercussions, did you? The navy is not warring against itself. We war against the enemy—foreign and domestic. Your shipmates are your family no matter what division they are in because once you leave this base, there are no divisions. It's one navy. If you don't learn it here, you're not going to learn it anywhere. Now what you're going to do is clean this mess up. You have till dinner. Do you understand?"

"Yes, Petty Officer."

"Division 027, make sure Payton's things are folded and put back up," Petty Officer Savage said as she walked out.

The RDCs left and the girls were livid. All they could do was complain to each other about how unfair it was as they cleaned up the mess. I felt so bad that they had to clean up my things as well but I felt even worse with the walking pneumonia. Eventually, I drifted back off to sleep.

When I woke up, it was dark and no one was there. The barracks were cleaned and everything was back in its place. I assumed everyone went to the galley for dinner; that worked for me. It was quiet and dark so I went back to sleep.

Golf

On Saturday, I was awakened by Petty Officer Savage.

"Payton, you got to get up and eat something."

They had gotten soup, some fruit, and crackers from the galley and someone had filled up my canteen.

"You have to try to gain your strength back. We have battle stations coming up and tests to take. We can't do this without you," the girls said. It felt good having friends that cared about your well-being and wanted you to get better.

I struggled to get off the top rack and sat at one of the tables in the center of the room. It actually felt good to get out of the bed for a little while and eat something. My body definitely needed it and it was the only way I was going to get better by Monday.

"We'll bring you something back from lunch too. You just concentrate on getting better."

"I will. Thank y'all," I said with the little energy I had left.

"You're welcome, Payton."

As I sat there eating my soup, everyone was studying for the exam. I knew I had to get better because I had to have strength for the week ahead. Failing was not an option—sick or not.

After sleeping till lunch and waking up to eat something, I started to feel better. I decided to study a little in my rack while everyone else was studying around the barracks. I felt pretty confident about the test but I was going to take full advantage of this rest time till Monday.

Sunday morning came and instead of going to church, I decided to stay in. I knew Carter would probably be looking for me so I told Rudy to tell him what happened and that I was sorry I wasn't going to be able to see him this week although this would probably be the last time I would get to see him because liberty weekend for their division was next weekend and then he would be graduating. Simmons's liberty weekend was this weekend so he wasn't going to be there either and he graduated next week. I guess it was good getting to know them while I had the chance and now because of this sickness and graduation,

I wouldn't get to see them anymore. But that's life sometimes; brings people into your life and removes them just as quick. I'm sure I was being overly dramatic but that's how it felt.

While some people were at service, others stayed and wrote letters, took showers, and read letters that were passed out from loved ones. I had two letters from Carter and two from Simmons. Since we'd been training all week, we didn't get mail from Wednesday. It was good hearing from them both. Simmons told me where he'd planned on going for liberty weekend. Him and the boys decided to stay out all weekend and hang out in the city. He told me how much he missed messing with me at church, how he missed my smile, and how he hoped that we could keep in contact. He promised to continue to write me for as long as I wanted him to. For some reason, I got the vibe that he was a playboy and that he talked to many other girls, so the line, "as long as you want me to," sounded a little rehearsed. I didn't care though because I wasn't looking for anything serious; sounded like we were both on the same page.

Carter was a totally different story. He was saying pretty much the same thing but in poetry form. He was very poetic and different. He was a gentleman but with spice, if there ever was such a thing. He sparked my interest and was very attentive. Well as much as you could be in boot camp. Maybe it was because we got to spend time together more and because of our little rendezvous on the bus but whatever it was, I liked it and I liked him more than I did Simmons. He was still pushing for us being together but I was still honest with him and with myself. I wasn't ready for a relationship. I just wanted to have fun at this point in my life and I didn't want to hurt anyone with broken promises. I continued to write him back all the while making my intentions very clear but he didn't care. He just wanted to be in my world and I liked him being in it.

After I read my letters and wrote back, I got more studying done. I was starting to feel like my normal self again. I knew that by Monday, I would be back at one hundred percent.

When the girls came back from church, everyone was checking in with me.

"She's studying. She must be feeling better."

"I am, Young; more than yesterday."

"That's good to know because we're going to need you during battle stations. We gotta rock this thing out together."

"Hoorah!" said Rudy. "Oh by the way, Carter looked so devastated when he didn't see you today. I told him what happened and he wrote you this letter during service."

He was so sweet. He was always thinking of me and didn't care who knew it. I opened his letter and it read, "Baby, I'm so sorry you're sick. I wish we were off this base so that I could take care of you. I'd rub your feet and make you some soup. I'd make sure you didn't get out of bed and did whatever you asked me to. I got you boo. I wish I would have seen you this weekend because next weekend I won't be here and then we're graduating but don't worry, I got you. You'll be seeing me again. Love, Carter." He always made me smile whenever I would read his letters because he'd always go off the deep end with his words but a girl likes to be shown that she's needed and wanted and he definitely made it known. I replied back to his letter and made sure it went out with today's mail. I wanted to let him know that his actions were appreciated.

"Payton, you always have two guys at the same time," said Simpson.

"Right. She doesn't know what one at a time means," said Torres laughing.

"Y'all are just jealous. They are just friends, nothing more. I mean, I grew up in the church where it was 900 women to every guy and here we are in boot camp and the ratio is reversed. I'm not ready to be tied down yet."

"Mmmhmm," said Rudy.

"I know you are not talking, Rudy. You're trying to get married straight out of boot camp."

"So, I love him."

"Love?" we all screamed; them more than me because I was still a little weak.

"Yes, love. Adams and I are together and he's the only one I want to be with. I don't care about any other guys. I was brought here at this moment and so was he. It's perfect."

"Ok, say that once you get to your ship and see all these dudes around and see if you feel the same way," said Young.

"I will still. I just know it."

We tried to talk Rudy down off the ledge but she wasn't having it. After all, she and Adams were cute together. Maybe it would last. It wasn't our choice to make. It was hers and Adams and they had already made their decision. We relaxed and studied for the remainder of the night. We knew next week was our make or break it week and we were determined to make it.

HOTEL

We had our PT test on Tuesday and from the looks of it, everyone passed. It seemed that getting in trouble as much as we did made the push-ups and sit-ups a breeze to get through. We had to work in pairs and count off while proctors of the exam were walking by and making sure no one cheated for the other. I guess they didn't have enough proctors for each person so we basically had to do their job for them. I was ok with it because at least I knew the person that would be holding my legs and counting off for me.

Wednesday came and it was test day. We were all loaded into Lieutenant Commander McGrady's class with our pencil and papers faced down. We were all pretty nervous but we had studied the material from front to back and knew we could pass this test. Our RDCs had gone and everyone had used the head and hydrated prior to the start of the test.

"Ok, recruits. You have four hours to take the exam. You won't need the entire four hours if you have been paying attention in all of your classes. If you do end up needing the entire time, well that means you are either over thinking it, which isn't good, or you haven't been paying attention, which also isn't good. Use your time wisely. If you have any questions, raise your hand. You can only use the head when you have turned in your test. I hope everyone passes so that you can enjoy battle stations. Good luck and you may begin."

We all flipped over our papers and began the test. At first, the questions were easy. It went over navy history and how to record time.

Midway through the test, it started to get harder. I couldn't remember all of the insignia and which one went with which person. I was putting so much pressure on myself to get everything correct that I started to freak out. "Calm down, Yasmine. You know this stuff. Just breathe and go one by one. You have four hours and only one hour has passed." A little pep talk always helped me out. I sat there for a moment and tried to remember our training manual and what page the insignias were on. Once I got the picture in my head, I was able to answer the questions with more confidence. I scanned the room to see how everyone was doing. Rudy was smiling and answering her questions while Simpson was biting on her eraser. She looked like she was deep in thought over a question that had her stumped. I wish I could have whispered to her what helped me but then I would be put out of the test for possible cheating so that wasn't an option.

We all continued with our test and at the two-hour mark, people started getting up and handing their tests in. I had two more questions to go and once completed, I got up and turned mine in as well. I noticed that those that were still taking the test, would look up every time someone got up to turn in their test and then they would look at the clock. They didn't want to be one of those people that took the full four hours to take the test because of what Lieutenant Commander McGrady said. Hopefully, they didn't rush the test though because that could be worse than utilizing the full four hours.

Those of us that were done could go use the head or just sit and wait until everyone had completed their test. Rudy and I decided to go take a break since we got done around the same time.

"How did you think the test was, Payton?"

"Harder than I thought it was going to be but I still feel good about it."

"Yeah, same here. There were some things on there that I don't think we went over."

"Or maybe we went over it on the day you were mesmerized by Adams," I said jokingly.

"You could be right," Rudy said laughing.

"Well at least we are done and all we have left is battle stations."

"Yes. Battle stations. I think I'm more nervous about that than the test."

"I think we all are. They talk about it all the time and if we don't pass, we have to stay here longer. I do not want to stay here any longer than I have to. I'm excited to get off this base and see what else the navy has for us."

"Me too, Payton. I'm ready to travel and start my new job."

"Oh yeah. What did you sign up for at MEPS?"

"I got culinary specialist. What about you?"

"Storekeeper. I wanted to do something in the field I went to college for so storekeeper it was."

"I got a couple of options based on my test scores and this one sounded like a good choice. Something that would less likely send me to war when that time came," Rudy said laughing.

"I know that's right. I didn't come in here to fight either but with supply, I'm sure we will be somewhere around the action. Hopefully, we will never get to that point."

"I hope not."

After we got done with our break, we headed back to class. There were still quite a few people still taking the test, so we sat back in our seats and waited until everyone finished. At the three-and-a-half-hour mark, there were about three people still testing. Those of us that were done looked around the room at each other with raised eyebrows thinking about what Lieutenant Commander McGrady said. I really hoped they had paid attention in class since staying back because of this test would be brutal.

The last person turned in their test two minutes before the timer went off. At least they could say they didn't take the full four hours.

"Ok, recruits. Has everyone turned in their exam?" Lieutenant Commander McGrady said as he scanned the room.

"Yes, Lieutenant," we all said.

"Ok, great! Well, I must say that it has been a pleasure teaching each and every one of you. Some of y'all got on my nerves," he said smiling. "But not enough to make me want to throw you out of my class. I wish you good luck on battle stations and an amazing navy career. I hope to see you one day in the fleet."

"Thank you Lieutenant. This class has been great. You are the best teacher that we've had here," said Rudy.

"Thank you Rudy and I will see you all again one day."

After he said that, our RDCs came in the door. It was a bittersweet moment because class time was over and we would never again step foot in his class. Besides battle stations and graduation, our time in boot camp was over. We no longer had jobs on the base and now class was over. It was starting to feel real; real scary as to what would be coming next but we still had a couple of weeks before we came face to face with our orders.

After the test, we headed to lunch and then back to the barracks. The girls headed to the guy's barracks so that we could go over how we felt about the test and what would be coming next.

"So, how was the test?" Petty Officer Smith said as he took one of the chairs from the common area's table and sat in it.

"It was harder than I thought but I still felt confident about it," I said.

"Yeah, I thought it was going to be easier than it was," said Adams.

"That's why we told y'all to study as much as possible and allowed you all to study together. It seems like it's going to be easy when you're in class but once they compile everything into one test, it can be harder. I know y'all like Lieutenant Commander McGrady but McGrady doesn't make the test. He only teaches the material. I'm sure if he created the test, it would have been much easier," said Petty Officer Savage.

"If he had created the test, we would have had five questions," Young said laughing.

We all laughed and agreed. We did feel better that the test was finally over and now we could concentrate on the battle stations alone.

"Ok, recruits. Let's talk about what's going to happen early Thursday morning. You will be waking up early because battle stations will begin at 0200. Everything that you have been training for over the course of boot camp will be tested during battle stations. Because this will be a long and arduous process, you will be hitting the racks early tomorrow. I advise you all to cheer for your shipmates because you all will need it. You will have to jog to each battle station and walking is not permitted. The firefighting station will be the last battle station you will have to endure and this will let you know how many people have fallen off throughout the morning. After battle stations are over, you will have a huge celebration in the galley. There will be all kinds of food waiting for you that you haven't had in a long time—steaks, shrimp, pasta, barbeque chicken, and all. Trust me it's not something you will want to miss out on."

"Petty Officer Savage, what happens to those that don't make it to the firefighting station?"

"They will have two opportunities to complete battle stations with another group next week prior to graduation and if they pass, they will be graduating with you, but if they don't they'll be kept back for a week but don't think about that. You all are in good shape and we have been monitoring your progress over the last four weeks. You all should have no problem passing battle stations. Don't go into it thinking you are going to fail because then you will. Think about all the food you will get when you pass."

We all looked at each other with smiles on our faces but worry in our hearts. This sounded like it was going to be one heck of an obstacle course with dire consequences. We were all about to find out just how much we had learned over these six weeks.

It was Thursday morning and we were awakened to Petty Officer Savage's voice of excitement. "Today is the day, recruits! Let's see what you got!"

We were happy that it was battle stations but were still very sleepy. Although lights off came early, it felt like we had gotten the same amount of sleep. Once we got out of our racks and put on our smurf suits, things started to feel different. We were excited and felt like we just had a shot of espresso or something. We got outside with the guys and got in line.

"Are y'all ready?!" shouted Petty Officer Savage.

"Yes, Petty Officer!" we all shouted back.

"I can't hear you!" shouted Petty Officer Smith.

"Yes, Petty Officer!"

"Are y'all going to pass today?"

"Yes, Petty Officer."

"Well let me hear you!"

"Ahhhh!" we all screamed and shouted and jumped up and down. We were ready to take on the day. It was dark outside and we didn't care who heard us. We were going to pass these battle stations and we were going to do it loudly.

"Rogers, start us off!"

"Here we go!"

"Here we go!"

"Hah hah!"

"Hah hah!"

"Here we go!"

"Here we go!"

"Hah hah!"

"Hah hah!"

We jogged and repeated after Rogers all the way to the first battle station, which was the swimming station. We all were laughing and screaming and just full of joy as we reached the front door. We got inside and changed our clothes. We were told that we were to do the same thing as training only there was a lifeboat in the middle of the pool. We had to climb up the ladder and jump off the platform just like we learned a couple weeks ago. We all did as we were told. We noticed that when our shipmates jumped off the platform and swam toward the lifeboat that something was pulling them down into the water. Um, that was not part of our training. When I jumped off the platform and started swimming toward the lifeboat, someone grabbed my ankle and pulled me under. It caught me off guard and I kicked whoever it was and got away, swam toward the lifeboat, and my shipmates helped me in while someone else was trying to grab my ankle. These were "sharks" that were grabbing us. The petty officers that assisted us during training were now sharks trying to drown us. This showed us that battle stations were not going to be as straight forward as we thought they were going to be and that there were going to be some surprises along the way. Most of us made it to the raft while a couple panicked and had to be led to the side of the pool.

Once we were all done, we got dressed and headed to the next station. Those that got led to the side of the pool were able to continue battle stations with us but would have to repeat the swimming portion next week. We headed over to this other building and walked inside. This one was a little different. It was very dark and there were sounds of exploding bombs and lights that flickered on and off and it was dusty. We had to put on gas masks and crawl around on the ground that felt like there was sand and rocks all over the place and drag this dummy who was supposed to be a fallen shipmate on a stretcher throughout this maze. We had to work in teams because this dummy and stretcher were heavy. We had to take it up this ladder into another crawl space and then down this tunnel and maneuver it down a ladder into safety. It seemed like this station went on forever because there were different stations within this one station. By the time we got to the end, we were all tired and we were only at battle station number two. We were beat and it was only 0430. We had a long way to go. We started jogging to the next station but everyone was so tired.

"Don't y'all quit on me now! We got a long way to go! Let's go recruits!" We heard Petty Officer Savage yelling while we were trying to jog to the next station. Some of us started to walk but then Petty Officer Savage came straight over to us.

"Walking is not an option! Pick up those feet and let's go!" We all started jogging as slowly as we could to show that we were attempting. We completed more stations and then headed to the gun a simulation station. This was the last one before firefighting.

By this time, the sun was up and we all wanted to die. We were tired and hungry and wanted to quit but quitting wasn't an option. Some people had already fallen off because of the jogging and they couldn't keep up. We were trying to cheer for each other but that required energy that we didn't have. Those of us that were still moving forward entered the gun a simulation battle station. This one wasn't as cumbersome as the others, which was a good break from what we had just completed. We went through the station and did everything we had learned during training only this time, instead of shooting at a paper target, we were shooting at terrorists in the woods. This a simulation was pretty cool. I wish we could have done this during training. It would have made it a little more exciting but I was sick during that time so it probably wouldn't have mattered.

After the gun battle station, I had nothing left. I wanted to throw in the towel and just give up. I couldn't jog anymore. My side was hurting and I was tired. I wanted to cry but that wasn't an option. The firefighting station was through the tunnel and behind the building that we were processed in when we first got here. We had been jogging all morning and all over this base. I literally had nothing left. As I neared the tunnel, I started walking. I knew it wasn't permitted but at this point, I didn't care. I was waiting for someone to tell me that I was done and to go sit down but that didn't happen. Instead, I heard someone yelling at me. As they got closer, I recognized the voice: it was Petty Officer Savage. She had jogged with us throughout the whole morning and monitored us during each of the battle stations. I hadn't seen her for a while but all of a sudden, there she was.

"Come on Payton! Let's go! You better not give up now! You're right at the end. Let's go Payton! Stop that walking and pick up your feet!"

"I can't. I'm tired."

"I don't want to hear that word ever come out of your mouth again! Can't is no longer in your vocabulary. Pick up your feet and let's go!"

I attempted to pick up my feet ever so slightly to make it look like I was jogging but that was obviously not good enough. She kept on me. I looked around to see if there was anyone else around me but there wasn't. I was all alone. Where did everyone go? Did they all pass me? Were they behind me? I was too tired to even look behind me. Petty Officer Savage would have probably yelled at me if I tried. She wanted me to move forward and fast. As I got closer to the end of the tunnel, I could hear yelling. Who was yelling now? Who had enough energy to be cheering? Once I got out of the tunnel, I found out whom. They were seamen who were now a part of the navy that were getting ready to get on the bus and go to their duty stations. They had graduated and were off to the fleet. They were all smiling with their dress blues on, seabags on their backs, and paperwork in their hands, and they were cheering me on.

"Come on, recruit! You can do it!"

"Let's go! You're almost there!"

"Don't give up! You got this!"

All I could do was smile. They were right! I could do this! I was almost there and I just needed a little pick me up to finish the race. Their cheers were exactly what I needed. I picked up the pace and started jogging again. The cheers got louder. I felt a tear roll down my cheek. I was happy that I didn't quit. I was going to make it! I was going to pass battle stations. I looked over at Petty Officer Savage and she was still yelling but with a smile. For once in my life, I was glad that she was there.

As I rounded the edge of the last building on base, I could see the opening of the firefighting station. Yes! I made it! It never felt so good to see the opening of a building. Once inside, I saw a lot of people I didn't know. It looked like every division that was processed in the same time we were, had battle stations today. I guess we were all processed in together and we would be processed out together. I spotted Rudy and Young and went to sit next to them on the bleachers. I could tell that a lot of people were missing. As I tried to catch my breath from all the jogging, I could tell that Rudy was worried about something.

"Where is everyone?" I asked Young.

"I don't know. I came in and said the same thing. I was looking for you but didn't see you."

"Yeah, I was about to call it quits. My side hurts and my knees are throbbing," I said as I looked over at Rudy. "What's wrong with you, Rudy?"

"I don't see Adams. Where is he?"

"I'm sure he's coming. There are a lot of people that are still trying to get here. You can hear the seamen out there cheering so you know more people are coming."

"Yeah, but I'm starting to get worried. It's been a long time."

"Look at me. I just got here but I made it. Just give it a little more time."

We all sat there looking at the door to see who all would come and join us. It was weird because the more we sat there, the more energy we felt. Maybe because it was the last station and maybe it was because we were now with our shipmates. Whatever it was, it was definitely needed.

After a while, people started coming into the door. Simpson and Torres came right behind each other and then there was Wright. After about fifteen more minutes, it looked like they were about to get started with the firefighting station. Rudy looked down at her feet trying to hold back tears that were forcing their way down her face, when Young shouted, "Look!"

As Rudy looked up, Martin, Allen, and Adams were all coming in together. It looked like Allen had hurt his ankle somehow and Martin and Adams were helping him in. Talk about shipmates. It was good to see them helping an injured shipmate make it to the last battle station. Rudy's face lit up which somehow made her stand up. She was happy to see him but knew she couldn't show any physical affection toward him. Adams helped Allen to his seat and then went to sit by Rudy.

"I'm sorry I'm late," he said as he nudged Rudy.

"You scared me. I thought you didn't make it."

"And be taken away from you? Not in a million years," he said smiling.

Those two were so cute together. Only time would tell what their fate concealed.

Soon after, the firefighting activities began and we had to break out into groups and line up one behind the other just as we did during training. We were all going to battle a fire and had to rotate front to back. I was glad that this last station wasn't as exhausting as some of the others. I'm sure they knew that we wouldn't have much energy to be battling a fire and climbing up ropes and everything else at the last station.

After the last person was able to turn the hose on and off, the fires all went out, a loud horn blew, and an announcement was made.

"Congratulations. You have all passed battle stations!"

We all let out this huge scream, yelled, ran around, and hugged each other. It was finally over! We had passed! Battle stations had been won! We didn't know what to do with ourselves. It felt so good to hear them say we had passed. Now it was time to eat.

As we continued to celebrate, there was another announcement. "Because you have passed battle stations, you are no longer recruits. You are now seamen. Welcome to the fleet! As you proceed to the exit, you will exchange your recruit ball cap for the one labeled NAVY. Good job! You all should be very proud of yourselves." We all erupted into more screams and cheers. I could see Petty Officers Savage and Smith standing there like two proud parents. We wanted to make sure that everyone knew that our RDCs were awesome and passing battle stations was the loudest way that we could say it.

We all headed over to exchange the recruit ball caps for the navy ones and although they were the same ball caps with different writing, they just felt different. We felt taller, stronger, and more mature in them. We had passed battle stations and you couldn't tell us anything.

We lined up outside and awaited instructions from our RDCs on which galley we were to go to for this feast. There were a handful of galleys on base but we figured we were going to the main one because it was the largest out of all of them.

"Ok, seamen!" yelled Petty Officer Smith. "You guys made me proud today. You deserve the navy ball caps that you are wearing. Now don't let me down. Continue being the sailors we have trained you all to be. You only have two more weeks in boot camp. Let's finish strong!"

"Hoorah!" we all yelled with huge smiles on our faces.

"Ok, shipmates! Let's eat!" yelled Petty Officer Savage.

"Shipmates?" I said.

"Yes, shipmates. You've passed battle stations and now I get to call you shipmates. You are no longer our recruits. You are now one of us. Now let's go eat!"

"Hoorah!" we all said. We were on a high that no one could take away from us. Just to think, a couple of hours ago, I was ready to quit but my shipmate, Petty Officer Savage, wouldn't let it be. It turned out that we had some pretty great petty officers after all but you couldn't tell that six weeks ago.

We were all cheering as we marched to the galley; heads held high and chest poking out. We were seamen now with our navy ball caps on. We arrived at the galley and there were two other divisions that had already gone through so we lined up behind them to see what was on the menu. We couldn't believe our eyes. Any and everything we could have ever wanted was being served—shrimp, pasta, steaks, loaded baked potatoes, and fried fish. They even had an ice cream station and soda. It was definitely a great end to a very grueling day.

As we went down the line grabbing everything we could, I saw a familiar face. It was Sanchez. He was serving in the galley. I was shocked to see him and was at a loss for words.

"Hi, Payton."

"Hi. How have you been?"

"I've been ok. Looks like y'all passed battle stations."

"Yes, we did. I almost didn't but I made it," I said with a smile.

"I knew you would."

"I'm really sorry about everything that happened. I didn't mean to get you into any trouble."

"I know you didn't. Can I still write you? I have some things I want to say and I can't do it here."

"Yes, I'd like that."

"Ok, well enjoy your celebration."

"Thanks and good luck next week."

"Thanks," he said as he smiled and served the person behind me.

It was good seeing him. He looked like he was doing well but I knew he wished he had completed battle stations with us. He should have been with us but life had other plans. I wondered what all he wanted to say. Did he blame me for everything that happened? Did he like his new division? Would he hate me forever? I looked forward to receiving his letter but today I was going to celebrate.

We all got our food and sat down to eat. We were extra loud as we talked about the different stations and how hard it got jogging to every station. I told them how I almost quit and other people had similar stories but we all made it in the end. We couldn't believe that we were no longer going to be called recruits. We had finally passed the ultimate test. We were on our way; our way to the fleet.

After we finished eating, we headed back to the barracks so that we could take showers and relax for the remainder of the day.

Everyone was so full, we just wanted to shower and sleep but they wouldn't let us sleep. We had to stay up till lights out. When we got back to the barracks, we were still pretty excited. Petty Officer Savage came and joked around with us too. She was telling us about Rudy almost passing out, me almost quitting, and Simpson acting like she wanted to crawl instead of jog. We laughed so hard we were crying. It was so cool that Petty Officer Savage now viewed us as shipmates and she treated us as such.

"Ok, ladies. I want to talk to y'all about something."

"Yes, Petty Officer," we said as we tried to calm ourselves down because we noticed the look in her face and it was a look that was changing the atmosphere.

"Now when you get to the fleet, you are going to see some things that you haven't really seen in here. The military has always been a man's career, but every day we are getting more and more ladies to join. That still doesn't mean that they see us as equals because they don't. In their eyes, we will always be the weaker sex; that's why you have to run faster, learn faster, and hold your own. That's why it's important that you don't allow your emotions to get the best of you because there will be plenty of situations where your emotions will be tested. You must stay strong no matter what happens."

It sounded like she was talking in code but we didn't have enough experience to crack the code just yet. We were listening and trying to figure out what she was saying at the same time. You could tell she wanted us to grab ahold of what she was saying behind the words but we didn't have enough information yet.

"Just remember that women need to stick up for each other. You're already going to be competing against the men. You don't need to have women against you as well. You remember in grade school where you learned, no means no. Well, make sure that's engraved into the forefront of your minds because you're going to need it. Now get ready to take your showers." She walked back into her office and we all looked at each other.

"What does she mean by we will need to remember the, 'no means no,' saying?"

"I have no idea Young, but she said it for a reason. There was a lot that she said but didn't say, if you get my drift," I said.

"Yeah, I thought that too. It's as if she couldn't come out and just say it so she had to tell us without actually telling us. I guess we will find out sooner or later what all that meant," said Simpson.

"I guess so," I said.

As we were talking, some people got ready for their shower rotations while others prepared to do the laundry. We had been up all day running and jumping and crawling through sand and rocks. We really needed to wash these clothes and get in the shower as soon as we could but with eight shower heads and around sixty girls combined it was going to take a while. We found out that a couple of people got sent back a week and some were going to be able to complete the station that they failed with the group that was going the following week. It should be easier for them this time around since they wouldn't have to complete the entire battle stations all over again and they had the upper hand because they knew what to expect. We were happy that they got to stay with our group and potentially graduate with us. We didn't need any more people dropping off. We missed Robertson and Brooks and hoped they were doing well in their new division.

We ended up resting practically the whole weekend. Since we were done with our PT test, our written test, and battle stations, we didn't have too much to do. No one wanted to go to chapel on Sunday because we were still a little tired from battle stations. We just decided to write any letters that needed written and read the ones that came in. When I got my batch of letters, I had one from Carter, Simmons, and Sanchez, respectively. I decided to read Sanchez's letter first. I was nervous at first because I had no idea what he would say but no time was like the present.

When I began to read the letter, it was as if I could feel the sincerity in his voice. He apologized for starting the fight and wished he had left the situation alone like I had requested. He also blamed me for getting him into trouble because he said that Petty Officer Collins told him that I said he was jealous and that he was the aggressor, none of which I actually said. He went on and on about how Campbell wasn't a good person and if he wasn't in the military and met him on the streets, things would have been different. He ended the letter wanting to keep in touch and wishing that he could have stayed with our division. I knew I had to write him back to clear my name and let him know that I did not tell Petty Officer Collins anything to that effect. I never liked Petty Officer Collins in the first place and I knew he would twist my words around. I just wished Sanchez would have walked away like I told him to.

I also received a letter from Carter. He told me about graduation and what they were planning for liberty weekend and that he had a surprise for me. Surprise? What was he up to? Was he mailing me something? I didn't have my orders yet so I didn't know where I was going. I couldn't send him my new address, and we only had two weeks left so hopefully whatever he was sending, I would get before we left. I was happy to receive a letter from him, though. I had missed him since I wasn't able to see him last Sunday because I was sick and all we had now were letters. Maybe one day we would see each other again but I wasn't sure when that someday would be.

When Wednesday came, we got to go to the NEX and got some things that we needed for graduation on Friday. The girls got makeup, perms, and curling products while the guys got cologne, hair products, and supplies. Everyone wanted to look their best for their family and loved ones. We even got to use the phone and call home. That was a first. They never let us use the phones. I guess since we were now seamen, we got to live as if this was our duty station for the next week. I called home and talked to my mom about graduation. I knew my family wasn't coming because my mom had never been on a plane before and they weren't going to make the drive all the way up here. I was ok with it. I was just glad that I was graduating.

After we got done at the NEX, we went back to the barracks. The girls permed each other's hair while others did a dry run with the makeup. Everyone was nervous yet excited about graduation.

We heard the ceremony was going to be long and we had to make sure we hydrated prior to the ceremony but not too much that we would have to use the head. We heard some people actually passed out during the ceremony because we had to stand the whole time. Now it seemed that we had something else to look forward to—trying not to pass out during graduation. Just when you thought you were in the clear, you get more information that made you freak out.

Before we knew it, it was Friday—graduation day. We all had our hair done, makeup on, and dressed in our dress blues before heading downstairs to join with the guys. You would have thought Adams had just seen Rudy for the first time. He was mesmerized by her. It's crazy what a little makeup can do. We had already heard the speech about dos and don'ts during the ceremony and that liberty weekend would commence after graduation was over. We were all ready to have a weekend to ourselves. Everyone wasn't leaving the base because some of us didn't have family coming to visit but we still got to enjoy a weekend to do whatever we wanted.

We arrived at the graduation hall and lined up by divisions. Some of our shipmates got to hold the flags that we won during battle stations along with our division 027 flag. We were very proud of our division. There were people standing around making sure we entered the hall at the exact time we were supposed to. Once we walked in, we had to do a marching presentation to present our flags to the guests and then go to our section on the floor and stand at attention until the last division presented their flags. Once they were in position, the officers called us to parade rest and we would stand there for the remainder of the ceremony.

No one told us how long this ceremony was supposed to last. Around two and a half hours, our knees started to buckle and one by one, we began to stumble. We tried to walk in place a little but that only brought about dirty looks from our RDCs. What did they expect us to do? Pass out? If they didn't let us move our legs around, we were definitely going to start dropping like flies. Three and a half hours in, it began to sound like the ceremony was coming to an end. It turned out to be a four-hour ceremony. This felt like it was the longest graduation I had ever been to; maybe because we had to stand up the entire time.

When you're sitting, at least you get to fall asleep a little but you don't have that luxury if you're standing up.

Finally, the commander said his speech and congratulated us all and congratulated the parents on raising navy sailors and then we were dismissed. Of course, we couldn't just run out of the place screaming like we did at battle stations. We had to wait until the lieutenant came over to us and said, "Attention," so that we could all stand at attention, and then yelled, "Dismissed." Some of our shipmates had already identified where their families were and ran to greet them while the rest of us hugged each other and tried to decide what we were doing for the weekend.

"Can y'all believe we are done?"

"Man, it's so surreal right now, Young," I said.

"I know right. What y'all planning on doing this weekend?" said Rudy.

"I have no idea," I said. "My family didn't come because it was too far so I may just hang out in the barracks."

"No. Come with us. My mom is here and she wanted to get us a hotel room for the night. Y'all can come chill in our hotel room with us," said Young.

"Are you sure your mom won't mind."

"Of course not, Rudy. We already talked about it."

"Ok, cool. I'm down," said Rudy.

"Me too," I said. "Where is your mom?"

"She's right over there. Come on so I can introduce y'all to her." We all went to meet Ms. Young and she told us about the hotel room that she just got. She wanted to walk around the base with Young but told us to meet her at the NEX around 5 pm. We all corrected her and said 1700 and just stood there laughing. It was amazing what we had learned in just six weeks.

It was around 1300 when the graduation was over so Rudy and I had some time to kill.

"I thought you would be hanging out with Adams."

"I am but we are hanging out tomorrow. His family came into town and he wanted to spend time with them today and we were going to spend some time with them tomorrow and Sunday."

"Aww, look at y'all. Meeting the parents."

"Yeah, mine didn't come either. I knew they weren't going to come. Once we find out where we are going next week, I'll let them know and maybe they will meet me there if it's closer to home."

"Yeah, my parents are the same way. They aren't going too far from home."

"I think our parents should meet then." We had a good laugh and went to get something to eat at the NEX. The NEX had a phone station as well as this fun center attached to it. You could play pool, darts, and video games or just watch some TV. We decided to hang out there until it was time to go with Young. It felt good to finally be graduates of boot camp. Next week we would get our orders and be on our way. Who knows where we would all end up? All we knew was that we had this weekend and next week because come Friday, we would all be getting bused to different places and start our navy adventure.

At exactly 1645, Young was at the NEX. She had to explain to her mom that she needed to be fifteen minutes early because that would mean that she was on time. Her mom didn't understand but agreed to have her at the NEX by 1645. We all headed out with Young and her mom. We had a lot of fun and ended up having McDonald's for breakfast the next morning. We all got the hotcakes platter and moaned every time we took a bite. We didn't remember their pancakes tasting this good but being in boot camp for 7 weeks made everything on the outside taste one hundred percent better.

Young's mom dropped off Rudy and I around noon on Saturday and we said bye to her and Young. Young was going to stay with her mom until she had to be back on Sunday so Rudy and I headed to the NEX.

I told her I would stay with her until Adams came and picked her up and then I'd head to the barracks.

When we got to the NEX, everyone was there making phone calls, watching TV, and playing pool. We decided to sit at a high top and talk and watch some TV. We didn't know what was going on in the world so it was good to catch up and see what we missed. As we were sitting there talking and having fun, Adams walked up.

"Hey ladies, I mean shipmates. What are y'all up to?

"Nothing. Just hanging out waiting for you to come pick up Rudy so I can go back to the barracks."

"Why are you going back to the barracks?"

"Because I don't have family here and I am not about to be a third wheel with you and Rudy."

"Aw, Payton. You don't have to be a third wheel," said Rudy. "We are all family now."

"Yeah, I get that but I'm sure you guys want to spend some time together and I am not getting in the middle of that."

"Yes, we are going to spend some time together and no I don't want you tagging along but I'm sure someone else wants to spend some time with you," said Adams as he looked over at the door and smiled. I saw someone walking toward our table but I couldn't make out who because of the bright light bouncing from the windows, but as they got closer, this huge smile came across my face. It was Carter. I jumped out of my seat and gave him this big hug. This was liberty weekend so we could show a little affection but not much. He held me so tight like he actually missed me.

"Boy have I missed you," Carter said.

"What are you doing here?"

"Well, I told you I had a surprise for you. I'm your surprise."

"You did a very good job. I can't believe you're here."

"Well believe it and I have a full day planned for us. Are you ready to go?"

"Yeah. What are we doing? Where are we going?"

"Don't you worry about that. Just come with me."

He grabbed my hand and we started to walk toward the door. Adams and Rudy were smiling at us as we told them bye and went on our way. He had a taxi to take us to another base that wasn't that far away.

"When I wrote you, I was on the base here. This is where I am stationed so I knew I would be able to come spend the day with you. I just had to make sure you were at the NEX so that I could come pick you up."

"Oh, so that means Rudy was in on it."

He laughed. "Yes, she was. I told Adams and he knew that you would be with Rudy, so we were all in on it."

"Wow. What a surprise. I'm glad you came to get me. I missed you and because I was sick, I thought I wasn't going to get to see you anymore."

"I know. That's why I had to make this happen. I couldn't take you leaving me without me seeing you at least one more time. I really do have feelings for you and I know you just want to keep this casual but I'm really digging you and I want us to be something more."

"Well, let me think about it. I can't make any promises," I said smiling.

"Yeah, yeah. I know. I heard you loud and clear but I can't help the way that I feel."

"I know and I like it but I just don't want to hurt you."

"And I appreciate that. We will just take it day by day and enjoy the time that we have."

"That sounds good."

We spent the day on the navy base in Great Lakes. It was a different atmosphere than the boot camp base. There were sailors marching around in fatigues and officers walking to and fro. We had to salute when they were in our eyesight. He gave me a tour of the base and we had some lunch. Then, he took me to his barracks and showed me where he would call his home for the next several months as he was here for school. Once his training was completed, he would get orders to his ship or next duty station. He said he had four months of schooling and then he wouldn't know where they would send him next. I didn't know where my schooling was yet or how far it would be from him. All I knew is that I had today with him and I planned on enjoying every minute of it.

We spent the entire day together and he made the day feel like time had stood still. I didn't want to leave him. I just wanted to stay with him until it was time for us to be shipped out but that wasn't an option. I had to get back to the base and because I didn't have to be back until Sunday at 1900, there was no rush for us to get back. We finally got back to the base around 2000 because he didn't want me out too late. We got out of the taxi and he had the taxi driver wait.

"I don't want this night to end."

"I know Payton. Hopefully, we can have more nights like this. Maybe you can come see me and I can come see you. We can make this work. I know we can."

"Oh, Carter. What am I going to do with you?"

"Keep me," he said smiling. He gave me a hug and then kissed me like he never wanted to let me go. We didn't care who saw or who was around. We didn't know if we would ever get this chance again so we took it and I'm glad we did. After our embrace, he looked into my eyes as he gently touched my cheek and then looked away. He got into the taxi, waved goodbye, and then he was gone.

As I walked back to the barracks, I felt really sad. It felt as if I would never see him again. Why did we have to meet here? Why couldn't we have met in the fleet? And, would it have even mattered because you can be separated in the fleet too? Orders change and so do duty stations. It just didn't feel fair but this is what we signed up for. I knew that I could still write him. He had given me his address with his last letter and I could write him from my school and let him know where I was. We could keep in contact just like Rudy and Adams. They seemed to have everything figured out. Rudy's thought process started to make some sense to me. Maybe this could work. Maybe writing letters and going to see each other here and there could actually work out in the end. I was starting to think on the possibility of it but then there was Simmons. He still sparked my interest and I didn't know much about him. He was more of a mystery. I wanted to get to know him too but Carter had this hold on me. I wasn't sure who would win out in the end and I was making no decisions tonight.

When Friday came, we were all standing at the same building where we stood at eight weeks earlier—the processing unit. This is where it all began and where it would all end. It was a bittersweet moment for all of us. No one shed a tear outwardly but I'm sure some of us were crying on the inside, I know I was. These people were now my family, my shipmates, and I didn't want to just leave and never see them again but that was the navy. You never knew where you would end up and who you would meet next. You could only try your hardest to keep in contact and let life happen.

I had received a letter from Sanchez and he apologized for saying things were my fault after he read about how the conversation really went down between Petty Officer Collins and I. He stated he would still write me as long as I wrote him back and he wished me well in the fleet. I received a poem from Carter and a letter from Simmons letting me know where he was stationed—at the Great Lakes base. Life has a funny way of finding humor in all situations. Good thing the base was huge because if it was small, he would have seen Carter and me last Saturday. I don't know why guys come in twos for me. I guess for the sake of options. That and this ridiculous ratio of guys to gals in the military but I'm not complaining.

There were several buses that arrived because some of us were going to different places. Some stayed in Great Lakes and were going to the base that I had visited, while others were going to California, Florida, Texas, or Virginia. To our surprise, Young, Torres, and I were going to Meridian, MS. I was glad that I would have some familiar faces to start this next journey with me. Adams was going to California, while Rudy was going to Florida. They promised to write each other and to see each other any free time they got. I prayed that their love would last because it started so innocently. That's something worth holding on to. Their love was a little different than Torres and Javier's. Although Torres was head over heels in love with Javier, by the time boot camp ended, they decided to take a break for a while. I'm guessing Javier couldn't take the distance or someone else caught his eye. Whatever the reason, Torres had her girls in her corner and we were going to make sure that she was ok. We all said our goodbyes, thanked our RDCs for training us, for keeping us in line, and for teaching us what it meant to be a United States sailor. We were proud of what we had become and it was only up from here.

As we were all loading onto our buses to embark on yet another unknown journey, I thought about all the good times and not so good times that I had on this base. I looked down the road that went from the processing unit all the way down to our barracks and wondered if I had made the right decision. This decision allowed me to meet some amazing people, learn that I had what it took to complete any mission that life threw at me, and that no matter what I thought before, I was not a mistake. I was someone's shipmate and I mattered. They needed me just as much as I needed them and with that, I knew that I had made the right decision. We sat on the bus getting ready to head to the airport when the doors closed shut. I looked out the window one last time to gaze upon the base that had groomed us for the last eight weeks and made us into sailors. I had learned a lot and gained some invaluable friendships that I would take with me wherever I went. I knew that this wasn't the end but only the beginning. The bus driver started the bus and I whispered one last time, "Goodbye boot camp. Thanks for everything."

COMMITMENT

Commit to the decision that you made,
no matter how hard it gets.

INDIA

The journey from boot camp was eventful. Once the bus arrived at the airport and we headed inside, people were clapping and saying, "Thank you for your service." We all smiled and said thank you. Young, Torres, and I looked for the directions to catch our flight to Meridian, MS. Once at the gate, we found three seats together.

"Meridian, MS? I've never heard of this place."

"Me neither, Young. I wonder what the base looks like?" said Torres.

"We will soon find out but it looks like our flight is delayed," I said.

"Well, at least we are away from boot camp. It feels good to finally be in the fleet, whatever that means."

"Right, Young," I said laughing. "They said it all the time but never really explained what would be different once we were in the actual navy. I guess we still won't find out for another six weeks," I said.

Our A-school was six weeks long. We had to go to school to learn the job that we signed up for when we were at MEPS. Because I had already taken some courses toward accounting, I decided to pick a career that would be the equivalent and I chose storekeeper. Young and Torres were going to be yeomen. Since we all were in the administrative field, we went to the same A-school.

Our flight was delayed for about three hours and then we had to fly to Atlanta where the flight was delayed again. My parents came and visited a while since we couldn't go anywhere and our house wasn't too far from the airport. It was good seeing them and hearing about what all was going on with Deonte and Lexy. When we finally boarded the last flight to Meridian, MS, the plane was so small that it made the ride very scary. This had to be a very tiny base if they only had small planes to get there. That meant that not too many people traveled to this part of Mississippi and once we landed, I could see why. The airport was so small that you could see the front door from the back door. It seemed to be one way in and one way out. You could view the entire airport just by standing in the middle of the room. Yes, this was a very small airport and I couldn't image the base being any bigger.

When we got outside of the airport, there was a van there to meet us. There were about fifteen of us that would be training here. We all loaded our seabags and garment bags onto the bus and took our seats. When we arrived at the base, it was 2200. It was dark and very quiet. As we rode through the base to our barracks, we noticed that there was little to no grass around. There was a lot of dirt, though. Young and I looked at each other and smiled. This was going to be a very interesting six weeks.

When we finally arrived, we were led to our barracks which slept three people. It was set up like four rack beds but one of the rack beds had a desk underneath it. We were all happy that we were going to rack with who we came with and didn't have to share a room with anyone else. It was definitely going to be a change from sixty to seventy girls to only three. This navy life seemed to be getting better.

We were informed that there would be a briefing in the morning and that classes would start on Wednesday. They were not wasting any time. This felt like a processing unit as well—get you in, get you trained, and get you into your place in the navy. It was fine by me because I wanted to travel overseas and the sooner I could get that process started the better. We didn't know how they wanted us to put up our things so we decided not to unpack, change into our PT gear, and lay down for the night. We were told that reveille would be at 0600, which was a change from the 0400 we had to do in boot camp. Yeah, things were different here and I could really start to get used to this place.

Reveille at 0600 came quick and we could hear the horn being played from our room. We got up, got dressed in our dress blacks, and headed outside. When we got outside, we noticed that there was a volleyball net with sand in this common area in the middle of the barracks that looked like Motel 6 hotel rooms. The barracks were three stories high and everything was brick, wood, and metal. Since the base wasn't that big, we knew we wouldn't have to walk forever to get anywhere.

We saw others that had arrived at the same time that we did and were walking over to another group of other newcomers, so we decided to follow them. Once we arrived with the others, we chatted for a bit before being called to attention.

"Hello, sailors and welcome to A-school. I am Petty Officer Murray and I will be giving you information about what will be happening over the course of these six weeks. You will have two days for processing and then you will start class on Wednesday. Because you only have six weeks here, things will go by like the blink of an eye. You have to pass your final test in order to graduate and obtain your orders to your next duty station. The weekends are yours to enjoy unless you have watch. You will have from Friday at 1700 to Sunday at 1900. If you are not in your rooms by 1900, you will be considered AWOL [Absent Without Official Leave]. If you are AWOL, you will be put on restriction and you will not be able to go anywhere. If you live close, you can bring your personal vehicles to get around but you must make sure to get them back before you ship off to your next duty station. Do I make myself clear?"

"Yes, Petty Officer," we all shouted. I only lived three and a half hours away from base so I could have my parents bring my car here so that I could get around. That would be so great. Finally, it was starting to feel like normalcy.

"Ok. Processing will begin on Monday. We will meet back here so that I can give you your checklist on what you need to complete over those two days. You will be given all the paperwork, passes, and school schedules at that time. There will be PT every morning. You are to arrive at 0700. PT will last for an hour, then you will shower and be in class by 0900. You will also have evening PT, which starts at 1700. If you are late, you will be considered AWOL and will be put on restriction. When you get to your classes on Wednesday, your instructor will also give you your job assignments and schedules. If you have any questions, ask. You are to adhere to all times listed on your schedules. You are to carry your schedules on you at all times. It's best if you put it in the same insert as your badge as you will not be able to move around on this base without your badge. If you are caught without your badge, you will be put on restriction. If you do not show up for your job or watch, you will be considered AWOL. At the end of these six weeks, you must not only pass your training class but also a PT test to show that you are fit for duty. You will also be receiving your watch hours during processing. If you are late for watch or don't show up, you will be considered AWOL and will be placed on restriction. You are not here long enough to get in trouble so don't. Do what you came here to do so that you can be on your way. We will be watching you. We will now break out into groups so that we can show you where everything is on the base. If you have any questions, ask them because if you find yourself somewhere you don't belong, 'I don't know,' will not be good enough. Do I make myself clear?"

"Yes, Petty Officer," we all shouted. This was going to be different from boot camp. We had a whole week to get processed in before training started but here we had two days. Since the base was only a hop, skip, and a jump long, I could see why it wouldn't take us that long to get everything done.

"Good. Now let's divide up."

We all got into groups of 10 and followed one of the other petty officers around the base. They showed us where the galley was, sick call, the gym, the school building, and our PT spot, which was the same parking lot we were just standing in with Petty Officer Murray. There was a Subway and a mini-mart where you could buy food, supplies, and rent movies. There was also this lake that we were told we would have to run around for PT. We had to run a mile and a half in thirteen minutes. Now the lake didn't look that big but for the number of times we had to run around it, I was sure it was going to feel bigger later.

We finished our tour and were dismissed back to our rooms. We were able to do pretty much whatever we wanted for the rest of the day and the next day. There wasn't too much we could do, though. We couldn't leave the base because no one had a car and we didn't know anyone yet so we couldn't go chill in anyone else's room so we decided to just walk around and get used to the base before Sunday.

"This is a pretty cool place," I said.

"Do you mean boring?" said Young. We all laughed.

"Yes, it looks boring but it's a little less restrictive than boot camp and besides, I can have my parents bring me my car and we can get off the base and go do things in the city."

"Yeah, that's a good idea," said Torres. "I'm glad you don't live that far from here."

"Yeah, me too. I'll give them a call and let them know that we made it and see if they can bring my car next weekend."

We headed to the front of the base where the Subway was so that we could use the phone. There were pay phones around the base that we could use at our leisure. I spoke to my mom and she said that they would drive down and bring my car. Yes! A little more freedom for me and the girls. But for right now, all we could do was hang out and try to get to know people. Unfortunately, because it was the weekend, there were not a lot of people that actually stayed on the base. I could see why. There was nothing to do and it took you literally thirty minutes to walk around the whole base, twice. We decided to head back to the room and get settled the best we could.

Monday rolled in and we were standing back in the parking lot waiting to get our next set of instructions. There were a lot more people now and everyone was looking at us like we had three heads. I guess they were trying to see who the newbies were. We tried to do the same thing over the weekend only all of them were gone. They would have to wait until later. We only had two days to get processed in and be ready for class by Wednesday. Petty Officer Murray arrived and gave us our instructions.

"I see that you all made it back and on time. Good. Now you will be divided up into groups again so that you can go to different processing units at different times. It will make things go by smoother and quicker. Each group leader has a stack of checklists that I mentioned on Saturday and they will be handing out copies. Your goal is to get everything completed and signed off on by 1600 so that we are ready for evening PT. What you don't complete today will be finished up by tomorrow. Any questions?" I'm sure we had questions but no one dared to be the first to raise their hands and ask. "Ok, good. Let's get divided up and you can be on your way. If you have any questions, ask your group leader."

Petty Officer Murray divided us up and went on his way. I guess here his sole job was to give instructions because so far that's all that he did—give us instructions and walk off. Our group leader informed us that each group was going to start from a different section of the checklist. We were starting from the top, the next group from the middle, and the last group would work their way up from the end. Hopefully, this method would ensure that we all got to different processing units at different times.

We started on our way and the first place was the administration building. We went in two at a time because the place wasn't as big as the administration building in boot camp. They couldn't house all of us at the same time so those that had to wait stood in line on the sidewalk until the other two came out. Once inside, they verified the information in our personal file folders, gave us base badges to wear, and informed us of the dos and don'ts of the base. We had to sign a couple of documents, received our watch hours, and then we were free to go. Wow! That's it. I see why they only gave us two days for processing. If all of the other places we had to go to today were this quick, we could have everything done by lunch.

After admin, we headed over to sick call. They gave us a tour and general information for coming to sick call and then we were on our way to the next place. There weren't too many places we had to go to seeing that the base was quaint but there were base rules that we had to go over and make sure we understood because if any of the rules were broken, there would be no excuse that we could use to justify

India

breaking them. After we went over some of the rules, we headed to the galley for lunch. Someone asked how many galleys we had here and our group leader laughed and said, "Only one. Where would the other one go?" He had a point. All of the buildings were pretty much in the center of the base and all of the dirt and grassy areas were used for either PT or recreational purposes. Like I said, this base was a hop, skip, and a jump long.

We got to the galley and it was bigger than I thought it was going to be. Probably because there was only one on base so they had to make sure they could serve a large number in rotations. When we got inside, we noticed that there were navy and marines sitting down and filed in line.

"Why are there marines here?" asked Young

"Back in the day, the marines were a part of the navy and now they still work very closely together. You will see marines and navy together once you get to the fleet. Here, we train together."

"Oh, cool," said Young and we all headed to get our trays. As we were preparing to find a table, we noticed that everyone was looking at us and smiling. Hopefully, this newness would wear off soon.

"So, Payton, what are you going to do now? Not only do you have navy guys on your roster now you can have marines too," Torres said laughing.

"I'm here to learn my job and be on my way. I don't have time to be messing with these guys. Besides, they look crazy."

"And attractive," said Young.

"This is true," I said laughing at Young.

We finished up our meal and headed to the next processing unit. By 1530, we were done with our checklist. We had everything signed off, received our base passes, and were informed about the process of having a car on base. I couldn't wait until the weekend came so that I could meet my parents with my car. Because we finished prior to 1700, we had a little downtime before PT so we headed back to our rooms to change into our smurf suits. I thought we were done with these outfits but it was apparent that we were going to be using them for our entire military careers.

"What do you think PT will be like here?"

"Same as boot camp, Torres. How much different can it be? Push-ups, sit-ups, and running. That's all we are going to do our entire navy careers," I said laughing.

"As long as they don't make us do any eight-count bodybuilders, I'm fine. I hate those things. Up and down and up and down. Can we stay on one level and be done with it?"

"Now you know that's not the navy way," Young said teasing Torres.

"Well, it looks like everything we do will be done in that same parking lot. How do they expect us to do sit-ups on the ground? It's still cold outside."

"I don't know but we are about to find out," said Torres.

And boy was she right. When it was time for PT, it looked like people were coming out of the trees. I'd never seen this many people on the base. We were all spread out in the parking waiting for the instructor to come, and guess who it was? Yup, Petty Officer Murray. He had others in front with him to assist with us.

"Ok, let's get started. We have some new people here so show them how it's done. Make space."

All of a sudden, the people who were accustomed to this place put their right arm up to their side to push over the person to their right and then did the same thing to their left. I guess this is what he meant by make space.

"Ok, fifty jumping jacks, let's go and count off."

"One, two, three, one. One, two, three, two." Hold up, what kind of counting is this? He said fifty. Counting like this was not going to get us to fifty. More like one hundred and fifty. We did as the others were doing and counted along with them. After we got done with the jumping jacks, we did push-ups, and then he announced Torres's favorite—eight-count bodybuilders. I looked over at her and she just rolled her eyes. I told her this was going to be boot camp PT all over again. After we got done with eight-count bodybuilders, our temperature changed. It was now hot and I felt like I was sweating everywhere.

"Ok, take off your sweatshirts, put them under your back and give me fifty sit-ups each. Find a partner close to you." He just answered the question I had earlier about the sit-ups; we will be doing them on the concrete just like everything else we had to do, great. Torres, Young, and I were close by each other so Young and I were partners, while Torres got a guy that was close to her. She looked over at us and raised her eyebrows as to say, "He's not that bad looking." We laughed and completed our sit-ups.

After we were done, we all stood up. We figured we were done and it was time to head back to the barracks but nope. Petty Officer Murray looked at his watch as if to set a timer, then he started jogging in place. After he got done messing with his watch he said, "Ok, let's go," and took off jogging down this road. Everyone followed him and we followed them.

"Where are we going?" said Young.

"How are we supposed to know? Just follow the group," Torres said.

We followed them down this paved road, which turned into a gravel road. It was as if we were going back behind the base. We were running between trees and bushes. It was a nice escape from the openness of the base that we were used to. I loved nature so I really enjoyed the scenery but I didn't enjoy the running. My knees started hurting but I knew I needed to keep up with the rest of the group. When we got further down the path, Petty Officer Murray turned right and started to go up this hill. A hill? I didn't know if my knees could take it but I pushed forward anyway. The hill was steep and a lot of us ran out of breath trying to make it to the top. As we tried to keep up with Petty Officer Murray we noticed that he had already made it to the top and was now heading back down the hill as others ran with him. A couple of us were lagging behind, I'm sure because we were new and had no idea that we'd be running this much.

Going down the hill was a lot easier than going up and it felt better on my knees. We started back toward the way we had started and when we got closer to the parking lot, I let out a sigh of relief hoping that we were done for the day. That was until I noticed we were running right past it. "Where are we going now and why aren't we done yet?" I thought to myself. I was tired and ready to call it quits for the day but I don't think Petty Officer Murray cared about what I wanted. We ran around the base a little more and then ended up back at the parking lot. We stayed there until everyone arrived and then we were dismissed. On the way back to the barracks, I could hardly move. My knees were aching really badly and I thought there were going to give out.

"Are we going to be doing this every day?" said Young.

"I'm guessing so," I said. "Looks like everyone else was aware of what was going on except for us."

"We gotta stay in shape in order to pass the PT test seeing that we can't leave here without passing," said Torres.

"That's true. So we may as well get used to it and fast but I don't know how much more of this my knees can take," I said.

The next day came and my knees were very sore. There were no hills to run up in boot camp. We only had long straight roads so this was definitely a change for my knees. I could barely get out of bed. A couple more days of this and I should be fine but today was going to be a struggle. We didn't have much to do because we had gotten everything signed off on the day before so we decided to walk around the base to work out our sore muscles. We knew if we stayed still the whole day, we wouldn't be able to walk in the morning.

Young and I ended up going to the gym while Torres stayed behind. She said she had gotten enough exercise for one day. I agreed but knew that Young didn't want to venture out alone.

"Did we not exercise enough yesterday?" I said.

"Yes, but I want to see what all they have. We don't exercise on the weekends, so I have to find another way to do it and I'm not going to do it on my own."

"The weekends are for resting. You are not supposed to be working out seven days a week. Even God rested one day out of the week."

"Funny Payton," she said smiling. "But I may need to get some more time in on the weekends."

"Ok, Young. Let's go see what they have."

We walked inside and the gym was just like the base, small. There were some exercise machines, weights, and a wall that was covered with a huge mirror. There were also some dressing rooms in the back and a desk with a guy standing behind it.

"Hi, ladies. Can I help you?"

"Yes, we are new here and we just wanted to see what the gym had to offer," said Young.

"Well, this is it. You can come anytime. We close at 8 pm and open at 5 am."

"At 8 pm? Don't you mean 2000?"

He smiled. "Sorry, I'm not military."

"How did you get on base if you're not military?" We assumed that anyone who was on the base had to be military. It was like our own little world.

"Well, you can work on the base and not be in the military. Sometimes it's preferred because you all come and go but we will still be here. I'm Tony and you are?"

"I'm Young and this is Payton."

"Hi, Young and Payton. So how long are y'all here for, six weeks right?"

"How did you know?"

"Remember, I stay. Y'all go."

Young smiled. "Funny."

They continued to talk about the people he'd seen come and go and where some things were around town while I checked the place out. It was a cool little place to go to when you had nothing else to do.

"I'm here every day, Monday through Friday, so come back and see me."

"I will," Young said smiling as we walked out the door.

We decided to head to the galley for lunch. It was weird not having to go at a particular time since we weren't in school yet but we knew as of tomorrow it would change.

"He was cute wasn't he, Payton?"

"Yes, he was. Look at you. Locking one in already?"

"I'm not locking anyone in. We are only here for six weeks and then they are shipping us off to somewhere else. May as well enjoy my time while I'm here."

"Touché." We laughed and headed into the galley.

When we got back, Torres was reading a letter.

"We got mail while y'all were out. I put it on your racks."

"Cool. I didn't know we would get mail this soon." They had given us our orders when we were in boot camp and we were able to write letters right before we left to let everyone know what our new addresses would be.

"I didn't think we would either but there was a mail delivery while y'all were out. I'm sure that this will be one of our jobs soon," Torres said laughing.

When I got to my rack, I had a couple of letters from family as well as letters from Carter, Simmons, and Sanchez. I decided to read Carter's letter first because I already knew how it would go; he'd tell me he missed me, maybe throw in a poem, and end it with we should be together. I had him down to a science. With Simmons, I never knew what his letter would entail. He was still a mystery to me. A part of me liked the mysteriousness of him because I couldn't predict what he would say next. His letters kept me on my toes and I was starting to be more and more intrigued by it. Sanchez was just a friend now. Because of everything that happened, he still liked me but I didn't want to go down that road again with him. Although we were in different places,

I knew it may be an issue if we ever were in the same place so I decided to keep him as just a friend. It was nice to have people to talk to and to check in on you. Although the military seemed like a big place, it could feel lonely at times. I decided to write everyone back and take it easy for the rest of the day. Besides, we had PT at 1700 and I was not looking forward to it.

PT finally came around and we started off just like the day before with our jumping jacks, eight-count bodybuilders, and push-ups but when we started jogging this time, we went in a different direction. I was hoping there wasn't a hill waiting for us. We got to the lake that we had passed by when we first got to the base. We were told that we had to pass the running part in thirteen minutes so today, we would be running around the lake. If we ran around the lake five times, that would be equivalent to a mile and a half. After Petty Officer Murray told us about the PT test, he took off running. We all followed him. The run started off smooth and before you knew it, we had finished the first lap. "This wasn't going to be that bad," I thought to myself and I kept at it.

Around the second lap, I noticed my knees started to hurt. Obviously, my knees did not like this running business and honestly I wasn't a fan of it either but I made the decision to come to the navy, so I had to stick with it. By the third lap, I didn't feel like I could run anymore. I started jogging a little slower as people were passing me by. I didn't care. If I had to make it to the fifth lap, I couldn't do it at the pace that Petty Officer Murray had set for us. When I got to the fourth lap, Petty Officer Murray shouted that we had five minutes left. He had already finished the laps and was waiting on the sidelines for everyone to get done. I didn't know how I was going to finish this last lap in five minutes. I had already stopped jogging and had started walking by this time. I caught my breath a little and started jogging slowly again. This wasn't the actual PT test so if I didn't make it, it wouldn't be the end of the world. Looks like I would have to start utilizing the gym after all.

When I got halfway around the lake, Petty Officer Murray blew his whistle. The run was over and I only had a little ways to go. He called everyone to where he was standing. "To those of you who finished, good job but for those of you who didn't, you better pick it up.

You only have six weeks here and it's going to go by fast. If you don't pass the running part of your PT test, you don't pass A-school." I see they like to use the fear tactic to get us to do things in the navy. I guess they say it's a system that works and if it ain't broke, don't fix it. It worked in boot camp and from the sound of it it's going to work here too.

After his speech, he dismissed us back to our room.

"What are we supposed to do now?" said Torres.

"We can go to dinner and then chill for the rest of the evening. It's not like we can really go anywhere and besides, we have class tomorrow," I said.

"Yeah, we do. Where is your class Payton? Torres and I have the same job so I'm sure we are in the same class," said Young.

"Well, there's only one building for classes so I'm sure I'm down the hall from y'all."

"I wonder what these classes are going to be like. Will they give us a test a week or what? We only have six weeks here so there can't be that much we have to learn," said Young as she got her things out of her locker to prepare for a shower.

"We are about to find out. All I know is that I have to pass this run test because I'm not staying anywhere longer than I have to."

"You're going to pass, Payton. Remember, we started this together and we are going to finish this together."

"Hoorah!" we all said. We all had our showers and then headed to the galley before calling it a night. Wednesday was approaching fast and I was eager to see what we would be learning.

Wednesday came and after PT and showers we headed to class. My class was on a different hallway as Young and Torres's. When I walked into class, I could already tell that the ratio of male to female was way out of balance. Once everyone got into the class, I noticed that we had sixteen guys and five girls, including myself. Wow! That's three guys to every girl with a spare left over. I've never been anywhere where the ratio of men to women was this astronomical but no complaints here.

As we took our seats, I noticed our instructor was writing his name on the board. Mr. Porter. From the looks of it, he was a civilian too. He was an older black man with a very low haircut with salt and pepper hair. He wore glasses and had this very calm demeanor about him. I could tell that he was going to be a good teacher.

"Hello class. I'm Mr. Porter and this is SK training. SK stands for storekeeper. There are a lot of acronyms in this class so it is extremely important that you pay attention. There are two restrooms down the hall and you can use them at your leisure. You are all adults and I will be treating you as such. There will be weekly quizzes and homework as this is a very short training program and I want to make sure that you are more than prepared for your final test in about five weeks. The person with the highest test score will receive a very special prize. I'm not going to tell you what it is but just know that you will want to take advantage of every opportunity to gain extra credit if needed. You'll be glad that you did. I will now be passing out your instruction manuals and homework booklets. Does anyone have any questions?"

"Yes, how long are these classes?" said one guy in the back. He seemed pretty confident to be asking questions on the first day like he'd been here for a while.

"What is your name young man?"

"It's Warren."

"Well, Warren, class starts at 0900 and ends at 1600. So you let me know how long you will be in my class."

"That's all day." We all laughed.

"Do you have anywhere else to go, Mr. Warren?"

"No sir, I guess I don't."

"Good to know. We will be going to breakfast and lunch together and you will have dinner on your own. Make sure that you are in class on time because after the bell sounds, you will be considered late and

I follow the military guidelines on tardiness. If you are found walking around the base during school hours, you will be stopped and questioned so you better have a good excuse as to why you aren't in class. I do want to say one thing. As you can see, there are a lot more guys in the class than females. Fellas, you are going to want to make sure you look out for the ladies of this class. You are all shipmates now and if anyone messes with them, they mess with you so get to know these ladies and make sure you look out for them here and when you see them in the fleet."

His last statement reminded me of what Petty Officer Savage said to the ladies during the last week of boot camp. It sounded like there was some sort of unspoken rule for the females in the military. I wasn't sure why we needed all this protection but I wasn't going to turn it down either.

We headed to breakfast and on the way back to the class, he gave us a tour of our training center. He showed us where the heads were, where we would be graduating from in the next six weeks, and where the marines' hall was. He informed us that they also trained in this building and we would pass them from time to time. We had already seen them in the galley so it would be normal to interact with them while we were here. We got back to class and started our lesson.

"As I told you, in the majority of this class you will be learning different acronyms that you will need to know once you are stationed on your designated ships. We will also go over some ship types and the specifics of your jobs. As storekeepers, you are like supply managers. You manage all the supplies on the ship. You will be the ones signing off on the inventory sheets once a shipment arrives, completing the monthly inventory, and issuing out supplies when needed. You will need to make sure you have one hundred percent accuracy on all of your inventories because if anything is missing, you will have to account for it. Because you are the holder of all supplies, you will have a lot of friends." We all laughed. "Everyone will want to get to know you because when they need new boots or flight gear, you are the ones they will have to come see so just keep that in mind."

That was good information to know. It was already easy to meet people, this would just make it that much easier. I was starting to look forward to getting into the fleet and knew that I needed to do whatever it took to pass the test.

We went over more of the training manual, headed to lunch, and back to class. The guys in the class were pretty cool. You could tell that there were some that were going to be like our brothers because there weren't many females in the class. They felt like they had to take care of us and besides, Mr. Porter said so. After class was over, Mr. Porter dismissed us and we headed back to our rooms to get ready for PT. When I got to the room, Torres and Young were coming right behind me.

"Here we go again. More PT," Torres said as she was putting her training manual away.

"You may as well get used to it, Torres. We have PT every day for the next six weeks," I said.

"I know but I'm tired. We just got out of class and now we have to go to PT."

"Yeah, but if you don't practice, you don't pass."

"But every day?"

"According to them, yes."

"There's gotta be a way around all this PT. I noticed that they don't even take roll call when we line up," said Young.

"We haven't been here that long and you're already noticing things?"

"Hey, in boot camp they said stay prepared. Anything can happen at any time. So I'm observing all situations—good and bad."

"That's a good idea. I need to be doing the same thing. Good that you're looking out, Young," I said as I patted her on the back and smiled.

We headed to PT and I got in my row, made sure I had enough space around me, and waited along with everyone else for Petty Officer Murray. For some reason, he didn't show up but someone else did.

We were all standing around talking and laughing when he showed up and he didn't look that amused.

"Attention!" We all stopped and stood in attention, eyes straight. "I'm Lieutenant Shaw and I will be taking over PT today. Petty Officer Murray will be back tomorrow. We are going to work out every inch of your body today so let's get to it."

We started off with our normal routine of jumping jacks, push-ups, sit-ups, and then he started having us do things we'd never done before. We were doing planks, rolling on our backs and doing scissors, rolling back over into eight-count bodybuilders, and some other exercises I can't even name. Who was this guy? Where did he come from and when did he say Petty Officer Murray would be back? After a five-minute break to hydrate, he took off running and didn't say a word. Looked back at us and said, "What are y'all waiting on?!" Um, we are waiting on you to tell us what to do. We all looked at each other and took off running behind him. We didn't know where he was going because he wasn't going the normal route that Petty Officer Murray used to take. He was just running. We were all over the base—in the front, in the woods, around the lake, behind buildings, just everywhere. We eventually found our way back to the parking lot and we were all leaned over with our hands on our knees breathing heavily. Who was this dude and why did Petty Officer Murray choose him as his replacement?

"Ok, good job. See y'all tomorrow." Hold up. I thought he said Petty Officer Murray was going to be back tomorrow. I had to ask.

"Lieutenant, didn't you say Petty Officer Murray was going to be back tomorrow?"

"What's your name sailor?"

Uh oh. What did I ask that question for? "Payton, Lieutenant."

"Well, Payton, looks like he may be away for a little longer so y'all have me tomorrow. See you later." He smiled and walked off like he didn't just do these exercises and run with us. It didn't look like it fazed him at all.

We all headed back to our barracks and I'm sure some of us wanted to crawl there. I know I did. Two days in a row with Lieutenant Shaw were going to be the death of me.

The next day, we were in class learning about the different ships. Mr. Porter was telling us about the difference between the USS and USNS ships.

"For the USS ships, these are primarily run by military personnel and depending on their type, they can be the largest ships in the fleet. They are like floating cities. If you go overseas, they can't dock like a regular size ship. They have to stay away from the dock and have a smaller boat come and take a few people at a time to shore, whereas with the USNS ships they are normally smaller and are manned by both military and civmars—civilian mariners. The military normally manages the civmars, although the civmars are doing most of the work. You both work together but the military is like the manager over the civmars and with these types of ships, you are able to pull right into port." Now that sounded like the ship that I wanted to be on—a USNS. Sounds like less work and more of the travel—a win-win.

We continued to go over the different types of ships and then had a fifteen-minute break to relax from everything we had been learning so far. During our breaks, we got to talk with the others in the class, hydrate, and use the head. Warren was the loud one in class and was always making us laugh. He was from the South Side of Chicago and wanted everyone to know it.

"Payton, where do you want to go when you leave here?" he said.

"I don't really know. I'll go anywhere overseas. I don't want to stay in the States. I came here to travel and that's what I plan on doing."

"Well you came to the right place because the navy travels all the time, especially with you being stationed on a ship."

"Yeah, that's why I'm here."

"Where did you grow up?" said Acosta. Acosta was from the Bronx. He was Puerto Rican and Dominican and had this very protective vibe about him like once you were down with him, he'd kill someone for you; like mob style, but there was also a sweet side to him. He tried to hide it but I could tell that it was there.

"Atlanta, GA."

"Oh, you're close to home. Do you plan on going there on the weekends?"

"Some weekends, but not every weekend. I have my parents bringing my car this weekend so I'm pretty excited about that."

"Boys, we got a ride," said Dixon who was another class clown. Dixon was from Kansas. He said he grew up on a farm but didn't want to take over the family business. He wanted to get as far from Kansas as he could after high school and that's what landed him in the navy.

"Oh, no you don't." I laughed. "I am not going to be the base taxi."

"We'll pay you."

"In that case, I may have to rethink this." We all laughed.

"Ok, let's get back to the lesson," said Mr. Porter and he began writing on the board. I liked the way that he taught because he showed us things and how it would relate to our jobs in the navy. He taught by the manual but also gave us some real-world scenarios so that we could visualize what we would be doing on the ship. It sounded like he had been on this base for a long time and had seen people come and go so he knew what he was talking about. He was a wealth of knowledge and I was glad that fate brought me to this class.

Class went by pretty fast and although it was only the first week, it felt like we had been there for a month. When we were dismissed, we were trying to find all kinds of ways not to have to go to PT with Lieutenant Shaw but no one could come up with anything.

PT was as crazy today as it was yesterday. It seemed that after PT yesterday, he went back to his barracks or wherever he slept and tried out some new exercises and experimented with them on us. He was a no-holds-bars type of instructor. He pushed everything to the limit and walked away like nothing had just happened. I didn't know where Petty Officer Murray was but I wished he'd hurry up and get back.

JULIET

Before we knew it, it was Saturday and my parents told me that they'd be at the base around 1500 to bring me the car. I was finally going to be able to get off this base and go do something in the city. I wasn't familiar with Meridian but I wanted to go ride around and check out the area. Young had been going to the gym to see Tony and I would go with her sometimes. He told me not to get too excited about going into the city because there wasn't a lot going on. He said there were a couple of shops and restaurants outside the base but that was pretty much it. People normally went to Alabama, Louisiana, or Atlanta on the weekends. Oh, great. So, I get to go back home on the weekends. At least it was better than sitting on the base with nothing to do.

My parents showed up around 1400 because they weren't aware that there was a time difference between Atlanta and Mississippi. I was at the galley at 1400 and since I didn't have a cell phone, I didn't know that they were waiting for me. By the time I got back to my barracks, I saw them standing outside of the car in the parking lot.

"Hey, what are y'all doing here so early?"

"We didn't know the time changed crossing over into Mississippi," my mom said.

"We had to register the car with the gate and they gave us some paperwork to give to you. They said you need to go to the administration building on Monday."

"Ok, Dad. I'll do that." We were on better terms now. I think the time away did us some good. We were fine when I was away from the house but were always at each other's neck when I was there. The military seemed to be the best for our relationship.

"Do you want to go grab something to eat? We have some time to kill before we get back on the road. You can bring a couple of friends with you and it'll be my treat."

"Sure, Dad. We can do that. Let me go tell the girls."

I went to the barracks and asked Young and Torres if they were up for some free food. Of course they were. We loaded in my parent's vehicle and went to this restaurant outside the base. It was our first time getting a look at what was outside of the base and Tony was right; there wasn't much out here to do. We had a good time talking and letting my parents hear about boot camp and how A-school was going. My dad shared some stories of his boot camp days and how different things were. We ended up staying out later than we expected and when we got back, it was dark. We said our goodbyes and I told them I'd probably be down there the next weekend if I didn't have watch. They said ok and got on the road.

"I finally got my car!" I said as we headed back inside the barracks.

"Yes! Now we can go somewhere on the weekends," said Torres.

"Right. Where are we going first?" asked Young as she headed to the head to change her clothes.

"We first have to see what our schedules for watch look like. That starts next week along with our jobs."

"Oh, damn. That's right."

"Language, Young," I said smiling.

"Girl please. You heard more than this from Petty Officer Savage and, did you hear your dad today?" she said laughing.

"Yes. That's him all day every day. It doesn't even sound like cursing anymore. It's like normal conversation now. I should have warned y'all."

Juliet

"For what? That's all we've been hearing since boot camp. Sounds like it's part of the navy way."

"I guess but I've kept myself from it the whole time I was growing up. I think I can stick with it in here too."

"Good for you Payton but there's no damn way I can. It's not a lot, though; just here and there and maybe over there."

"You're crazy, Young." I laughed.

"Just a little," she said as she got in her rack. We all turned in pretty early since we were all full and our eyes were heavier than our need to go anywhere.

Wednesday came and I had watch from 2400 to 0300. That was a hard watch because I'd normally be asleep during these hours. The good thing about it was that I got to walk around to make sure there was no one else walking around the barracks. It gave me time to wake up a little because that cold morning air was hitting me in my face. I walked around, kicked a couple of rocks, and shined my flashlight whenever I got to an area that was pitch black. We had light poles around the base so it was pretty bright, but there were some areas that were in some pretty dark places that we had to search to make sure they were free of contraband. Who would hide stuff around the base anyway? You had barracks. Find a good hiding spot there but to think about it, the room searches that they did while we were in school were pretty invasive and if they found anything that was not supposed to be in our room, they confiscated it and put a chit, which was the navy's way of saying a warning letter, on our beds alerting us that we needed to come to the command station.

The command station was where we had to check in if we wanted to go on leave, if we were late, or to check in and out for watch and work. No one wanted to go to the command station because that's also where restriction happened. You did have a couple of people that liked to be put on restriction because they figured if they got in trouble enough, they'd be kicked out of the military. For whatever reason, they no longer wanted to go to the fleet so they would try to find ways to prolong it. For some, it was working but for others, after a while, they were still shipped out to the fleet whether they liked it or not. You were property of the government now. You didn't have a say into what you wanted or where you were going. You may have been given options but you weren't really given options. You were going to go where they wanted you to go. No ifs, ands, or buts about it.

As I walked around the base, I noticed someone walking toward me. If they hadn't been dressed in uniform, I would have probably been scared but I knew it was Hicks coming to relieve me. I made sure I got the name of the person that was set to relieve me just in case they overslept or decided not to show up. After I was relieved from duty, I had to go back to the command station and check out before heading back to my barracks. I only had a short amount of time to sleep before I had to get up and get ready for PT.

By Friday, I couldn't believe that we had made it to the end of our second week of class. We were learning so much and had already taken two quizzes of which I got a 96 and 93. It was the running joke that I was going to be the person that would end up with the highest grade in the class. Oh, it wasn't a joke to me because I wanted whatever prize Mr. Porter told us about at the beginning of class and I was going to work my butt off to get it.

Our class was going really well. We all got along and we were even hanging out after class. We had our own little group section during PT and wouldn't let anyone else take our spot. The guys were also adhering to the instructions of Mr. Porter by protecting us; even from the guys that we may have wanted to talk to. They were like our older brothers protecting their little sisters. If we wanted to hang out with anyone outside of our class, we would have to sneak to do it but I'm sure they would find out about it and come get us. We were having fun in A-school although we knew that in four weeks, we'd be separated.

The weekend came and went. I had gone home over the weekend to see what the family was up to. Everyone was still doing the same ole same ole and had a million questions about the navy. I didn't have a whole lot of time to stick around since we had curfew on Sunday but it was good to see Lexy and Deonte. Deonte was still acting like a fool and Lexy was still trying to find her own way out when she graduated. She said she didn't want to go to the military though, but that she'd find something to do. I told her that she had time to decide and when the time came, she'd know exactly what to do.

On Tuesday after class, I had duty—crossing guard duty. I didn't know why this was even a thing. There weren't many people on the base let alone cars. If people didn't know how to cross the street on their own, then they didn't need to be in the navy. The speed limit on the base was five miles per hour. Even if someone hit you, you weren't going to die. You may have gotten a bump but that's it. No matter how much I tried to rationalize how ridiculous this duty was, I still had to do it but the good thing was that when you had duty, you got out of PT so I was fine with it. I just wished it was something more exciting but we were in Meridian. There wasn't a lot of excitement to be had.

The majority of my time was spent standing on the sidewalk waiting for people to walk up to me wanting to cross the street. If there were no cars in the area, I would walk into the middle of the crosswalk, stand in parade rest with one arm in front of me letting the oncoming car know that they needed to stop. Of course, the guys in our class would come and bother me while I had duty. Walking back and forth across the street making me work but at least they were giving me something to do.

I was an hour and a half into my three-hour shift when some sailors came up to me wanting to cross the street. There was a car a little way down the road so I proceeded into the middle of the crosswalk and alerted the driver that he needed to stop to let my shipmates go by. As my shipmates were walking across the street, I noticed that he wasn't stopping. He was actually speeding up. Who was this dude? Did he not know the rules of the base? We were told that no matter what, if there were people in the crosswalk, we are not to move from our post until they were clearly on the other side of the street and on the sidewalk. They weren't aware that a car was heading straight toward me and at a higher than normal speed. I wanted to get out of the center of the street but I had to make sure they were on the sidewalk before I left.

As he got closer and closer and closer, my eyes got bigger and bigger and bigger until I gasped because it was too late for me to get out of the way. All of a sudden, he stopped. My mouth laid wide open at the audacity of this guy to come within an inch away from hitting me. After I was sure my shipmates were safe across the street, I proceeded back to my post. As he passed by, I looked in the car and it was Lieutenant Shaw. He smiled and said, "Good job," and continued on his way. I stood there saying to myself over and over, this dude almost hit me. What was he thinking? It threw me off for the remainder of the evening. I couldn't believe that he almost hit me.

Thursday came and we were preparing for our weekly test that we took every Friday. We always had a fun game, which Mr. Porter would initiate for us to remember the acronyms and prepare for our test. His class didn't feel like we were a part of the military. It just felt like we were in college and at that point in time, nothing else mattered. We laughed and joked and teased each other because of test scores. By this time, Warren and Hunter were really like my big brothers. Hunter was about the same height as Warren but he was this geeky white guy that wore glasses. Warren always messed with him but they acted more like best friends than anything else. We were always hanging out and joking around. Acosta had taken a liking to me and wouldn't let anyone else talk to me. It was so funny. All he had to do was give them this look as to say, "I wish you would," and they would back up and walk away. I didn't have to worry about anything. I was covered and so were all of the girls in the class. The guys had our backs and we had theirs.

During our fifteen-minute break, Fisher and I went to use the head.

"These guys are crazy," said Fisher.

"Yes, they are."

"What do you think this prize is going to be?"

"I don't have a clue but I want it. At least if I win it and I don't like it, I can pass it along to someone else."

"That's a good idea. I think I'm like five points away from you, Payton. You better not mess up."

"I'm not playing with you Fisher. Leave my prize alone."

"That's going to be our prize," she said laughing. Fisher was cool. She was from Connecticut and was the tallest girl in the class. She was only 5'6" but that was taller than the rest of us. When we got into the head, there were two marines already there. One of them was crying while the other was comforting her.

"Are you ok?" said Fisher.

"Yeah, she will be ok," said the marine who was comforting her friend.

"Do y'all need anything?" I said.

"No," said the one that was crying. "It's just hard in here, that's all. So many people told me not to go to the marines but I didn't listen. I should have listened. Just be glad that y'all chose the navy."

We didn't know what had happened to her but we were sorry that it happened. They stayed in for a little while longer and then left.

"What do you think she meant by that, Payton?"

"I don't know Fisher, but I hope she's ok."

"Yeah, me too." We finished in the head and returned back to class.

When we got back to class, it was time to go to lunch. I was glad because I was hungry. I didn't eat much for breakfast so it was definitely time for another meal. We all lined up and marched to the galley. When we got there, there were a couple of classes already there so we scoped out what tables we would be sitting at, got our trays, and headed over. The girls normally sat together since it wasn't that many of us and we could girl talk while we ate. Not too long after we sat down, a group of marines came in. It was guys and a couple of girls. Fisher and I noticed the girls from the head earlier. The one that was crying still looked a little sad but she looked better than when she was in the head. I wanted to go over and ask her what happened but I decided against it.

The girls and I were talking and laughing when a couple of guys from the marines came over.

"What's so funny ladies?" one of them said smiling.

Before we could even open our mouths, some of the guys in our class stood up.

"That's none of your concern," said Warren.

"I'm not talking to you. I'm talking to them," said another one of the marines.

"You talk to them, it's just like you're talking to us. So any questions that you have, you can direct those over to us."

"That's ok, we'd rather talk to these beautiful ladies."

Acosta walked over to the guys and said, "I'm only going to tell you this one time, leave the ladies alone or we're gonna have some problems. Besides, you have ladies of your own. It would be wise if you talked to them instead."

"Yeah, leave our ladies alone and go deal with your own," said Warren.

We all just looked at the guys knowing we shouldn't get up and intervene. We knew that if anything broke out, we would not want to be in the middle of it. The marines looked at the guys in our class, looked back at us, and then walked off. For us to work alongside the marines as close as we did, you'd think our interaction would be different but it was like we were on two different teams and the guys in our class weren't having it.

"If they mess with y'all again, let us know," Warren said. Then all the guys sat down and resumed their conversations. It was so surreal but Mr. Porter told them to protect us and because they either felt we were in danger or just didn't want the marines talking to us, they took matters into their own hands.

The rest of the day went by as normal. We went back to class, learned a little more, and headed back to our barracks for PT. When we got to PT, it was a pleasure to see Petty Officer Murray. I didn't know where he'd been and I didn't care. I was just glad that he was back. We did the same set of exercises we did on the first day we had PT and followed him as he took off running down the path. I had still not run the mile and a half in thirteen minutes but I wasn't giving up. I was getting closer to the time but was always right at fourteen minutes. I had to go faster somehow but I felt like I was doing the best that I could. I decided to go to sick call and see if there was something they could do about my knees because every time I ran, halfway through, my knees would start hurting. Hopefully, Mr. Porter would let me go during class.

Friday morning after we came from breakfast, I asked Mr. Porter if I could go to sick call and see if there was anything they could give me for my knees. He gave me a pass to go and get them looked at. When I got to sick call, they told me to make sure that I hydrated. "I'm here for my knees, what does hydrating have to do with that?" I thought to myself, but I went ahead and hydrated anyway. When the nurse called me to the back, she examined me then left out. I was sitting in the room for a good thirty minutes before her and a medical lieutenant walked in.

"What seems to be the problem, sailor?" said the lieutenant.

"Every time I run for PT, my knees start bothering me. I'm trying to pass my PT test but halfway through the run, my knees ache and it slows me down."

"Ok, let me have a look." She had me to roll up my pant leg and she examined my knee cap. She rotated my leg and then moved my knee cap around. I jumped because my knees were very sensitive at this point. After she finished, she had me to roll my pant leg back down.

"Do both knees feel the same when you're running?"

"Yes," I said.

"I'm going to prescribe you some ibuprofen. This should help with the pain and before you go to PT, make sure you take two."

"Ok, thank you Lieutenant."

"You're welcome."

I left sick call with my prescription and headed back to class. Everyone was working on their test and I hoped I had enough time to take mine.

"You should have no problem finishing your test," said Mr. Porter.

"That must mean this test is easy then."

"For you, I'm sure it is."

I took my test booklet and scantron and took my seat. Forty-five minutes later, I was done with my test and so was the majority of the class. There were some people that were still testing and they had fifteen minutes left. After the fifteen-minute mark, he made everyone put their pencils down and turn in their test. One more test down and we had three more weeks to go. Petty Officer Murray was right, time was flying by here. Our PT test was only two weeks away and so was the main test. I wasn't worried about the main test but the run was still going through my mind. I was hoping the medication would help me moving forward.

After class, Acosta caught up with me and walked with me to my barracks.

"Payton, why do you walk so fast?" he said smiling.

"I didn't know I was walking fast. What are you up to, Acosta?"

"Nothing. Just wondering if you were going home this weekend."

"I hadn't planned on it. Why?"

"Because I thought we could spend some time together so that I can get to know you a little better without the whole class in my face."

"Ha, is there something wrong with the whole class being in your face?"

He smiled. "You know what I mean."

"Well, I'm not going out of town and I will be here all weekend. What do you want to do?"

"I was thinking we can go grab a bite to eat and then just walk and talk."

"Ok. What time do you want to meet up?"

"How about in an hour?"

Juliet

"Ok, sounds good. I'll meet you by the phone booths by my barracks."

"See you then."

"Ok," I said as I walked to the barracks. Young and Torres were already there getting changed.

"Where are y'all going?"

"Some of the people from our class are going to the movies. A couple of people have cars so we're all riding together. You wanna go?" said Torres.

"No, a guy from my class wanna hang out."

"Here we go again," said Young throwing a pair of socks at me.

"We are just hanging out." I laughed

"What happened to Carter and Simmons?"

"They are still there. We still write each other but they are just friends."

"You and all these 'friends' of yours," said Young with her air quotes.

"Y'all need to get y'all some friends so that you can leave me alone."

"I'm working on it," said Young.

"I'm waiting till I get to the fleet," Torres said. "Maybe I will be there for a while and don't have to keep moving around. Then I can really see what's out there."

"Girl you are a trip," I said as I proceeded to the head. "Y'all have fun and bring me some popcorn back."

"I am not bringing you back any contraband," Young said laughing as Torres and her walked out the door. Young and Torres had become my best friends and I didn't even want to think about where we would end up in the next couple of weeks. I hopped in the shower and got ready to meet up with Acosta.

I met up with Acosta at the phone booths and we headed to the activity center on the base. The activity center was the local hangout for us. It had a couple of pool tables, darts, video games, and TVs. You could also order food and drinks. We got a table and learned more about each other. He told me that he had a sister that was still in the Bronx and that he had a niece. His mom and dad were still together and they lived in the Bronx as well not too far from his sister. I told him a little about me and we ate and played some pool. After a couple of hours, he said he wanted to walk me back to the barracks because he didn't want me out too late by myself. It was sweet of him but I could definitely handle my own. We decided to take the long way back to the barracks. As we were walking, he started to ask questions about my status.

"So why are you single?"

"How do you know I'm single?"

"I just assumed seeing that I don't see you with anyone around the base."

"I could have someone back home."

"Well, do you?"

"No," I said laughing.

"You're funny. I think you're beautiful and I would love to stay in contact with you when we leave here."

"That would be nice but I have to tell you that I keep in contact with some other friends from boot camp as well." I didn't have to tell him but I just wanted it to be clear that I had other friends.

"That's cool. They can't compare to me. I'll have you soon enough." What is with these guys? Everyone is trying to lock me down but I'm trying to fly. I want to be as free as a bird but every time someone looks at me, they want to put chains on my legs. I don't understand. I assume that it's that they see what they like and they want to make sure no one else gets a hold of it either. Well, I'm not ready to be locked down just yet. There's so much of the world to see and I was just getting started.

"Oh, is that right?"

"Yeah, that's right. You'll see."

"Ok. We shall see."

He walked me back to my barracks and gave me a hug goodnight. We hung out more throughout the weekend and I got to know him a little bit better. He told me about this girl that he used to date and how she cheated on him. See, that's why I don't want to be locked down to anyone just yet. I don't want to cheat on anyone and that's why I'm real with them and myself. It doesn't make any sense to cheat. If you want to be with the person, then be with them. If you don't, then don't. There's no in between. The more he talked, the more he sounded like he was still wounded from the breakup but he assured me that he was over it; but his eyes told another story. I vowed to be his friend and told him that he could talk to me about anything but that I wasn't ready for a relationship. He said he understood and that he'd wait but I told him that I didn't want him to wait. I wanted him to live his life in the navy and we would just have to see where life would take us. I'm sure he wanted me to say something else but I had to stay true to myself and what I knew I wasn't ready for.

The weeks seemed to fly by and before you knew it, it was time for the PT test. I was dreading the run because I hadn't passed it the whole time I had been here. The push-ups and sit-ups were no problem and we had just finished those two tests. We were now all standing in line waiting for them to tell us when to start running around this lake. Oh, the lake. I remember when we first got here and it seemed so peaceful. Now, in my mind, it was marked life or death. I had been taking my ibuprofens and they were helping a little with my knees but they still were a little painful halfway through the run.

Petty Officer Murray was assigned to watch the running part of the PT test and I could still hear him saying, "If you don't pass this run, you don't pass A-school." Oh, I was going to pass one way or another. As I was daydreaming about when we first got to the base, I heard, "Go!" Everyone took off running and so did I. I decided this time I would start off jogging a little and then speed up at the end. I noticed that whenever I took off running like everyone else, I got tired quickly so I thought this idea would help me out in the long run because I could speed up at the end and recoup those sixty seconds that I'm always short by. The first four laps went by fast and I still had a good pace.

As I rounded the lake heading into my last lap, Petty Officer Murray said that we had three minutes left. Three minutes? What happened to the five-minute warning? I felt my heart drop down to my stomach. I knew it was time for me to speed up. I started moving faster than I ever had before. I ran down the stretch and then round the end of the lake and went down the final stretch. As I was midway through the final stretch, I felt someone's hands on my back like they were pushing me to go faster and I quickly looked back to see if anyone was behind me but I didn't see anyone. I started to go faster than I had before and rounded the last corner of the lake to get to the finish line. I tried to push myself to go a little bit faster but I felt like I was about to fall to the ground so I kept my pace. I got closer and closer to Petty Officer Murray who was standing at the lap checkpoint. I just knew he was going to blow that whistle before I got to him but I kept running. People were passing me but I didn't care. I just needed to get to him before he blew that whistle. I got closer and closer and closer and then it happened. Five steps after I passed him, he blew the whistle. Ahhh! If we were allowed to cry, I probably would have. I stopped running and fell to the ground. I couldn't believe it. I had finished before the whistle and my knees were killing me. I just laid there on my back trying to catch my breath and holding my knees. Warren, Hunter, and Acosta ran over to me to see if I was all right.

"Payton, are you ok?" asked Hunter.

"Yeah, I'm all right. I passed!"

"You did, then you fell. Let us help you up," said Acosta.

Acosta and Warren helped me to my feet and sat me in a chair that Petty Officer Murray had out there for him.

"Are you sure you're ok?" said Acosta.

"Yes, I'm fine," I smiled. He would go get me new knees if he could. "I just need to rest a little but I'll be all right."

"I'm going to get you some ice packs from the galley," he said. There was no stopping him. He took off.

Petty Officer Murray came over. "Payton, why are you sitting in my chair?"

I looked at him like, "Really Petty Officer? Really?"

He smiled and said, "At least you passed this time."

"Yes, I did and now I can leave A-school."

"Not until you pass your test."

"I'm not worried about the written test. This was the only test that I was worried about and now it's over. Thank God!"

"Yeah, you better thank somebody because you almost didn't pass."

"Almost doesn't count, Petty Officer Murray."

"You're right," he said as we walked away to check on the others. By that time, Acosta had come back with two ice packs and placed them on my knees.

"I got it, Acosta. Thank you for getting them for me."

"You're welcome. Let me know if you need any help to your barracks."

"I think I can make it there. I just have to sit here a little longer."

"Ok, I'll sit with you."

He was not going to leave me by myself. After a couple more minutes, I was able to get up and walk back to my barracks, with Acosta close by of course. I decided to take two more ibuprofens before I had to go to watch later on that night. I was planning to tell whoever was in the commanding center tonight that I was not going to be able to do a lot of walking. Either I was staying in the command center or taking a seat on one of the benches in the courtyard. My knees were really hurting me and I was not going to make it worse.

Thursday came and we all had come back from breakfast. Everyone was on edge because of this major test that we had to take.

Mr. Porter handed out the test and had us place it face down. "I want to say good luck to all of you. You all know the material, just take your time. You have the remainder of class to finish your test. We will be having bag lunches today so if you don't finish before lunch, you will have after lunch as well. I know you all can pass this test and remember there's a prize for the person with the highest overall score. Anyone can win it at this point; except for a couple of you." We all smiled and looked around the room because we knew who had the lowest scores on the tests throughout the weeks. He sat down at this desk and said, "You may turn your papers over and begin." Everyone turned over their papers, took a deep breath, and began the test.

It was very quiet in the class as everyone was concentrating on each and every question. There were so many questions and so many acronyms. I just knew I was going to mess up and combine the acronyms. I knew I had to just take my time and try to remember where things were in the training manual. That's how I was able to pass my test in boot camp. I envisioned the page numbers and what was on that actual page and was able to see the page clearly. I knew if I did the same thing here, I would be able to see the actual acronyms and answer the questions correctly. After a while, I asked to use the head because I needed a break. He let us go one at a time so that we wouldn't be sharing answers in the hall. I went to the head to splash some water on my face. On the way there, I saw two of the marines that were at the galley the day they got into it with our guys.

As I passed by them, one of them said, "Where are your bodyguards?"

I smiled. "They are taking a test. Why? Do you want me to go get them for you?"

"No, I wanted to talk to you. You're very attractive and I just wanted to get to know you better," said the other one.

"I don't think that's a good idea."

"Why not?"

"You were there the other day in the galley, right?"

"Yeah, but they don't scare us. We just left them alone so that we didn't get in trouble."

"And that was a good idea just like it's a good idea that y'all just walk away now."

"I'll walk away but I'll see you later," he said as he looked at me and walked down the hall.

I shook my head and headed into the head. We needed more women in the navy to balance things out but from the looks of things, there weren't that many women in the marines either.

I eventually went back to class and continued my test. I finished right after lunch and sat there with my head down while everyone else finished. Fisher finished around the same time I did and looked at me and smiled. I shook my head at her as if to say, "You can't have that prize. It's mine." People started to finish an hour after lunch and two and a half hours after lunch, everyone was done.

After Mr. Porter took up the tests, he sat on his desk and said, "So, how was the test?"

"Man, Mr. Porter, that test was hard," said Warren.

"Yeah, half of that stuff I never saw before," said Hunter

"That's because you don't pay attention," said Fisher.

"I do pay attention to those things that interest me."

"This whole class should interest you, Mr. Hunter, as this will be your job in the fleet," said Mr. Porter.

"How did you do, Payton?" asked Acosta.

"I think I did well."

"Yeah, I'm sure you did," said Warren as he threw a piece of paper at me.

"Now come pick it up," said Mr. Porter.

We all laughed and continued talking about the test and what was next.

"Mr. Porter, when are you going to tell us who won the prize and what the prize is?" asked Fisher.

"I'll reveal that on Monday along with what you need for graduation next Thursday. There are a couple of things you will need to do before then and some things I would need to pass out. You will also be receiving your orders for your next duty station."

I couldn't believe graduation was next week. I had made some good friends here and now it was time to leave them. That was the only thing I didn't like about the navy. It allowed you to meet people and then took them away from you. I was going to miss my friends.

Another hour and a half had passed and Mr. Porter dismissed us for the day. He told us that we were all going to meet up after class on Friday and go to the activity center and that he was going to join us. We were all excited to see Mr. Porter outside of his work attire and to hang out with him a little before we were off to another place and he was graced with his next class.

Monday came quick and it was our final week of A-school. It was definitely bittersweet. We had come here six weeks ago and somehow we were smarter and more mature and getting ready to head off into the fleet. We got to class and everyone was looking forward to seeing what this prize would be. We all took our seats and Mr. Porter addressed the class.

"First, I want to say that it was such a pleasure gathering with you all last Friday. I had a lot of fun and I'm going to miss this class. You all were one of my best classes."

"I bet you say that to all of your classes, Mr. Porter," Warren interjected.

"I actually do not. I've had some headaches but you all are by far the best class I've ever had."

"Thank you Mr. Porter. You're not too bad yourself," said Hunter. Those two always had something to say.

"Thank you Mr. Hunter. And to get back to what I was saying before, I have your orders in my hand but I must first say that you all passed your tests."

Juliet

We all busted out into cheers and high fives and hugs. It was good to hear that everyone passed. No one had to stay another week or retake the test or anything. That really showed how awesome Mr. Porter was as an instructor. He'd been here for a while and knew what it would take for all of us to pass.

"And the person with not only the highest grade in this class but the highest grade in the school from all classes is our very own, Ms. Payton."

I couldn't believe it. I knew I was neck to neck with Fisher but I had no idea that I would get the highest grade in the whole school. Everyone was cheering and applauding.

"So, what does she get?" said Warren. Always with the questions.

"Ms. Payton will receive an advancement from E-2 to E-4 within 30 days of reporting to her duty station so now you all will be calling her petty officer. She has also received orders to a USNS ship and will be leaving for Italy in March."

"Are you serious?" I asked.

"Yes, Ms. Payton. You deserve it," Mr. Porter said with a smile. I couldn't believe it. I would be promoted to E-4 in a couple of months and I was about to go to Italy. This could not be happening right now. I didn't know what to say. I was at a loss for words.

"Good job, Payton. You deserve it," said Acosta. Everyone chimed in right after him.

"Thank you everybody," I said still in shock. I still couldn't believe what I had just heard. Mr. Porter passed out our orders and made sure to tell us to keep up with them because some people would have to fly out on Friday and some of us weren't leaving right away. I wasn't set to leave until the end of March because my ship had already set sail to cross the Atlantic and was unloading supplies at different ports. I had to wait until they were on their way back to Augusta Bay, Italy, and that was going to be in another three weeks. I had never heard of Augusta Bay, Italy, but I was about to be able to go see it first-hand.

"Mr. Porter, since I can't fly out till the third week of March, do you think I could wait at home until that time?" Everyone that I came with was going to be gone by the time I was set to fly out and I didn't want to stay on base if I didn't have to. Besides, I still had my car. I could take it home and just wait there until it was time for me to go to Italy. It would be better to fly out of a major airport like Atlanta Hartsfield than the little one in Meridian.

"I'm sure you can. After class, go by the administration building and talk to someone there."

"Ok. Thanks Mr. Porter."

We spent the remainder of the day talking about our time in boot camp and who was going where. We were exchanging information so that we could write each other and stay in touch once we got to the fleet. When we were leaving class, I saw the same two marines standing in the hall. As we walked by, they looked at me, smiled, and waved. I smiled, shook my head, and kept walking. "What was that about?" asked Acosta. "Nothing for you to worry about," I said as we walked out the door.

I went to the administration building before making my way to the barracks to get ready for PT. Although we were done with the PT test, it didn't stop us from having PT. We were going to have PT up until Wednesday. Graduation was on Thursday and that was the only reason why we weren't having it then. When I got to the room no one was there but as soon as I got dressed, Young and Torres walked in looking all sad.

"What's wrong with y'all?"

"We are going to different places?"

"Where are y'all going?"

"I'm going to San Francisco and Young is going to Florida. We both fly out on Friday."

"Aw, ladies. We knew that this could happen. We just have to make sure we write and stay in touch.

Juliet

"Where are you going, Payton?"

"Well, Young, I got the highest grade in the school so I got orders to go meet my ship in Italy."

"What?! You're the person they were talking about in class today with the highest score in the entire school?"

"That would be me," I said with all thirty-two of my teeth showing.

"Congratulations Payton. Who knew we had a nerd living with us," Young said laughing.

"Ha ha, shut up, Young. I'm just extra smart that's all."

"More like extra, extra," said Torres. "I'm so happy for you. Italy. Wow! That's going to be nice. When do you fly out?"

"My flight doesn't leave until the end of March, so I have three weeks. My ship is over there now but they are in the middle of the Atlantic doing some training exercises. I went to talk to the people in the administration building to see if I could go home until it was time for me to fly out and they said that I could but that I better make sure I didn't miss my flight. So, I will be meeting them there. I'll leave to drive home on Friday after you all leave."

"Sweet," said Young. "See, that's the kind of orders I need."

"I'm still blown away by it all."

"I bet you are but it's going to be great. You are going to have so much fun. I wish I was going with you."

"I wish you both were going with me. We have been together since boot camp and now we have to separate. It's not fair but this is what we signed up for, I guess."

"Yeah it is and it sucks."

"Yes, it does, Young. It truly does. Last week for PT together ladies, let's go make the best out of it."

"Hoorah!" said Torres and we headed out to PT.

Graduation day came and my parents and grandmother came down to attend. I still couldn't believe I had the highest grade in the school. When we walked down in our dress blacks to the training center, I saw that they had put my name on the marquee with my grade and job. I smiled when I saw it and headed to class. We were all gathered in our class until the ceremony took place. We took a lot of pictures. It was amazing to see the shot of all the girls and then all of the guys. There was no comparison at all. We all thanked Mr. Porter for how awesome he was and some of us wrote him letters just thanking him for all that he had done for us over these six weeks. I made sure to give him my contact information so that we could stay in touch.

The time came for us to attend the ceremony. It wasn't packed like it was in boot camp. There were about sixty people there and we were sitting in a small room inside the training center. It was a little larger than our classroom but was vastly reduced in size from the auditorium in boot camp. We were all just excited that we were graduating together.

The ceremony was nice and quick. We all got our awards and I received three because of my educational achievements throughout the weeks. It felt pretty good to be acknowledged for the hard work that I had endured to get to this point. Afterward, I took pictures with my parents and grandmother and we took some more outside before my parents had to head back. I told them that I was going to head back the next day because I wanted to see my friends off. They said ok and got on the road.

Friday came and we all got packed up. Young, Torres, and I decided to write each other letters but promised not to read them until we got to our duty station, or for me, home. I was going to miss them so much but we couldn't cry. For the navy, that wasn't an option. We gave each other a hug and we looked around our barracks to make sure we hadn't forgotten anything. The room looked a lot smaller now as if we had grown so much after only six weeks. We were finally going to the fleet. Training no more and navy lives set to start.

Juliet

I walked out with Torres and Young and I saw the guys from class as they got ready to get on the van headed toward the airport. I gave Warren and Hunter a hug and then Acosta. He hugged me and said that he wished he didn't have to let me go. I told him that maybe we will see each other in the fleet one day and that this wasn't goodbye but I'll see you later. He said ok and boarded the van. He looked so sad. When everyone got on the van, the driver did a final check and then got in the driver's seat. I stood there until they passed me by. I saw Acosta one last time, waved, and headed to my car. Besides pictures, I would never see Acosta again. He ended up getting married and having a daughter of his own. I was glad that I kept our friendship innocent and that the love he was waiting to give to someone was finally accepted by someone who deserved it. I looked around Meridian one last time and remembered all the good times we had here. After my daze, I smiled, looked up at the sky, and got on the road.

KILO

Three weeks flew by and before I knew it, I was in Augusta Bay, Italy. This place was so beautiful and full of life. The buildings were vibrant in color and the people were just as colorful. Everywhere I went, people were laughing, smiling, and talking. It was contagious. I decided to walk around the city and partake of this contagious atmosphere of happiness.

I had made it to Augusta Bay ahead of my ship because I was told they got into some bad weather on their way across the Atlantic and that it would be a couple of days before they returned. That was fine by me. I needed to get caught up on my sleep anyway. I had major jet lag and if it wasn't for having to use the head, hydrate, or eat, I wouldn't have gotten up at all. I needed to get accustomed to this new time zone before I would be of any use to anyone. I had just come back from getting something to eat and decided to write Simmons a letter before I went back to sleep. Carter was no longer talking to me because of what happened during the three weeks I was at home.

When I had gotten home from A-school, I had a couple of weeks to spare so Carter wanted to come see me but Simmons wanted me to come see him. From the sound of the request, it was a simple choice but I didn't choose the simple answer. I chose the complicated one. I didn't want Carter to come see me because I didn't want to have to make any excuses or lie about why I wasn't going to be at home for the entire weekend so I decided to go see Simmons instead. I figured it was a huge base in Great Lakes and there was no way I would see

Carter while I was there and I was right. I didn't see Carter one time but what I didn't anticipate was that Carter and Simmons both shared a good friend. Carter and Simmons weren't friends but Simmons had a friend named Tucker and so did Carter and when I was up there, Tucker saw a picture of me in Carter's room and told him that I was at the base but that I came to see Simmons. Oh, the webs that we weave. Carter decided to make sure that he didn't run into me the whole weekend that I was there and when I got back home, he called me and told me what he knew. He said he couldn't fault me for going to see Simmons but because I never told him about Simmons, it was like I was trying to hide something. I wasn't trying to hide anything but I didn't see the need to tell everyone that I was conversing with whom I was conversing. Nevertheless, he decided that he no longer wanted to talk to me because it hurt too much. I had to respect his decision. Simmons also found out through Tucker that I was also talking to Carter but once he found out that Carter no longer wanted to have anything to do with me, he decided to stay around. It was crazy for a while but now I was in Italy writing Simmons.

After a couple of days, I received word that my ship had finally arrived. I gathered my things and got into the van to be taken to the dock to meet my ship. The ride to the ship was very eventful. In Italy, they drove wherever they wanted—on the streets, on the curb, in the grass. They didn't care. If they needed to get somewhere, pedestrians were not going to stop them from getting there. I held my breath a couple of times hoping the driver didn't hit anyone and I got to the ship without any accidents.

When I saw the ship, everything that I had learned felt like it had departed from me. How was I supposed to greet someone when I first walked on the ship? Who was I supposed to show my ID card to? Where is my ID card? All of these questions were running through my head but I knew I just needed to relax and just get up the ramp of the ship. When I got onto the ship, I was met by Petty Officer Willis.

"Hi Payton. I'm Petty Officer 2nd Class Willis. You will be reporting to me. Right now, I will show you to your rack and then give you a tour. I'm sure you are tired so I will let you get some rest before you start duty. It normally takes a couple of days before you get in sync with the time but if you have any questions, let me know."

"I will, Petty Officer Willis."

She showed me to my rack so I could put down my things. Surprisingly enough, she was also my rack mate. I didn't know how that was going to work but I would have to deal with that later. She gave me a tour of the ship and showed me where the galley and heads were. Those were going to be the most important over the next couple of days because I didn't plan on going anywhere else.

After the tour, she showed me the process of using the head as we didn't have one in our actual rooms like we did in boot camp and A-school. The head was down the hall and across the walkway and because males and females were always around, there was a specific protocol we had to follow in order to take a shower. We had to make sure we had everything in our white mesh bag, wear our PT gear, and shower shoes as we headed to the head. She informed me that I could take a shower without shower shoes but she wouldn't recommend it. We were to take showers of seven minutes or less as everyone had to also utilize the showers but on the weekends you could take longer showers. Sounded like boot camp.

After she gave me the whole spill of head etiquette, she left me alone. I did as she said and headed to take my shower and get in my rack. I was still very sleepy and needed a couple of days to sleep it off. Good thing they understood and afforded me those days. The only time I got up is when I was hungry. I went to the galley to eat and then went back to my rack. I knew eventually I would have to meet my new shipmates.

After a couple of days, the jet lag seemed to wear off and I could function normally without falling asleep. I was able to meet the others on the ship although I didn't remember what everyone's name was. It was going to take me some time but at least I was awake enough to see their faces. Petty Officer Willis showed me my work station in the office part of the ship before leading me down to my storeroom. The work office was a small space on one of the top levels of the ship. There were two sections that we were to work in with one of the sections leading out to the outside of the ship. There were windows everywhere and you could see the ocean all around. It was such an amazing view. I had never seen anything like it.

When we headed down to the storeroom, it seemed like it went down forever. There were three different levels to this one storeroom. The first level was considered the main level. That is where we would be the majority of the time but because the ship wasn't big like the carriers we were told about in A-school, we had to store things below the deck of the ship and that's why it had so many levels. I met the civmars in my group. There were four of them—Elle, Ralph, Leo, and Julio. They didn't go by last names like we did so this was going to be a little different than what I had been learning this whole time. It shouldn't take too much getting used to seeing that I had only been in the military for five months at this point. I still knew how to call people by their first name.

"Hi and what's your name?" asked Elle who was an older white lady. She looked like she was around retirement age but she worked because she wanted to. She seemed nice enough.

"Hi, I'm Payton."

"It's nice to meet you Payton. We will be doing most of the work done here although you will have your own work to do. If you need anything or need to know where something goes, just let us know. We've been here a while so we can help you out."

"Thank you Ms. Elle."

"You're welcome."

After I met the civmars, Petty Officer Willis took me back to the office and started to inform me of what I would be responsible for on the ship. It started to sound like an actual job. We got up in the morning, went to orders on the deck to get our assignments for the day, and went to work. We had PT during the day and our normal breakfast, lunch, and dinner. It didn't sound like it would take too much getting used to.

After I learned what I needed to do in the office and found out how the normal day to day operations went, I headed back down to my storeroom just so that I could get a feel of things. Julio showed me around and took me down to the other two storerooms. He stated that we didn't have to go down there too often but sometimes we had to and that there was asbestos on level two. I didn't know what asbestos was but since he felt the need to mention it, I thought it would be a good idea to find out what it was, but that would have to wait until later because right now, I was learning about what my responsibilities were going to be on the ship.

Lunchtime came around and I was still getting used to everyone.

"Hey Payton. Do you mind if we join you for lunch?"

"No, not at all."

"I know you don't remember us but I'm Crawford and this is Burns. I'm one of the other petty officers on the ship and so is Burns. We all do pretty much the same jobs but in different areas on the ship."

"Oh, ok," I said trying to eat and talk at the same time.

"How old are you anyway because you look really young?"

"You don't ask a woman how old she is. You're so rude," said Burns, who was an older woman with a strong accent. Her accent sounded like she was from the islands; maybe Jamaica. She looked to be in her mid to late thirties but I could've been wrong.

"Oh, I don't mind. I'm twenty years old."

"Oh, you're a baby," said Crawford.

"I guess so."

Everyone on the ship that I had met so far looked like they were way older than I was. There were some that looked to be around twenty-four to twenty-eight but I couldn't really tell.

"If you have any questions or have any problems with anyone, let me know," said Crawford. "I have to look out for you since you're the baby of the ship."

There was the navy motto again—look out for the women. They said it so much that I started to think that there must be a reason behind it. What is happening to the women that everyone always has to look out for them? Or maybe it was because I was new to the ship and from the looks of it, the youngest one. Maybe he thought that he should take me under his wing and teach me the things I should know. Whatever it was, I was going to use it to my advantage. I learned in A-school what to do on a ship but until you are actually on a ship, you really don't know what to do. I was going to make sure that if I had any questions that I found Petty Officer Crawford and asked.

When lunch was over, I returned to the office to finish up training with Petty Officer Willis. My primary job was to manage the civmars, complete inventory checks, and help balance the books; all things that I could do without being micromanaged. I stayed in the office for the rest of the day and when 1600 hit, we were considered off. We had to go and get dressed for PT and I wondered where on the ship we were going to exercise. The whole deck of the ship was covered in what I can only describe as tar smashed with some sort of tool and left to dry. The deck wasn't smooth at all and some parts protruded from the flat surface. I was continually tripping over them so I knew PT was going to be a challenge.

Once I got dressed, I decided to follow everyone else to see where they were going. Everyone moving in the same direction was a good sign. We all ended up on the flight deck. We didn't have a huge ship and the flight deck was probably the largest part of the ship that we could all fit in to exercise. PT was brutal. We were doing jumping jacks, sit-ups, and push-ups on the deck. I later found out that the material that they used to cover the deck was called nonskid. It was to ensure that things stayed in place on the deck of the ship. That may have been true but it wasn't a good idea to do PT on it. My knees were already not agreeing with me with all the running that we had to do, now they were shouting because we had to get down on all fours to do fire hydrants. They could really come up with some interesting exercises. Exercises that I had never heard of or done in my life.

We got done with PT and we were on our own for the remainder of the evening. I decided to take a shower before going down for chow. On my way to the head, I met someone else.

"Payton, right?"

"Yes, and you are?"

"I'm Freeman. Just to save you some time, most of us are petty officers and the majority of everyone else are civmars. We do have a couple of seamen on board, including yourself, but from your file it looks like you will be a petty officer soon."

How did she know what was in my file? I thought paperwork in the navy was G-6 classified.

"Yes, I should be receiving my promotion within thirty days."

"That's great. That's the goal. Move up fast so that you can delegate the work. Yes, we all have jobs to do but if you can delegate some of your work out, it will make life much easier."

"Thanks. Good to know."

"Anytime. Once it's time for liberty, I'll come scoop you up. We can hang out together. I don't want you having to always hang out with the Mr. and Mrs."

"Mr. and Mrs.?"

"Crawford and Burns."

"Oh, are they married."

"No, but they act like it. They act like the old married couple on the ship and neither one of them is that old. Burns is always mad about something and wants to monopolize all of Crawford's time when he isn't working but you will catch on. By the time your promotion rolls around, you will have figured out what really goes on here."

"Interesting. Well, I can't wait."

Freeman laughed and went to her rack. This was already turning out to be one interesting ship.

After I went to the galley and headed back to my butt, I was beat. All I wanted to do was go to sleep. Petty Officer Willis wasn't in the room yet so I decided to try to get some sleep before she came in so that way maybe I would be zoned out and wouldn't hear a thing when she entered. Great thought process but it didn't work out the way I wanted it to. When Petty Officer Willis came in, I didn't hear her. I didn't even know she was in the room until I heard this loud noise that soon went away. Then there it went again and then it went away. It was silent for a moment then the noise got louder. What was she doing? I woke up to see if she was moving furniture around which I couldn't see how that was possible because everything was bolted down to the deck. It was still dark in the room and she was in her bed. I figured out what the loud noise was. It was her snoring. I couldn't believe it. Was she going to be this loud all the time? If so, I was going to have to change rooms because there would be no way that I was going to be able to get any sleep. She was loud. I'm sure the whales outside heard her too.

Within the next couple of weeks, I was starting to get in the flow of things. I was remembering names and putting things away in the bins that they went in. It didn't feel like I had only been there for less than a month but that's the same way it felt in boot camp and A-school. The military had a way of making you grow up faster than expected. Freeman and I were hanging out all the time and became really good friends. She'd fill me in on what all happened before I came aboard and let me know some of the dos and don'ts of the ship. I was happy to have someone who had been in longer than me and could let me know how things worked. I needed that because if they left me out on my own, it was not going to end well. Sort of like last week. It was my turn to put the flag up for reveille and I put it up upside down. I didn't even notice it until I was standing there saluting the flag and someone came running down to me and told me that it was upside down. I had to hurry to take it down and flip it around all without the flag touching the ground which was a big no-no. You did not allow the flag to touch the ground because that was a sign of major disrespect. How did I know? Because I let the flag touch the ground and got yelled at so bad, I thought I had killed somebody. But I learned not to let the flag touch the ground anymore. Lesson learned. Some things were going to take some getting used to, while others only took one wrong move to make right.

We were now in Cyprus and were out in the city sightseeing. Cyprus was such a gorgeous place. I see why people would vacation overseas and get away from the States for a while. Life overseas was much more family-oriented. People went out to eat and stayed out. No one was getting fast-food and rushing back to the next activity. People just lived over here. It was as if no one had anywhere to go and they just enjoyed life. I felt the same thing when we were in Augusta Bay, Italy. I guess it was a theme for Europe and so I did as the Europeans.

The end of April rolled around and it was time for my advancement ceremony. We all were called to the flight deck so that the captain could present me with my E-4 award. It was a nice and quick ceremony. I was now a petty officer of the United States Navy. We had some seamen on the ship for whom I was now responsible, who didn't take the news all that well because they now had to listen to me—a twenty-year-old who had only been on the ship for a month—but hey, I didn't make the rules. In the military, you were awarded based on your years of service and your ability to pass the advancement tests. In order to take certain advancements, you had to have been in your position for a certain amount of years. That didn't qualify for my advancement as it was an educational advancement and they had other requirements that applied. All I knew was that I worked hard to be where I was and I was given what I deserved.

After the ceremony, everyone was congratulating me as we were heading back to our stations around the ship. I worked closely with Petty Officer Willis when I was in the office as our desks were right next to each other. I would try to get off early so that I could hurry up and go to the galley, get my shower, and get to sleep before she got into the room but she would always wake me up with her snoring. I started beating on her rack every time she got louder and louder. If I couldn't get any sleep, then she wasn't either.

One morning, I went into the office and she said that she wanted to talk to me. We went outside of our office and stood on the outer part of the ship. The people in our office were looking and trying to figure out what was going on. Was the new girl getting in trouble already? It wouldn't be the first time. I had already gotten written up for laughing during morning attention. It wasn't my fault though.

Freeman said something and I started laughing at her and I got in trouble for it. I was sure that wasn't going to be my only write up because I smiled all the time and that was frowned upon when we were standing at attention. I tried to stop but when my mind starts to wonder, I can't always control where it goes.

"Payton, you have got to stop hitting my rack in the middle of the night."

Why was she calling me outside during the day while we were working to talk about our rack life? This was something that could have waited until we were back in the room or in the morning while we were in the room together.

"Well, I can't sleep."

"You need to try to get to sleep before I get in there."

"I do. Do you not notice that I'm in the bed every time you come into the room but you wake me up every time with your snoring."

"That's not something that I can help."

"Then I'm not going to stop beating on your rack. I have to sleep too and it's not fair that you are the only one that gets any sleep at night."

"Maybe we need to change your room with someone."

"I think that would be best because I don't think that I need to be racking with my petty officer anyway."

"Ok, I will see who wants to switch and I will let you know."

"Ok, thanks."

She obviously already had someone in mind because before our shift was over, she told me where my new room would be and that I could start moving my things over before we even got off for the day. I loved how fast things moved in the navy. Hopefully, my new rack mate didn't snore like she did.

I was moving my things into my new room when my new rack mate showed up. "Hi, you're Payton, right?"

"Yes, and you're Mohammed, right?"

"Yes. Girl, I want to thank you for speaking up about changing rooms because my rack mate was a rack mate from hell. She leaves her stuff all over the place and she snores. Do you snore?"

"No, and she sounds like my rack mate."

"I don't know why they had you in there with your petty officer in the first place. That had to be violating some kind of rule."

"I would have thought so too but she got mad because I kept hitting her rack in the middle of the night. If I wasn't going to sleep then she wasn't either."

"Oh, you're a rebel already."

"Ha ha, just a little bit."

"I can tell. We are going to get along great."

Mohammed helped me with my things and helped me get set up. Mohammed was a Muslim. She wore her head wrap but when she took it off she had long locks. She said the best thing about wearing her head wrap was that when her hair needed to be re-twisted, no one could tell. She was so funny and we had a good time together. As we were getting things settled, she told me that her rack mate and mine were actually best friends so it sounded like it was a win-win for the both of us. Now they could snore alongside each other.

I was still getting used to delegating work to the seamen and they eventually got over the fact that I was young. We all became good friends and hung out in the different cities together. Pena, Wells, Keller, Freeman, and I were always together. We went to a lot of places. Our home port was Augusta Bay, Italy, and whenever we went outside of Italy to unload supplies, we came right back to Augusta Bay until it was time to go back out again. We went to Israel, Greece, the coast of Africa, Spain, all over Italy, and of course Cyprus. I couldn't believe that I was in all these places that I only read about a year ago. I guess the saying is true—envision yourself where you want to be and watch God take you there.

There were many times where we were out to sea and there was no sight of land anywhere in the distance. It was just us and nature; whales swimming in the distance and flying fish coming in and out of the water. We even had dolphins that would swim aside the ship. Maybe they thought we were one big dolphin seeing that we were the same color as they were. It was very serene and peaceful. There were other times where we had to pull aside another ship and cast lines to them in order to give them supplies and fuel. It was so cool to see us taking pallets of food and supplies and sending them across the ocean and onto another ship. I had never seen anything like that in my life. At night, we couldn't go outside of the ship because we would risk terrorists knowing our location because it was pitch black in the middle of the ocean and once we opened the hatch, the light from the inside of the ship would radiate the darkness and anyone would be able to see our location. I learned that by also venturing out in the middle of the night just to see what it looked like when it was total darkness outside. We live and we learn.

When I applied to be an SK, I had no idea how much work it involved or all the cool things I would be able to see. The good thing about it was that when we pulled into port, we had to work and we worked hard. We had to unload pallets, go over the inventory with the receiving ship, and make sure the receiving ship loaded all the pallets and signed off on the inventory worksheet prior to us being considered off to go out and enjoy the city that we were in and because our ship was smaller than a lot of the other navy ships, we always got to pull into port and spend a couple of days in the city. I got to explore the culture of these different cities and take mental notes of how they were different from the States. It allowed us to broaden our minds and unleash the adventurous spirit that we held inside of us. It also allowed us to be a part of something that was bigger than ourselves. It allowed us to be alive.

We had made it to mid-May and had less than a month before we would be heading back to the States. We were out in the middle of nowhere making our way to our next destination. I was in my rack reading because I was on break when I heard the sirens going off. I figured it was another man overboard drill because we had those from time to time and the civmar swimmer we had on the ship would dive into the water and perform trainings of rescuing someone who had mistakenly fallen overboard. I got up and looked out the porthole and I saw a ship coming toward us. I didn't think much of it but I knew to follow protocol during drills. I went above Mohammed's rack because she slept on the top rack and got out my life jacket and put it on as I proceeded to the location of my lifeboat. When I got outside, everyone was on the starboard side of the ship looking at this ship that was heading straight toward us.

"What are they doing?" said Freeman.

"When are they planning to turn the ship?" I said.

"What are they even doing out here? We didn't have any unloads today," Pena said as she was putting on her life jacket and walking toward us.

The ship was getting closer and closer. We were still blasting our sirens to alert the ship that they were heading straight toward us but it didn't seem like anyone on the ship was listening. We were told that the captain was trying to get in contact with the ship through radio transmission because it was one of our ships. It was a carrier and if it hit us, it would tear our little ship to pieces.

"What are we going to do?" yelled Pena.

"Hopefully they'll turn the ship in time," said Wells.

We were all terrified that one of our own was about to run right into us and all we could do was watch it happen. We couldn't move our ship fast enough to get out of the way of a direct hit. That's how close they were. As I sat there praying that God would intervene and turn this ship around, we noticed that the ship started to turn slightly.

The captain must have gotten a hold of someone and whatever he said must have worked. We saw some of the sailors from the other ship come out and look at us. I'm sure they couldn't believe how close they were to us either. They were much closer than the other ships that had pulled alongside of us for a cross water supply delivery. The ship kept coming closer and turning at the same time. They were so close, it was as if I could jump from our ship and land on theirs. Just in the nick of time, they were fully turned and riding alongside our ship. We all cheered and hugged each other. No man overboard today. Once the news made its way to us, we were told that someone was drunk at the wheel. I really hoped that wasn't the case because incompetence could have cost us our lives. We didn't come here to die and we surely didn't come to die from friendly fire. I was certain that someone was going to be in a lot of trouble. I was just glad that it wasn't for killing us.

Closer to the end of our tour, we found ourselves in Athens, Greece. The people were so nice and the food was extremely flavorful. I had never had a gyro like they made them in my life. They actually put french fries in their gyros and the sauce was so tantalizing on my tongue. I think I may have eaten like three of them because they weren't big like you may find in the States, they were smaller and cheaper.

"Lil bit, you better slow down on those gyros," said Julio.

"But they are so good."

"Tiny can put some food away," said Freeman. "I've seen her do it."

"Why is it always the little ones that eat so much?" said Frank, who was one of the civmar boatsmen on the ship. He looked out for me too because he said I reminded him of one of his sisters. The civmars went out to sea when we went but when we got back into port in Virginia, I was told they would all go home until it was time for us to go out again but that our ship was about to be dry-docked for a couple of years for maintenance and when the ship is dry-docked, we had to get off the ship. Many people got apartments because the navy allotted us pay to help with living costs or you could live in the barracks on the base. I had already decided that I was going to get an apartment. I hadn't even been to Virginia yet but I knew I wanted my own space and besides, if the navy was going to foot the bill, why not?

"When are we going shopping?" I said because I loved the European clothes and who knew when I would be back over here again. Our tours were six months long and I was told that we only did a tour once a year and sometimes they were in different parts of the world.

"You can buy things as we walk around but don't buy too many items since it's your first tour. You don't want to spend all your money. Buy some things now and then save up for when we get back to the States so that next year, you can buy more," said Freeman.

That sounded like a good plan to me. They knew more than I did because they had done tours before. This was my very first one and I came in mid-way through. We hung out in the city for the remainder of the evening and I bought some things and brought them back to the ship. The leather in Greece was very affordable so I brought some things back for Deonte, Lexy, and my parents and also picked up some things for myself. I tried not to go overboard but it was hard with their prices being so low.

Once back on the ship, we relaxed for the remainder of the evening because we were heading back out to Augusta Bay in the morning. On our way there, we hit a big storm. I was down in the storeroom with the civmars watching them wrap up the pallets and I started feeling really sick. Because our ship was small, we were able to feel every wave. There were several times where we had to tuck our sheets into our mattresses and tie our things down to our dressers to avoid falling out of the bed and our things flying across our rooms. It felt like we were in another big one. The civmars weren't phased at all. They were still laughing and joking around but when Julio looked at me, he knew something was wrong.

"Lil bit. Are you ok?"

"I'm ok, I think."

"You don't look good," said Elle.

"I'll be ok."

Just then, the ship rocked and I threw up all over the step that I was standing on.

"Lil bit, go to bed," said Julio.

"But I'm ok. I can't go to bed. I have to work."

"It's fine. If anyone comes looking for you, we will cover for you. You only have a couple more hours anyway."

"Ok. Y'all know where to find me if you need me."

"Yes we do. Now go to bed."

Our civmars were great. They looked out for us and I did the same thing for them. They knew that I wasn't going to be any good to them for the remainder of the day if I continued to feel the way that I felt. I had to continue to hold on to the bars that we had around the ship so I didn't fall on my way back to my room. Getting back to my rack felt like the longest walk in history but once I was there, I felt better. I tucked my sheets into my mattress and made sure my things were also tied down and got into the rack. Before I laid in my rack, I looked out the porthole to see what was happening outside and all I could see was the ocean one second and then the sky the next. The weather was really rocking our ship and that was why I was so sick. I got in my bunk, closed my eyes, and slept for the remainder of the day.

Our last night in Augusta Bay, some of us decided to go to the beach and have a mini beach party. We had some food and drinks and someone had a radio. It was such a beautiful night. Julio decided to teach me how to dance salsa. He was of Cuban descent and Pena was Dominican. I was trying to get them both to teach me Spanish because I took it in high school and used to be able to speak it but if you don't use it, you lose it.

"You have to do your feet like this," said Julio as he showed me some moves.

"My feet don't go that way," I said jokingly.

"They can if you teach them to."

"We are on sand and you are trying to teach me salsa."

"You can learn salsa anywhere. Once you feel it on the inside, your body moves with the rhythm."

"That's true with any music. Music has a way of bringing all cultures together. It's a way of life all by itself."

"You're wise."

"If you say so."

He continued to teach me how to dance salsa as we all laughed and enjoyed our last night in Italy. I was glad that I was able to fly over here to meet the ship instead of flying into Virginia and waiting for them to come back. This was going to be an experience that I would treasure forever.

It took us three weeks to cross over the Atlantic and thank God we had some good weather coming back. It was crystal blue skies and deep navy waters. From time to time, Pena and I would go lay on the flight deck and just look up at the sky and talk. The flight deck was a quiet place to just think or read. Sometimes we just needed to get away from the ship and this was the only place that seemed to be far enough away.

"What are you going to do when you get back?" asked Pena.

"I don't know. I've never been to Virginia."

"I want to go get my son. He's in New York with my mom."

"So why don't you? We are about to be dry-docked so you will have at least two years on shore duty before we get new orders."

"Yeah, but what happens after two years?"

"That's a long way away. Why even think about it right now?"

"Because it will be here before you know it. I'm going to visit when I get back."

"That's a good idea. I don't know what I'm doing. I'm going to have my parents bring me my car and then at least I will be able to get around."

"You have a car?"

"Yes. I got one when I was in high school. It gives me trouble here and there but at least I have one."

"Yes, that's going to help you a lot around the base because the base is huge—one of the biggest in the fleet. There's so much to do on base that you really never have to leave it."

"That's cool. Sounds like I won't be bored then."

"No, you won't. Besides, you have all of us. You can't be bored with our crew."

"Ha ha, you are so right."

We stayed out there and talked about what we wanted out of life and how long we planned on being in the military. It was good to just be outside, feeling the breeze on our faces, and enjoying the time that we had.

When we were close to the coastline of Norfolk, Va, we all had to put on our dress whites and stand shoulder to shoulder all around the ship. That was how we pulled out of port and how we came back in port. It was surely a sight to see. As we made our way in, all the family members that were waiting for their loved ones started to cheer. Some people were crying, some kids were running around while the parent was trying to catch them, and some little babies were asleep in their stroller. The families were happy that their loved ones had made it back safely and we were glad too.

After we were dismissed, the majority of our ship's personnel took their things and went with their families that were waiting for them, but I went back to my room to change. I didn't have family that was waiting for me but I did have family that was telling me to hurry up so that we could go venture out onto the base.

"Payton, you should come over later if you don't have anything to do," said Freeman who had an apartment off base.

"Ok. I don't know what we are about to get into but I'll let you know."

"Ok, see you later."

We had liberty weekend when we returned. That was all of us except those that had watch. We all rotated watch duty and I was glad that I didn't have duty this weekend. We knew we had to go back out in three weeks for war games but then we were going to be on shore for the next two years. I started to wonder if I could get orders to be stationed overseas. I really enjoyed myself over there and the military bases there felt like European culture. They were strict to a certain point but they were also a little more relaxed than boot camp and A-school. Those were the only two bases that I could compare anything to. It was time to venture out onto the Norfolk base and see what they had to offer.

I was still talking to Simmons and found out that in a couple of months, he was going to be stationed at the Dam Neck base in Virginia. The navy was bringing people back together instead of ripping them apart. It was music to my ears. Dam Neck was about a thirty-minute car ride from Norfolk so it would be easy for me to go see him when I didn't have duty and vice versa. That was one good thing I had to look forward to.

Once we got dressed, Pena, Wells, and I went out on the base. We went to some of the activity centers to see who was there and then went to get something to eat. We stayed out late and found our way back to the ship around 0200. Good thing we didn't have to wake up early in the morning. The only problem was that my body was used to waking up early so sleeping in late wasn't even an option. I got up that morning at 0700, went to the galley for breakfast, and headed back out to see what the base had to offer.

Three weeks went by and we were back on the water. We had all-hands meetings in the mornings and had to meet in the conference room at the back of the ship. The lieutenant and captain attended these meetings so we made sure to get there or else that meant extra duty and since we valued our free time, we made sure to arrive before them.

"Tomorrow is war games. Many of you know what war games are but we have some newbies on the ship so I will go over what it is and what is expected of you. The marines use our ship for their war games. We will be considered terrorists. You are to act like terrorists when they come aboard the ship. We won't know what time they are set to arrive as their mission is surprise attacks. If you see them before they get here, then their mission has been compromised, which means they have failed their mission. During these war games, you are to play along. You are to resist capture, try to get away, and even refuse to go with them. This is what terrorists would do and your participation is mandatory. When we help them with their training, it helps the military against enemy attacks. Understood?"

"Yes, Captain!"

Pena whispered to me. "This sounds fun."

"It does, doesn't it?"

"I'm going to act like I'm not going with them and that I can't hear anything that they are saying."

"I'm going to resist and say, I'm not going anywhere. You can't make me go with you. Get out of my way," I laughed. Pena was new to the ship as well and neither of us had been in war games so we were ready for what was about to happen, so we thought.

The next day started off like any other day. We were all eating in the galley and were talking and being our loud selves. After lunch, we hung out around the ship waiting for the marines to come. We were told we wouldn't know when they were to arrive and we were to go about our day as normal. I went out onto the deck and sat on one of the ladders that went from the inside of the ship to the outside. All of a sudden, this metal piece that looked like a claw was thrown inside of the ship on my right side and then the left. These metal pieces had rope attached to them. My eyes got big and I turned around to see this marine in camouflage staring at me with a gun in my face.

"Get on the bulkhead!" he screamed but I was frozen. I couldn't move. Fear gripped my body and wouldn't let go.

"Get on the bulkhead now!"

Still nothing. As he was screaming, four other marines scaled the side of our ship and were now pointing guns at me. I recognized these guns. They were M16s and they were a couple of inches from my face. I know what I said, that I was going to resist, but did they really expect for me to play games with them with M16s in my face? They were all shouting at me to get down and down I went.

One of them pushed me and then pulled my arms together behind my back. I thought I was going to die. I was suddenly in fear for my life because, what if these guns were loaded, which I was guessing that they were, and it happened that they fire by mistake? My head would have been blown off.

After they tied my hands behind my back, one of them called to another and said, "Terrorist has been apprehended." He took me to the back of the ship while one of his teammates followed and the others went to find the other terrorists. When I got to the back, Pena was there looking terrified and so was Freeman. I couldn't believe what was happening. He threw me to the ground and had me sit with the others and said that we better not move or we'd be shot. Move? I wasn't even going to blink. I didn't want any mishaps.

One by one, they brought those captured to the back of the ship. After they completed their sweep of the ship, the marine in charge called to the others and said, "all clear," and went to talk to the captain. After they completed their briefing, they cut us loose and prepared to be on their way. We couldn't see their faces because they wore masks that only showed their eyes but as one of them walked passed me, he said, "I told you I'd see you again," and looked at me and I could tell from his eyes that he was smiling. I recognized his voice from A-school. It was the marine who wanted to talk to me but I told him it wasn't a good idea. I watched him as he went down the ladder and back on to their speedboat. I now knew what war games were and I didn't want to have any part in them. Next time, I was going to sit in the back and tie my own hands and just wait till it was over. It wasn't worth putting my life in danger to help them with their war games. I was all for being government property but this was way beyond the call of duty.

When we got back to the base, my parents agreed to drive up to Norfolk to drop off my car. They said that I needed to think about getting a new one because this one was on its last leg. I didn't want a car note but I knew if I didn't get one soon, I wouldn't have a car to get around in. I decided to go over to Freeman's house because although the base was big, it was lonely if you didn't have anyone to hang out with. I knew Freeman had a boyfriend and I didn't want to drop in unannounced so I'd hang out with her when he had duty.

"Payton, what's going on?"

"Nothing, Freeman. What are you doing over here all by yourself?"

"Girl nothing. Trying to figure out what I'm cooking for dinner."

"There's a lot you can cook. What do you have taste for?"

"Fried chicken."

"Oh, I love fried chicken. I can make some since I'm here."

"Payton, do you cook?"

"Ma'am, I'm from the South and in our house, after a certain age, if you didn't cook, you didn't eat. My whole family can cook—guys and girls."

"Good thing I invited you over then. Have at it. Everything is in the kitchen."

"Cool."

I ended up making fried chicken, rice, and green beans mixed with potatoes. I made enough so that when her boyfriend, Boyd, got off duty he had something to eat as well. After we ate, we hung out on her balcony watching the kids play in the street.

"I'm going to have to invite you over more often."

"Ha ha, I'm down. I don't have anything to do on the base anyway."

"That's why I got an apartment. Sometimes it's nice to get away from the base and feel normal for a minute."

"I can understand that. I'm thinking about getting an apartment too once I can."

"I highly recommend that you do. You'll like having your own space."

We stayed out there and talked all night about where we grew up and our journey into the navy. Everyone had a different story as to why they came in but I was glad that we all made the decision. It allowed me to meet some great people that I may not have met any other way. Yes, there were already interesting things happening but the bad didn't outweigh the good, yet.

A couple of months went by and we were preparing to go to dry-dock for two years. I had ended up buying me a new car. My old one couldn't take it anymore and the drive back and forth to Atlanta was proving to be too taxing on it. I decided to buy a car in Atlanta because all the dealerships in Norfolk would hike up their prices since it was a military town and I was not about to be paying double for a car. I received my loan from Navy Federal and took my funds to Atlanta. I liked my new car and loved the new car's smell. Now my shipmates and I could ride around without my car getting overheated and smoking, which was so embarrassing.

We had some new civmars on the ship since we were in port and our normal ones were out with their families. I was in charge of this one guy because he needed to do some work in my storeroom. I held all of the level one material for the ship. These were high priority parts that were a sum of 1.4 million dollars so I had to watch him to make sure that he did his job and that my inventory continued to be one hundred percent accurate. Everyone was at the all-hands meeting to go over what the next several months would look like and to see where everyone who didn't have an apartment would be staying on the base. I wanted to be a part of the discussion but knew I had to stay in the storeroom and watch him.

The storeroom had four aisles of supplies and at the end of each aisle was a walkway that connected all of the aisles together. There was some maintenance work that he had to do down one of the aisles. I stayed closer to the front of the aisles toward the steps that led into my storeroom. As I was putting some supplies away, he started making small talk.

"Why do they have you here all by yourself?"

"This is my storeroom and everyone else is in a meeting."

"Is that right?"

"Yes, it is."

"You're not scared of being down here all by yourself?"

"No. Why should I be?"

"I just asked," he said as he started to walk closer toward me. "Do you have a boyfriend?"

"I don't think that's any of your business and I think you should stop talking and just finish up what you came down here to do."

"Oh, you're sassy, huh?"

"No, I just want you to hurry up and get done so that I can go to my meeting?"

I had turned around to put something on one of the back shelves and when I turned around, he was about three feet in front of me.

"Why are you here?" I said questioning why he was so close to me when the hole he was patching was in another area.

"I just wanted to make sure you were ok."

"I'm fine. Please move out of my way. I have work to do."

"I'm not going anywhere," he said as he walked closer to me. I noticed that I was stuck in a corner and he was blocking my only entrance to go down one of the aisles. "I see something that I like."

"I think you need to go back to work," I said as I tried to push past him.

"Nah, you're not going anywhere."

He pushed me against the wall and grabbed my wrists with one of his hands. "I said I saw something that I liked and I'm not going anywhere until I get a taste." I tried to struggle to get free but he was stronger than I was. "Just relax and let it happen," he whispered in my ear. I could feel his hands start to go down my pants. I closed my eyes and felt his breath and the tip of his nose on my neck. I tried to scream but no words would come out. I just froze. I felt something wet on my face. I thought it was a pipe above us that was leaking but when I opened my eyes, there were tears streaming down my face.

I couldn't believe this was happening to me. Why wasn't anyone checking in on me so that they could stop this from happening? I didn't know what to do but I knew I wasn't going to just let this happen. Because I wasn't fighting, he loosened the grip he had on my wrists and I saw an opportunity to try to fight back. It was as if something in me just clicked. I pulled my wrist down fast and it caught him off guard. We struggled and somehow I was able to get past him. I took off running as fast as I could and I could hear him behind me. I rounded the corner and headed toward the steps. As I got to the steps, I felt his hand grab my butt trying to pull me back down and I fell on the steps. I let out a scream but immediately got back up and ran down the hall toward the all-hands meeting. I busted in the door and saw Crawford. He saw the look on my face and rushed into the passageway and tried to get me to calm down.

"Payton, what's wrong?"

I couldn't speak. I was hyperventilating and I couldn't catch my breath. Tears were streaming down my face and I just kept seeing his face.

"Payton, talk to me! What happened?"

I tried to formulate words. "He-He-He."

"He what? Who is he?"

"He tried to rape me."

Crawford's eyes got big. He went into the all-hands meeting and got the lieutenant and the captain and they all ran down to the storeroom were the civmar was. I stood in the corner of the passageway when Lieutenant Gibson came to get me.

"I need you to come down here and tell me what happened."

"I can't go down there."

"It's ok. We won't let him hurt you."

But in my mind, he already had. Why did I need to go down there where he was to tell them what happened? I could stay right where I was. Lieutenant Gibson walked me back down to the storeroom where I was now face to face with my attacker. He stood there with this smug look on his face. They made me tell them what had just happened while he stood there smiling at me. After I was done, they let me go back upstairs. I couldn't believe what had just happened. I kept replaying my actions in my mind to see if I had said anything that could have led him on but I couldn't find anything.

After about fifteen minutes, they led him upstairs and I jumped. I don't know why I jumped, I just did. They escorted him off the ship and tried to reassure me that this wasn't my fault. They told me that if I needed a minute, I could go to my room and then come to the all-hands meeting whenever I was ready. I went to my room and laid in my bed crying. I replayed what had just happened in my head over and over again trying to make some sense out of it. Why did this happen to me? How did he know he could do this to me? How did he know that I didn't have a covering; no one that was looking out for me? How did he know that my biological father wasn't there and that my stepfather was verbally and physically abusive? How did he know these things about me to take advantage of me?

I didn't know how to deal with these emotions. I felt filthy but knew that if I took a shower, no scrubbing in the world would get his breath off my neck or his voice out of my ear. I looked at my wrists and wanted to cut them off. Anywhere that he touched I wanted it removed from me. My brain wouldn't stop playing it over and over again and I could still hear his voice. I vowed in that moment to not ever allow another man to take advantage over me. I was going to protect myself at all cost.

After a while, I got up and joined my shipmates in the all-hands meeting. I sat in the back next to Pena in order to not disturb what was going on. She could tell that something was wrong.

"Payton, are you ok?"

"Yes," I said as I continued to look straight ahead.

"No, you're not. What happened?"

"Nothing."

"Are you sure?"

"Yes, I'm sure."

She didn't ask me again. She just looked at me with this worried look in her eyes and continued listening to the meeting.

After the meeting was over, Crawford pulled me to the side and asked me if I was ok. I told him that I was and that I had to go. I didn't drink much before but I felt like I needed something to shut my brain off. I went to a liquor store, got a bottle of Paul Masson, and went to this park that had a lake and sat in my car and started to drink. The more I drank, the quieter the voices got. I got out of my car and went toward the lake. I just stood there staring at the water wondering what would happen if I got in. Would I try to swim? Or would it be better for me to just let it happen? Up until this point, I was happy with my decision to join the navy but with one quick swoop, it was taken away from me. How do I move on from this? I took another drink. I didn't want to think about anything anymore. I just wanted to die. Why did God allow this to happen to me? Didn't they say He took care of His children? At that moment, I didn't like Him. I didn't feel like myself and I didn't want to feel anything more.

LIMA

I didn't know what happened but I woke up inside of my car. It was lights out and I had no idea what time it was. I turned on my car and my clock said 0800. What! I couldn't believe I slept that long. I was late for watch. I rushed back to the ship and stumbled up the ramp. My head was pounding but I couldn't deal with it right now. I had to get to watch. When I got to watch, Wells was there.

"Payton, where have you been?"

"I'm sorry. I'm here."

"Girl, you are drunk."

"No, I'm not. I'm fine."

"No, you're drunk or have a pretty bad hangover. The captain is here today so I advise you to go take a shower and drink some coffee or something before we switch."

Reluctantly, I agreed. I got in the shower and just stood there. I allowed the water to run over my face for what seemed like hours. In my mind, I was back at home and in college; hanging out with Jason and Veronica. We were driving in his car and he was smiling. He looked so happy and for that moment, so was I. The water turned cold and woke me up out of my daze. I got out, got dressed, brushed my teeth, and gargled with some mouth wash before heading to watch. I was glad that the captain didn't come out of his room because I would have gotten in a lot of trouble.

"Ok, I'm here. You can go now."

"Are you sure you're ok because I can stay longer if you need me to."

"No, I'm good. Thanks Wells. You saved my butt today."

"Don't worry, you'll owe me one," she said smiling as she gave me the room keys and headed off the ship.

Watch was going to be easy because everyone was gone and we didn't have anything to do since the ship wasn't going anywhere for a while. It was the perfect time to just be. I tried to think about what had happened the day before but nothing would populate. I couldn't recount the event, I no longer heard any voices but I still felt that something wasn't right. Why couldn't I remember anything? I didn't know what was happening to me but I wasn't going to fight it. I was just going to let it be.

After watch, I decided to hang out with Pena and Freeman at Freeman's apartment. We decided to chill out on the balcony before heading in to watch a movie.

"Hey Payton, what was wrong with you yesterday?" asked Pena.

"What do you mean?"

"You were looking weird and acting weirder."

"I was?" I was trying to think back on the previous day but nothing was registering. I didn't remember talking to Pena. "I don't remember."

"Yeah, I asked you if you were ok and you said yes but you didn't look at me."

I was perplexed as to what she was talking about. "Are you sure that was yesterday?"

"Yes, do you not remember?"

"No, I don't. Weird."

"Yes, it is. Anyway, what movie are we watching?"

"I don't know. Freeman is picking the movie."

We continued to talk and joke and hang out over Freeman's until it was time to head out.

"Y'all can stay over if you want. Boyd isn't here. They are out for three weeks so if you want to stay here instead of the ship, y'all can."

"I'm going to go back to the ship. I got some things to do," said Pena.

"I'll stay," I said. "I'll go back to the ship tomorrow to get some clothes. It'll be good to be roomies for a couple of weeks."

"Cool. I don't like being here by myself anyway. Stay as long as you want."

It was good having somewhere else to go. I wasn't sure what was going on inside of my head but when I was getting off of watch earlier, I got this sinking feeling as I passed by my storeroom. I couldn't remember anything but I felt different now about those steps.

By September, I had moved in with Freeman. Boyd's ship was doing a tour in the Mediterranean so they were going to be gone for six months. Freeman didn't want to be by herself so she said I could move in and we would split whatever bills that came in until Boyd got back. I had already planned on getting an apartment at the beginning of the year so this worked out perfectly. Our ship was dry-docked so we weren't living on the ship anyway. We had different jobs around the base and would hang out with our other shipmates any chance we got.

Simmons had arrived in Virginia and we were also hanging out. We had been off and on because the distance proved to be too much and I was meeting guys on the base and he was meeting girls where he was. We decided to just be friends while we were away and see what happened once he got to Dam Neck.

He called and told me that he had just gotten there and I decided to go see him. When I got there, he looked the same but more muscular. He was waiting outside for me and I decided to park in the back so that I could surprise him.

"Somebody has been working out I see," I said smiling.

"Hey baby," he said and jogged over to give me a hug. When he grabbed me, I jumped. "Are you ok? Did I hurt you?"

"No, I don't know why I did that. It's good seeing you," I said smiling but perplexed that I had just jumped for what seemed like no reason at all.

"I missed you."

"Yeah right."

"I did. You didn't miss me?"

"Only a little."

"Sure," he said as he grabbed my hand to walk me inside. I pulled my hand back quickly and looked at him. "Are you sure you're ok?"

"Yes, I'm sure." I quickly changed the subject. "How was Great Lakes?"

"It was fine. It started to get boring after a while. I was ready to go a long time ago but the school was eight months so I had to stay put. How was the tour?"

"It was a lot of fun. We got to see a lot of different places and the food was amazing. I can't even describe how good it was. Besides us almost getting hit by another ship, the tour was good."

"What?! How did y'all almost get hit by another ship?"

"They said someone was drunk at the wheel but I don't know how true that is. I mean, it's a big ship. I'm sure there was more than one person in charge of steering the ship."

"You never know."

"That's true. So, what are you about to do?"

"I don't know. I thought we could go get something to eat and just hang out and see what's on the base."

"Sounds good to me."

"Ok, let me change and we can head out. It's really good seeing you."

"It's good seeing you too," I said as I sat on his bed while he went to the head to change.

We hung out for the rest of the day and I laughed so hard with him that my stomach hurt. He was always making me laugh because he said he loved my smile. He made me feel good. It was like an escape from reality. After I dropped him off, I headed back to the apartment. I used to like riding in silence but all of a sudden that changed. I no longer enjoyed total silence and had to have some music playing on my ride. I blasted my Carl Thomas CD and headed back to Norfolk.

By October, Simmons and I were just friends. We had too many ups and downs and I believe we both got tired of fighting so we decided it would be best if we just stayed friends. We still hung out from time to time but the pressure of being in a relationship was removed and it made me feel more at ease. I needed to be able to do whatever I wanted, whenever I wanted and when you have a person telling you what they want you to do instead, that is only going to lead to heartache. We still called each other to check in, mostly when we were bored but I was glad that he was still a part of my life, however small it was.

I had a couple of people that I was dating but it was nothing serious. They were time wasters when I was bored and just wanted company. Whenever they started the "relationship" speech, I kindly told them that I needed some space. I didn't want anyone having that kind of control over me. I wanted to be my own person, free to come and go as I pleased. Freeman and I had a good time being roommates. We would hang out after work and have a drink. We always had a reason to drink. It was what we did in the navy. When we didn't have anything to do, we hosted gatherings. We would have our shipmates over, cook, dance, and play music all night long. We were just living life to the fullest with no care in the world. That was until October 12th.

I was at work that morning and was messing with Mason. He was a guy I met while working at my new command center. He was talking about what he was planning on doing that weekend when we got a phone call. "Oh no!" someone screamed and hung up the phone. It was out of the ordinary because no one ever slammed down the phone the way that she just did. She went into the Lieutenant Commander's office and closed the door. Everyone was looking around trying to figure out what had just happened. When she came out of the office, she went over to another petty officer's desk and they began to talk. Word spread fast and all of a sudden, people were running around and making phone calls. We didn't know what had happened but we knew it was serious.

"The USS Cole was just bombed!" someone said out loud.

What! What did they mean by bombed? Where were they? Was anyone hurt? I'm sure whoever yelled that out was not following protocol because pandemonium broke out.

"I know someone on that ship," said Mason as he tried to call one of his other friends on the base. I didn't know anyone on the Cole that I knew of. I started to think about my shipmates from boot camp and A-school. Any one of them could have been ordered to that ship. My heart dropped to my stomach and I froze. I stood there in the middle of the floor not knowing which way to move. What if we were next? What if they were planning to come to Norfolk and bomb us? We didn't have all the information as to where the ship was located or where it was going. All we knew was that they were bombed.

They locked down the base and no one could get on or go off until they released the lock. Some people were crying while others were still trying to get a hold of someone on the phone. I didn't know what to do. I just sat in my chair and watched everyone run around frantically. It was as if they were running in slow motion because that's how they looked in my mind. I eventually got up and went to ask the lieutenant if there was something that I needed to do. "Not right now. We don't know how serious things are at the moment." From the sound of it, things seemed pretty serious. I went back to my desk and waited for orders.

Over the next couple of days, we got names of those who were on the ship, those that had died and those that were injured. They said it was a terrorist attack and that the majority of the people that died were in line for lunch. I couldn't believe it. They were standing in line getting ready to sit down for a meal and that was it. Their lives ended. I kept thinking about our tour and how we had almost got hit by another navy ship and now a terrorist group had bombed one of our own. I had only been in the military for eleven months and it seemed like something was happening every month. This was no way to live. I was always on edge, drinking to stop the thoughts, and was always at sick call because of my knees. This was crazy. One minute, we would be living life to the fullest and the next, people were dying. It was already taking a toll on me but I had no idea just how much.

When March rolled around, Freeman's boyfriend had come back in town and I finally got my own apartment. I went to Rent-A-Center to get some furniture and my parents had come down to bring me my bedroom set and some of my other things from home. I was still on edge but at least I was able to get away from the base when I didn't have to work or have watch. It was my escape from the world. I met more people and we were hanging out all the time. My apartment started to be the hangout spot when we didn't have anything to do and because I loved to cook, there was always someone there.

I had watch on Friday and decided to meet up with Pena after work because she said she had some news for me. She was already on the base and because I lived fifteen minutes from it, I didn't see any need of going home and then coming back. We met up at the activity center and grabbed some food.

"What's going on, Pena? What is this news that you have to tell me?"

"I found out today that I'm pregnant."

I almost spit out my soda. "What?! Pregnant? By who?"

"Someone on our ship but I don't want to say any names because I don't want to get him in trouble."

"In trouble? This isn't something that he can hide. You're going to get big at some point and then what?"

"I don't know yet. I just came from sick call and needed to tell someone. I don't know what to do. They said that I wasn't going to be able to be on the ship anymore and that I would have to sign over paternity rights once the baby comes."

"Wow! Pena, I'm sorry to hear that."

"Thanks Payton. I have a lot to figure out."

"Well, let me know if you need anything. I'm here."

"Thanks Payton."

We continued to eat and talk about what the next steps for her would be. I couldn't imagine having a baby and having to sign over my parental rights to someone else. I didn't know how she was going to do it but I was going to find out who it was because they needed to take responsibility.

By April, I was having physical therapy appointments for my knees every week. I had to do shock therapy, water aerobics, and weight training. They were trying to strengthen the muscles that kept my kneecaps in place because the kneecaps themselves had started to pop out of place whenever they wanted to. If I was running and they got weak, down I went. It got so bad that even when I was walking, it would happen. I got to a point where I didn't know when the next time would occur, so I expected it at all times.

They gave me some knee braces so that at least when they got ready to go out, the cushion that surrounded my kneecap would hold it in place long enough for me to catch my balance. They were effective but I couldn't wear them under my clothes because the braces were big and bulky and I was petite. I would only wear them during PT and when I was resting at home. I was meeting with my doctor today to go over a plan. I arrived at sick call, checked in, and waited to be called.

"Payton."

"Yes."

"Please come with me."

I got up and followed the corpsman to the back. When we got in the room, I was told to wait until the doctor arrived. I didn't like coming to sick call but it was starting to become my home away from home. My appointments had increased and it seemed like nothing was working. I was looking at the different pictures on the wall when I heard a knock at the door.

"Payton."

"Yes, come in."

"Hi, Payton. How are we today?"

"I'm fine, Lieutenant."

"That's good to hear. I received your paperwork from your physical therapist and as I was looking at your chart, I noticed that they started you on shock therapy, correct?"

"Yes, that's correct."

"Is it working?"

"Not that I can tell. My kneecaps are still popping out of place. I don't think anything is working."

"Ok. Unfortunately, we are doing everything that we can without doing surgery but nothing is keeping the kneecaps in place. I'm going to have a meeting with the physical therapist to see if there is anything else that can be done but for right now, I'm placing you on limited duty. I don't see any other option for you. Once I speak with the therapist, I'm thinking you will only have two options: you can stay in the navy on shore duty, meaning you will not be able to go overseas or travel anymore because the medical facilities here are much better than overseas or you will be discharged from the navy on either an administrative discharge or a medical discharge. Both discharges are honorable. If you decide to stay in, you will have to change jobs because you are now unfit to do the job that you signed up for."

Is this what my navy career came down to? Stay in the States and change my job or get out? I didn't join the navy to stay in the States. I joined so that I could get away from home, travel, and get money to pay for college when I returned. None of his options seemed like a good fit for my overall goal.

"What is the difference between an administrative and medical discharge?" I asked.

"Basically, one you will be paid for and the other you won't."

Well, that sounded like an easy choice to make. I'll take paid for 100, Alex.

"Ok, so what do I do now?"

"I'm going to get you signed up with TPU, which is the temporary processing unit. Once we have made a final decision on if you're staying in or getting out, TPU is where you would start the process on being discharged, but for right now you'll just be on limited duty and TPU will find you a job where you don't have to put stress on your knees so much. When you leave here, take this chit over to TPU and they will process you in."

"Ok, thank you Lieutenant."

"You're welcome, Payton. Sorry we couldn't do more for you."

"Yeah, me too."

I got up and headed over to TPU. I was just told that I was unfit for the job that I signed up for and that I could leave. My head was spinning and I decided not to make any decisions until I heard back from the lieutenant. Maybe he'd come back with good news but from the sounds of it, that was highly unlikely.

When I got to TPU, they had me go down this hall to the administrative room to get signed in. As I was walking down the hall, I noticed this guy who looked like he was up to something. We locked eyes and he smiled. He seemed like the type of guy that I would be interested in but I knew I needed to go get signed in so I kept walking. Once I was in the administrative room, there were others waiting to get signed in as well. I got behind the last person in line and waited.

As I waited, the guy came back down the hall and looked at me. "What are you in line for?" I looked at him with one eyebrow raised as to say, "Why do people normally line up for?" but I didn't know him so I thought I'd be nice.

"I'm signing in to TPU. What are you here for?"

"Same."

"Great."

"You seem cool. We should hang out."

"Ha, just like that?"

"Yeah, why not? From the looks of it, you're not going to be in much longer anyway."

Well, he had a point but did he have to be so weird about it?

"Ok, I guess."

"You guess? Are we hanging out or not?"

"Yeah," I said smiling because now I was intrigued.

"Ok, cool. I'll be around. Let me know when you're done."

"I'm not about to be looking for you."

"Who approached who?"

"You approached me."

"Right. So I'll be around and I'll know when you're done."

"But you just said…"

"Don't make this difficult. I'll see you later."

He smiled and walked back up the hall. I laughed because I couldn't believe how this conversation just went. He's crazier than I am. We may just get along.

Once I got signed in, they sent me to this other room to be assigned to a new job for the time I'd be attached to TPU. When I walked into the room, there was another line. I shook my head and got behind the last person. By this time, my stomach was growling.

"Man, I'm hungry."

"Me too," said the girl in front of me. "I don't know why they have us standing in all these lines. If we are on limited duty, then don't they think we need to be sitting rather than standing? My back is killing me?"

Wow. Someone who shared my thought process.

"I was thinking the same thing. Hi, I'm Payton."

"Hi Payton. I'm Daniels."

"Nice to meet you Daniels. So, what alignment are you here for?"

"My back. They want to do surgery but I don't want them to. I don't trust them to operate on me."

"Me neither. My knees are my issue and now they are trying to see if there are any other options other than picking another job or getting out."

"Normally when you come here, they've already decided. I don't know of many people that have come to TPU and are not getting out."

"Are you for real?"

"Yup."

I had no idea that my lieutenant was already planning on discharging me. He surely fooled me into thinking it was my decision.

"I just want this line to hurry up and move because I'm hungry and I need to eat something quick."

"I'm with you on that one. Say, let's go to get something to eat when we leave here?"

"Cool."

We finished up and were both assigned to escorts. We would have to escort those that were in the brig to their medical and dental appointments. It sounded like an interesting job. I already had it in my mind to ask them what they were in the brig for in the first place. What trouble were they getting into to be thrown in military jail? We had to make sure that we gave our paperwork to our current unit to let them know that we wouldn't be there moving forward because of our limited duty status.

As Daniels and I were walking down the hall, the guy from earlier walked up to me. "Where are you going? I thought we were hanging out."

"You didn't say what time."

"You're right but I did say when you're done. Are you done?"

"Technically no because I have to go back to my old unit and give them my paperwork," I said smiling.

"Ok. I will let that one slide but we're hanging out later. What barracks are you in?"

"I'm not in the barracks. I have an apartment off base."

"Me too," said Daniels as we looked at each other and smiled.

"And who are you?" he said.

"Um, who are you?"

That's right. I never got his name. All this conversation and I didn't even know who this dude was.

"I'm Turner."

"Well, Turner, I'm Daniels. How do you know Payton?"

"She's a good friend of mine."

"Good friend? We just met today." I laughed.

"But I can already tell," he said smiling.

"We are about to go get something to eat. Would you like to join us?"

"I wish I could but I can't. They still need me around here."

"Ok then. We will see you later."

"Ok. Later ladies."

We smiled and walked off. He was a funny dude but I had a good feeling about him.

Daniels and I went to Subway and talked like we were old college roommates. We found out that we were both from Georgia and that we lived about an hour away from each other. She had a son and lived in a townhouse off the base. She was married before but was going through a divorce with her husband who was also on the base. She told me how the military was treating her since she was divorcing from an officer and how anything that she said was dismissed. They didn't care that she was also a military member. The only voice that mattered was her husband's. I felt for her. I couldn't relate to going through her situation and with a child. She also stated that she was stationed on the USS Cole and was flown off four days before the bombing because of an injury with her back and she was still feeling guilty about it; like she had let her shipmates down by not being there in their time of need. I told her that while we do not know why as many people died as they did, there was still purpose for her life. Maybe God positioned us both to be at TPU at the same time just so that we could meet. His divine connections are truly unmatched.

We hung out after lunch and had to separate to take our paperwork back to our current units. We exchanged phone numbers and addresses. I knew I had just made a lifelong friend. I could just feel it. When I got back to TPU to turn in my signed paperwork of release from the last unit, I saw Turner. He must have seen me too because he started heading straight toward me.

"I like how you disappeared earlier."

"I didn't disappear. You saw me leave."

"You know what I mean."

"I don't know what you mean. What are you doing here anyway?"

"Why are any of us here? Trying to get out of the military."

"I'm not trying to get out. I am trying to stay in."

"I'm sure a part of you wants to get out."

When he said that, it pulled on some internal strings. Was I looking for a way out? So many things had happened that I didn't know if staying in was the safest thing for me.

"You always have something to say, I see."

"That's true. So where are we going?"

"Going when?"

"Now, later, sometime soon."

I laughed. "Turner, where do you want to go?"

"It doesn't matter."

"It does matter."

"No, it doesn't. I just want to go somewhere and find out why we're such good friends."

I looked at him and smiled. "Ok, let's go."

We decided to go to Applebee's right off the base. That was one of the go to spots when we wanted to get away from the base although almost everyone there came from the base. It just felt different. We found out that we were a lot alike. We had a lot of similarities and when we shared stories of the people that we dated in the military, he said I sounded just like him only a female version. We stayed out all night talking. Although at first glance he seemed like someone I would date, after I got to know him, I knew that he was going to be one of my very best friends.

Over the following weeks, we hung out even more. Either he was at my place or I was at his. I was still dating guys so I would ask for his advice here and there. He would say the exact thing I was thinking. He told me that he would never set me up with one of his friends because of how I treated guys but he treated females the same way; probably why I never hooked him up with any of my friends either.

Escort duty was going well and Daniels and I were hanging out and going to the club some weekends. It was good to get out and have some time to ourselves. I knew she needed it every now and then. It was our way of destressing from a long work week, watch duty, and insomnia. Because we were always up and down, it was hard to sleep when we were supposed to. A lot of the time, we'd stay up until we had no choice but to go to sleep but that could easily be two days later.

Friday rolled around and I decided to go to this house party that a couple of the guys I met on the base were throwing. There were several different groups that I hung out with and depending on my mood was which group I would be calling. Reed and Morgan were two guys from the base that were always throwing parties. I knew that if I went to their party, I could eat and drink for free. Ward rode with me to their townhouse because she didn't have anything to do either. I met Ward through Wells and she was a lot of fun. She was from Maryland and was bigger than life. She didn't care who you were, she was going to tell you what was on her mind. She used to always say that she was a black girl on the inside but that her outside hadn't caught up yet. We had a lot of fun together and when I wanted to hang out, but not by myself, Ward would come with me.

We got to Reed and Morgan's place around 1500 because they needed help cooking. When I got out of the car, their neighbor was checking the mail. He was a tall light-skinned brother with curly hair. You could tell he was mixed with something. As Ward and I started down the driveway, he stopped me.

"Excuse me, can I talk to you for a second?"

"What do you want to talk to her for?" said Ward

"Ward, I got this. I'll be in in a minute."

"Ok, let me know if you need anything."

"I will," I said laughing. Ward was short but that didn't stop her from voicing her opinion, no matter how tall you were.

"Hi, I'm Mario. What's your name?"

"I'm Payton. I mean, Yasmine. Sorry, it's a military thing."

"I know. Everyone around here is in the military."

"That's true."

"I know you're about to go to a party my neighbors are throwing but can I get your number and call you sometime?"

"Yeah, you can."

"Wait one second. Don't go anywhere."

"I'm not."

He went to his car and grabbed a little piece of paper and a pen.

"Is that your car?" I asked

"Yes," he said smiling.

I didn't know what kind of work he did but he looked to be around my age and was driving a Mercedes. I knew he wasn't in the military because they weren't paying that much. I wrote down my number and handed it to him.

"Here you go."

"I'm going to call you."

"I hope so," I said as I walked back down the driveway.

When I got in the house, Reed was standing at the door.

"Payton, what's up?"

"Nothing much. What are y'all in here doing because I don't smell any food cooking?"

"That's because we were waiting on you. What took you so long? Ward's in here eating up the chips."

"I met your neighbor."

"Who? Sergio?"

"Who is Sergio? I met Mario."

"Uh-Uh Payton. You can't talk to that dude. He's bad news."

"Why do you say that?"

"Just trust me."

"Who is Sergio?"

"Sergio is his brother."

"Oh, ok. I'm a big girl. I can take care of myself."

"Don't say I didn't warn you."

"Ok, I won't say it," I said jokingly as I walked to the kitchen to get ready to fry some chicken wings.

The day turned into night and we were still partying with Reed and Morgan. Their parties never ended before 0300 and people normally stayed over. I had too much to drink and so did Ward so we ended up staying over too. When we got up the next morning, Reed was already up. He had just come inside from checking the mailbox from the day before. He handed me a note and said, "I'm telling you to leave that dude alone." It was too early in the morning to know what he was talking about. When I finally got my eyes all the way opened, I read the letter, "I see you stayed over all night." It was Mario. I didn't think anything of it. I woke up Ward so that we could get ready to head back to our places. We grabbed our things and headed to the car. When I got to the car, I checked my phone and noticed I had a missed text. It was Mario saying how much it was a pleasure meeting me and how he'd like to take me out sometime. I texted him back and said, I'd like that, and then we drove off. Maybe there were some neighbor issues the two of them had between each other and that was the reason Reed didn't want me talking to him. I didn't know what was up but I was old enough to handle myself.

Later on that day, I decided to hang out with Mario. He came to pick me up and we went to Applebee's. The same one everyone else went to. I was trying to see if Turner was there so that I could get some advice from him about Mario but he was nowhere to be found. I wondered what chick he was out with this time. Mario was a gentleman. He opened my car door and pulled out my chair. He told me to order whatever I wanted and not to worry about paying. I wasn't worried anyway because I had no plans on paying.

"So, Mario. What kind of work do you do?"

"Are you asking because of the kind of car I drive?"

"Yeah, that's one reason."

"So, what's the other reason?"

"Because I want to know. Why are you being so secretive?"

"I'm not being secretive. I just wanted to know where the question was coming from. If you must know, I own my own business and it's been very lucrative so it's afforded me some luxuries."

"See, was that so hard?"

"No, it wasn't. I've just met girls who were only interested because of the type of car that I drive."

"Remember, you stopped me, not the other way around."

"I know but I still gotta be careful."

"Understandable."

"So, what are you doing staying in those apartments all by yourself?"

"What do you mean by those apartments?" I knew my apartment complex wasn't that great but they were safe. I had just moved in and besides the creepy old man one building over from mine, it was cool.

"You know what I mean. They don't look that safe for you."

"I can take care of myself. They are safe enough."

"If you say so."

"I know so. I heard you had a brother named Sergio."

"Who told you that?"

"Your neighbor."

"Must have been Reed. I don't like that dude. They just moved in not too long ago and have been irritating me ever since with their loud parties at all times of the night."

"I can see that. So why did you leave a note on my car?" I figured I'd go ahead and ask now rather than waiting till the end of the evening.

"I was just looking out for you. I know I don't really know you but you shouldn't be over there at all times of the night."

"I know Reed and Morgan. They're good guys and they're not trying to do anything to harm us."

"That may be so but when you mix flirtation with alcohol, anything can happen."

"Sort of like now," I said as we were two drinks into dinner.

We enjoyed the rest of our dinner and headed back to my place. I invited him in as I wanted to show him that my place was safe and that there was nothing to worry about. He came in for a brief moment and said he had left something in his car and that he'd be right back. He walked back in but didn't appear to have gotten anything and hung his jacket up in the closet. We sat on the sofa and talked about his childhood and how he and his brother grew up with not much of anything. I told him my reasons for joining the military. He was easy to talk to and didn't seem like he was trouble. After more small talk, he kissed my cheek, pulled me close, put his hand on the small of my back, and that was that.

The next morning as he was leaving, he told me that he wanted to hang out again and that he would give me a call. I said ok and headed off to work. When I got to TPU, Daniels informed me that we had two people to pick up from the brig. We picked up the paperwork and headed there. On the way, I decided to tell her about Mario. I told her about dinner and that Reed had warned me about him but I had no idea what it was about because I didn't get any bad vibes from him.

"I'd listen to Reed if I were you. He's his neighbor so he sees things that you don't see. It's true that guys are prideful and like to protect their own but it sounds like Reed knows more than he is saying."

"Yeah, I get that but I need more information."

"I'm telling you, you should listen to Reed. Besides, didn't you say he was light-skinned?"

"More like high yellow." We both laughed.

"Those light-skinned boys are always up to something. I don't trust them because they're sneaky. My husband is white so he's as light as it gets." We busted out laughing. Daniels was my girl and I had to take what she said into consideration. It had only been one date, I figured I'd give it a couple of weeks to see if anything changed.

Once we got to the brig, there were two with their feet chained. They didn't look like bad news either but they were in the brig so we couldn't put anything past them. We showed the paperwork to the petty officer behind the desk, he signed off, and we loaded them into the van. We were to take them to their appointment, wait for them to get done, and bring them back to the brig. On the way to medical, I decided to ask one of them what he did.

"You don't look like a trouble maker. What are you in the brig for?"

"Drugs," he said as he looked straight ahead like he was trying to figure out where we were going. He was a young white guy with frumpy clothes and he wore glasses. I couldn't believe they let him get away with looking the way that he did but maybe the standards were more relaxed in the brig.

"Ok, you have to elaborate."

"They found drugs in my stuff and brought me here. I think they are going to kick me out."

"How did you get drugs on base?"

"It's easier than you think. They don't pay us enough so some of the guys sell drugs on the side. I found out who and that's where I got my drugs from. Before I got into the navy, I did drugs but when I talked to the recruiter, he said that they would help me get off of them. It worked in boot camp because no one had any but as soon as I got to the fleet, it was everywhere. It was easier to get than out on the streets. So I started using again and now they're kicking me out."

"Why didn't you try to get help?"

"Man I did, but it was always some issue with watch or duty. I'd tell them when my appointment was but they would never let me go so I stopped trying."

"I'm sorry that happened to you. I hope you can find some help when you get out."

"I doubt it. I tried that before and I relapsed. I thought joining the military would be my way out but I guess not."

We rode in silence for the remainder of the trip. I was thinking about the reason why he came in the military and where he was at now. I wondered if anything could be done to help him. Was there a way for him to stay in? It didn't matter how much I thought about it, there was nothing that I could do. I was to take him to his appointment and bring him back and that's exactly what I did.

When I got off, Mario had texted me and said he wanted to see me. I told him that I'd be home shortly and had to shower and change. When I got to the apartment, he was sitting in the parking lot. Did he not have anything else to do with his time? When he saw me, he smiled and got out of the car.

"What are you doing here already?"

"I was waiting on you."

"I can see that."

"I wanted to check out your neighborhood during the day to see what kind of activity was going on."

"I told you my apartments are safe. There's nothing going on here."

"Yes, I can see that now."

We proceeded to enter the apartment.

"Are you hungry?" he asked.

"Yes, I can eat. Give me a minute to take a shower and get changed and we can go."

"Ok."

I handed him the remote to the TV. "Here, make yourself at home."

"I plan on it," he said smiling.

I grabbed my clothes and headed to the bathroom. I was in the shower and thought I heard my front door open. I thought to myself, "Maybe he had to go out to the car to get something." Regardless, I was enjoying my shower and wasn't about to jump out to check and see. After about thirty minutes, I was ready to go. We went to this Cuban restaurant and they had a live band. It was a very nice atmosphere and we talked just like last time. After our meal, we headed back to my place and sat on the sofa and watched a movie. He ended up staying the night. When we went to lay down, he said that he had forgotten something in his coat pocket. I didn't think anything of it.

When he came back, he had a gun and a big one. The look on my face told him that he had some explaining to do.

"I know but I keep this for protection."

"Protection from whom?"

"From anyone who is trying to do me harm."

"Again, like who?"

By this time I was standing straight up trying to figure out why he had a gun in my bedroom.

"Sit down, let me talk to you."

"Nah, I'd rather stand."

He could see that I wasn't budging so he sat on the bed and started to explain.

"Remember when I told you I had my own business. Well I'm a street pharmacist."

"Oh, here we go. Just say that you sell drugs. I don't know why y'all always make it sound bigger than what it is."

"Ok, I sell drugs and in my line of work, there are some people that want what I have. I would never put you in danger but if I don't sleep with this under my pillow, I don't sleep."

"Sounds like a personal problem."

"Don't be like that."

"Be like what? Do you see how big that gun is? What if it goes off in the middle of the night?"

"How is it going to go off in the middle of the night with the safety on?"

"I don't know. Stranger things have happened."

"Not to me."

"They have to me."

By this time, he had put the gun on the bed and came and stood in front of me and put his hands around my waist. "I promise you, nothing is going to happen to you. Last time you didn't even know it was here."

"Wait. You had it here the other night too?"

"Yes, and you had no idea."

"I don't think I can deal with this."

"Why, because I'm trying to protect myself? I told you, nothing is going to happen to you. I promise. I like spending time with you and I don't want that to end. If we keep getting to know each other, you'll see that I'm harmless."

We talked some more and I was asking him all kinds of questions. Eventually, I got tired of talking and wanted to go to sleep. I decided to let him and the gun stay. He did have it here the other night and I didn't know anything about it. What's the worst that could happen?

A couple of days had passed and I had gotten over the whole gun incident. He didn't know that I had a gun of my own that I kept in the glove compartment of my car. My dad had given it to me for protection when he brought my things up for my apartment. If I ever needed to use it, I knew where to locate it. We were sitting on the sofa one night and he got a phone call. The call literally took 5 seconds.

"What kind of conversation was that?" I asked.

"When someone wants something, it doesn't take that long," he said smiling. "You want to ride with me for a minute?"

"Sure," I said as I put on my shoes and jacket.

We rode to this store parking lot and I was looking around because the neighborhood looked a little sketchy. I knew my apartment wasn't that great but it made my complex look like luxury apartments. After a little while, another car pulled up and someone got out of the passenger side and came to the window where Mario was. Mario rolled down the window, handed him something, and the passenger handed Mario something and said, "I need a little more."

Mario said ok and the passenger walked back to the car and they drove off. Did he just bring me out here to do a drop-off? I was stunned. I literally could not comprehend that he just brought me with him to give someone some drugs. Didn't he tell me the other day that he wouldn't put me in danger? Yet he thought it was cool to have me ride with him to a questionable neighborhood to drop off some drugs. My mind was running the whole ride back to the apartment but I never said a word.

When we got back inside, he proceeded to go to the coat closet and retrieve a weight scale and a little black bag. He sat the scale on my coffee table and then took some contents out of the bag. When I looked over at them, I noticed that they were little white rocks. My dad was a cop so I'd seen them before but I was thrown off to see that they had been in my closet this whole time. I was shocked and at a loss for words. I just sat there looking at him measure them, place them in a bag, put the rest back in the black bag, and put them back in the top of my closet.

"Do you want to ride with me?"

I just stared at him and shook my head.

"Why are you looking at me like that?"

I looked at him like he was crazy for asking me that question. I tried to find words to say but the only thing that came out was, "You do know that I'm in the military, right?"

"Yes, I know and I'm not going to do anything to get you in trouble. Like you said, your apartment is safe. The other day when I came over here and got here before you, I drove around your complex to see what was going on and you were right, it was safe. No one would ever know that I was here. That's why I can leave my stuff here and know that it will still be here when I get back. This is the perfect setup. No one knows I'm here so I can do my drops from here."

I just stared at him trying to make sure that I was hearing what I was hearing. I felt myself shaking a little bit and didn't quite know what was happening because I'd never felt this feeling before. If I had my gun, I'd probably have shot him and dealt with the consequences later. As I continued to sit there, he said, "Ok, I got to make this run. I'll be right back." He kissed me on my cheek and left.

I sat in that one spot looking at the place that he was once standing and trying to formulate a thought. Nothing was coming to mind. I felt my heart racing and my hands shaking. I was angry; furious even. I couldn't believe that he had drugs in my house. I had gotten over the gun thing, but he had drugs in my house. He thought it was ok to bring drugs into my house and he was so nonchalant about it, as if it was normal. Besides getting up and gathering his things, I sat in that same spot until he came back. When he knocked on the door, I had his stuff in my hands.

"You have to go!"

"What? What do you mean, I have to go?"

I let him in because I knew I was about to get really loud really quick and I didn't want to wake my neighbors.

"You need to get your stuff and get out of my house!"

"Why, what happened since I was gone?"

"Um, let's see. You took me on a drug run then came back and took drugs out of my closet and told me that this was the perfect place to stash your mess. Are you kidding me? I'm in the military! If anyone found out that I had drugs in my apartment, I would be kicked out! Do you understand how serious this is?!"

I was livid and there was nothing that he was going to say to get me to calm down or change my mind.

"Baby calm down."

"No! I'm not your baby."

"Why are you so upset? I told you what I did."

"Yes, but what you do on your own time, is on you! When you include me into your foolery, then it's on me too and I can't be involved with this. I'm already on the brink of getting out and you are trying to get me kicked out! Not going to happen! Get all your shit and get the hell out of my house!"

I couldn't believe the words that had just come out of my mouth. I never cursed before but somehow the anger that I felt rose up and I couldn't put it down. I scared myself because of how angry I was since I couldn't think enough to calm myself down. I had to just let the anger play out. I wasn't in control anymore. My anger had taken over the wheel and my calm self was now riding in the trunk.

He walked toward me and I could feel my arms tighten up. The closer he got, the more my anger rose. All of a sudden, I felt my arms go back and then with all the force that I had, they flew forward and landed in the center of his chest. He stumbled backward and looked at me like I had lost my mind. He was right because I didn't know where my mind had gone. I was no longer thinking, only reacting. He caught his balance and raised up like he wanted to hit me back but I stood my ground and was ready for whatever he wanted to do.

"I was just going to get my gun from under your pillow."

"Well say that next time."

I let him pass me and watched him as he walked out of the door. I paced around my apartment for a while trying to calm myself down. I kept shaking my hands hoping that whatever I was feeling would come out through my fingertips. After about an hour, I was able to catch my breath and slow down my heart palpitations. I was too amped up to sleep so I stayed up all night sitting on my sofa.

The next day, I went to work and then had watch from 1900 to 2200. Whenever I was on watch, I would keep my phone in my car because I didn't want to be distracted. When I got off and got home, I decided to check my messages. I had twenty text messages and five voicemails. They were all from Mario. I figured he was trying to apologize and get back over here but I was highly mistaken. The text messages were stating that I needed to call him back ASAP and that if I didn't, he'd be over. Did you really need twenty text messages to say that? I didn't even listen to the voicemails because

I figured they all said the same thing. I decided to give him a call. When he answered, he just started yelling.

"Where is it?!"

"Where is what?"

"You know what the hell I'm talking about!"

"If I knew what you were talking about I wouldn't be asking you questions."

"I checked my bag and I'm missing some."

"Missing some of what?" I wished he'd talk in complete sentences because I didn't have time to be going through this back and forth.

"My stash! I'm missing some. I did a count and some are missing! What did you do with them?"

"I never went in your bag. I didn't even know it was in my closet, remember?"

"I don't believe that. You saw me going in that closet. You were the only one there. I know you got it!"

"I don't have anything of yours! Whatever you had in there, should still be in there!" I felt my insides rising up again and my hands began to shake. My heart started beating faster with every word I spoke.

"All I know is that I'm missing some. I know you stole it and you better give it back! I tell you what, you bring me my shit or I'm coming and shooting your apartment up. You don't fuck with nothing of mine!"

"Oh, really!" I said as I got off my sofa and stood up. "Dude, you know where I stay! I'm here now if you're bad! You don't scare me! Bring your ass over here because I got something for you!"

"You're dead! Just know that! You're dead!"

"I'm ready when you are!" I hung up the phone and went to my car. I reached in my glove compartment and took out my .380 Smith and

Wesson and went back in the house and locked the door. I checked to make sure my gun was loaded and sat it on the table. I sat on the sofa opposite of the door just in case he started shooting at my front door. I started shaking my hands again trying to make myself calm down but at that moment, I didn't know if I wanted to calm down. He said that I was dead and that he was coming to shoot up my place so there was no need for me to calm down. I looked out toward my patio door and waited. I was on the ground floor and my patio led to the street so he could easily shoot up my entire living room and bedroom if he wanted to. I wasn't going to take no one threatening my life. If I was going to die tonight, someone was going to know who it was that I was fighting against.

The night turned into day and the day into night. I didn't receive a phone call and no one came to my door. I saw my creepy neighbor walking back and forth pass my patio but no one else. The next day, I had watch, so I had to leave the apartment. I got dressed and walked out the door; my .380 in hand. I looked around to see if I recognized his car but I didn't see him. I went to work and came back, still nothing. I figured he may try an element of surprise and try to shoot me when I least expected it so I stayed on guard. After about a week, I went on with my life. If he was going to get me, then hopefully I would be somewhere near my gun.

After a week and a half had passed my phone rang. I had locked Mario's number in my phone so that I would know when he called. When I checked, it wasn't him. Maybe he was calling from someone else's number. It didn't matter because I was not going to live in fear. I answered the phone very defensively.

"Hello!"

"Hi, is this Yasmine."

"Yes it is. Who is this?"

"This is Sergio, Mario's brother. I wanted to let you know that Mario found what he was looking for and wanted to apologize for threatening you. He said he didn't mean you any harm and that he was mad. He wants to talk to you." His voice was very soft and calming as if he knew his brother and was apologizing for him. But I didn't care. I just wanted to be done with it all.

"Sergio, tell your brother I don't care what he wants. Good that he found what he was looking for but tell him he better not ever call my phone again!" And I hung up. I sat on the sofa shaking my head and thinking that if I had just listened to Reed and Daniels in the first place, none of this would have happened but no, I had to be hard headed. Sometimes finding things out the hard way could lead to the end of your life. Lesson learned.

MIKE

I spent the next couple of weeks watching my surroundings and circling my apartments before I pulled in. I wanted to make sure he wasn't still trying to gain entry back into my life. I told Daniels what had happened and she joked about the warning that she gave me in regard to light-skinned brothers. We could always talk about any and everything. She'd tell me when I was being foolish and vice versa. It was like we were sisters but with different mothers. I'd go over to her place sometimes just to get away from my apartment and play with her son, Tyre. He was so cute with his curly hair and light brown skin like he came into the world sun-kissed. I joked with Daniels that he was light-skinned too so she better watch out. It was always fun getting together.

But tonight, I couldn't. She was going over her cousin's house for a while and it seemed like either everyone had something to do or I didn't want to be bothered with them. I hadn't seen Turner in a while, so I decided to call him up and see what he was up to.

"Hello. Who dis?"

"Is that how you answer the phone?" I said laughing. "It's Payton."

"Payton! What's going on? What are you doing?"

"Nothing, I'm bored. What are you doing over there?"

"The same."

"Ok, I'm coming over."

"Cool."

I hung up the phone, got dressed, and headed to the barracks. On my way there, I was checking my rear view to make sure I wasn't being followed. I didn't know why I was checking because it was dark and I couldn't tell if someone was following me or not. I was paranoid but had no reason to be because I hadn't received a phone call or text from Mario since I talked to his brother.

I arrived at Turner's barracks, headed upstairs, and let myself into their common area. When I knocked on his door, he responded with, "Who is it?"

"You know who I am. I told you I was coming over," I said as I walked in the door. He was sitting in a chair next to his bed reading a magazine.

"You really are bored. You're reading."

"Funny Payton. I like to read. What have you been up to?"

"Oh, nothing." I didn't want to go into the details about the last couple of weeks. I was trying to get past it and didn't feel like rehashing all of the details. "I was at the house bored and needed to get out."

"You can always hang out here."

"I know. That's why I'm here."

"Oh, be quiet."

We laughed and talked about when he was getting out and how long he had to wait until he got the final sign off. I still didn't know what my status was. All I knew was that I was still on limited duty and escorting prisoners around. It was an easy job so I had no complaints. As we were talking, his phone rang. He answered and said, "I'm here," and hung up the phone. Were all guys' conversations five seconds long?

"Who are you expecting? Do I need to leave?"

"Nah. My homeboy's coming to pick something up right quick."

Mike

I heard that before. I hoped he wasn't into the same thing that Mario was into too. As I lay across Turner's bed, his friend walked in. I sat up and looked straight at him. I didn't know what had come over me. I'd never seen anyone that captivated all of my attention like he had. He was tall, brown-skinned, and very attractive. He talked to Turner for a bit and then went to his drawer and picked up his brush. I looked over at Turner and my eyes motioned for him to introduce me. He shook his head no and smiled. I shook my head yes. He rolled his eyes and then said, "Evans, this is Payton." I smiled and said, "Hi." He said hi back and finished talking to Turner and left. Something within me said, "It's him." I didn't know what that meant but I took notice. I had never believed in love at first sight but something had just happened. I didn't know what exactly but I knew I needed to find out.

"Who was that?"

"Who? Evans?"

"Um, yeah!"

"Oh, that's my homeboy. He came to borrow my brush."

"And you weren't going to introduce me?"

"Payton, no. I know how you are with dudes."

"Man, hook that up!"

"No," he said smiling.

"Yeah you are. For real, Turner. Stop playing."

"You like him like that?"

"I don't know him but I want to get to know him."

"That dude ain't cute." He laughed.

"Ha ha, um, handsome is the word and very. Puppies are cute."

"So, you like my boy, huh?"

"Just hook it up and stop playing."

"Ok, girl. Geesh. I'll let him know."

"Thank you," I said as I threw his pillow at him.

I hung out with Turner for about another hour before I headed back home. I thought about Evans the whole ride back to the apartment. I didn't know who he was but I was mesmerized. Who was this guy and why hadn't I seen him on base before? Crazy question because the base was massive. There were plenty of people there that I had never seen before. All I knew was that I saw him tonight and I was going to harass Turner until I talked to him. Who would have thought that a guy messing with me in a hallway would lead me to him?

Three weeks had passed and Turner was still playing games. He was messing with me about how much I liked Evans but wouldn't tell me what was going on with him. He was irking my nerves and making me laugh at the same time. He had texted me to say that he was coming over because he left something at my apartment one day. I said ok, although there was nothing there that he could have left behind.

By this time, Pena had moved in with me. She was getting further along in her pregnancy and was looking like a cute penguin. She had also gone up to New York to get her son and he was staying with us too. That was my little man. I took him everywhere that I went when I had a day off. He was going to stay until Pena had her baby and she had to decide what she was going to do—stay in or get out. It looked like we were all facing the same questions.

I was playing with my radio when I heard a knock on the door. When I went to answer it, I was pleasantly surprised. It was Turner and Evans. It caught me off guard and I got really nervous but I didn't let it show. I acted like I normally did.

"Hey guys, come on in."

"Payton, you remember Evans?" Turner said smiling as he walked by me.

"Yes, I do. Hey Evans."

"Hey. You got a nice place here," he said as he walked into the living room.

"Thank you."

"What do you have in here to eat?"

"Turner, you better get out of my fridge if you didn't wash your hands," I screamed from the living room.

"Man, she's always cooking."

"Is that right?" said Evans.

"Yes, that is," I said as I went back over to mess with my radio. "We are having a cookout in a couple of weeks. Y'all should stop by."

"You know I'm coming," said Turner.

"Yes, you're always here. I know you'll be here."

"I don't see what I came here for. I don't know where I left that thing."

"What are you looking for?"

"That thing."

"Yeah, that narrows it down. If I find that "thing" I'll let you know."

"Ok, thanks Payton. Evans, let's go."

As they walked toward to door, Evans turned and said, "See you later, Payton."

"Ok," I said as I smiled and closed the door behind them. I was sure Turner didn't leave anything at my place but as long as he brought Evans with him, he could come and check anytime.

It was the day of the cookout and I had gotten up early to make sure the apartment was cleaned from head to toe. I made sure Pena cleaned her room because I knew with our little apartment and how many friends we had, people were going to be all over the place. Around noon, I started cooking. I made baked beans, collard greens, macaroni and cheese, pot ribs, chicken, and hot dogs on the grill. It was going to take me a while to cook all the meat because I had this tiny little grill that I put in the grass right outside my patio. I wanted to make sure the food was done before everyone got there. That was the plan anyway but people started coming early because they didn't have anything else to do and wanted to come and hang out. Everyone who was coming through was responsible for ice, drinks, alcohol, and buns.

Around 1700, we were all listening to music and having a good time when my phone rang. I didn't recognize the number so I answered cautiously.

"Hello."

"Hi. Is this Payton?"

"Yes, it is."

"This is Evans." A huge smile ran across my face. "Turner gave me your number, I hope that's ok."

"Yeah, that's ok."

"Turner had to go out of town but I was wondering if I could come through?"

"Of course you can."

"Do you need me to bring anything?"

"You can bring something to drink."

"Ok, I'll see you in a bit."

"Ok."

My day had just gotten ten times better. Evans was coming through and I would get to know him a little better without Turner interrupting. Things were turning around for the better and I was happy about it.

When he got there, he knocked on the door and I went to open it. No one wanted to open my door although they kept going in and out all day. I got to the door, let out a breath, and opened the door trying not to seem too nervous.

Mike

"Hi," I said trying to control how big my smile was. "Come on in."

"I brought this. I hope it's ok." He'd brought a big bottle of vodka.

"Yeah it is. I don't drink it but someone will. Come in and make yourself at home."

When he got inside, I introduced him to everyone the quickest way possible.

"Hey everyone, this is Evans." Everyone said hey and that was that. I knew he would mix and mingle and get to know people. I was still cooking on the grill and had to be outside to watch it. He came in and out and made himself comfortable. After I got done cooking and talking to everyone, I noticed he was sitting inside on the sofa. I decided to go over and talk to him for a bit.

"Are you ok?" I asked.

"Yeah. Did you cook everything?"

"Yes. I love to cook."

"I can tell. Thank you for letting me come over. Turner had to go out of town suddenly and he gave me your number and said I should come by."

"I'm glad he did. I hope you're enjoying yourself."

"I am." He had a cup in his hand so I knew something was helping him enjoy his time. As I was sitting there talking to him, Ward screamed from the front door that Reed, Morgan, and the crew left and took the bottle that Evans had brought with them. I didn't know why people wanted to play games with me but it wasn't going down today.

"Excuse me, will you?" I ran outside and confronted Reed.

"Where is it, Reed?"

"Where is what?"

"You know what I'm talking about. Don't steal anything from my house especially when you didn't bring it."

"I don't know what you're talking about," he said as I could clearly see he had something behind his back.

"Give it here!"

He pulled the vodka from behind his back and gave it to me. "I was only joking."

"Well don't and don't come back over here either."

I left and went back inside. When I walked in, Evans looked back at me. I smiled and held up the bottle that he brought and placed it back in the kitchen. I continued to mix and mingle until everyone left. I had been on my feet all day and just plopped on the sofa to rest. Pena and Max were in my room watching TV. I looked in the kitchen and saw that Evans was still there cleaning up and getting ready to take out the trash.

"Oh, you don't have to do that. I got it."

"It's ok. Where is your dumpster?"

"When you go out of the door, go right and then left and it will be down on the right."

"Ok, I'll be back."

I couldn't believe he stayed and was helping clean up but I was glad that he did. I didn't get to spend a lot of time with him because I was hosting the entire night and now I was beat. He came back and asked if there was anything else that needed to be done. I told him no and he came and sat on the sofa next to me. I wasn't sure what Turner had said to him to get him to come over but whatever it was, I was glad he did.

"Do you do this often?" he asked.

"Yeah, this is the gathering spot. People like to hang out here."

"I can tell. I really wanted to thank you for letting me come."

"Anytime. You're always welcomed."

"Really?"

"Yes, really. With or without Turner," I said smiling.

He smiled too and we sat there talking for a while. He eventually got up and said that he should be going. I said ok and got up with him. As he was walking toward the door, I tugged on his shirt. He turned around and looked at me and I stood there looking at him. He came close, kissed me on my cheek, put his hand on the small of my back and that was that. By this time, Pena and Max were in their room.

The next morning, I woke up to the smell of breakfast. I got out of bed and found him in the kitchen cooking.

"Oh, you cook?"

"I can do a lot of things," he said smiling.

I smiled and went to sit on the sofa. "Do you need any help?"

"Nah, I got it."

He made us two plates and handed mine to me. We ate breakfast together and talked. When we were done, he said that he really had to go. I said ok, gave him a kiss, and watched him walk out of the door. I didn't know what it was but I knew that he was the person that I wanted to be with. I had never felt this way about anyone. It wasn't the fact that he stayed over, it was something more. I just knew that he was the one for me and that I didn't want anyone else.

After I got up off the sofa and got myself ready for the day, I texted those that I was dating and told them I was done. There was nothing more that I needed from them and there was no need for them to come back over to my place. I made it crystal clear that it was over and I didn't want to have anything else to do with them. Simmons was the hardest because we had not only dated but we were also friends, but I knew if we stayed friends then he would always think that maybe there would be a possibility later on down the road. That possibility was shot, killed, and buried. I knew what I wanted and I went after it.

Evans got used to coming over but he would always come over with Turner and when Turner was ready to go, Evans had to go with him. It irked me because I wanted Evans to stay. Every time they got ready to leave, our conversation went something like this:

"Stop suffocating that man, Payton."

"I'm not suffocating anybody. You're just mad, that's all."

"You're right. I don't have anyone that I can hang out with so he doesn't need anyone either."

"Too late for that."

"Argh."

And then they would leave. It was funny because I knew Turner was serious but eventually, Evans was going to have to make a decision and I knew he had to make it on his own.

The decision came quicker than I thought. Within three weeks, he was coming over without Turner. We had made a decision to be exclusive and not date anyone else. What he didn't know was that I had already made that decision the first day that I saw him. It took me a minute to make it official but from that first day, I just knew. It was something about him that commanded my attention and although I wanted to be free and live my life to the fullest, if it meant that I couldn't be with him, I didn't want that life anymore. Living life to the fullest now meant being with him and only him and however long I would have had to wait would not have been long at all.

Eventually, we were spending all of our free time together and that meant being homebodies. Besides going out to get something to eat, we stayed in the house watching TV and just being together. I hated being away from him; like it literally hurt my heart to be apart from him. It felt like whenever he would leave me, he would take a piece of my heart with him and it would hurt me to tears. I didn't know what the navy had in store for me but I knew I didn't want to go anywhere without him. I had an appointment to speak with the lieutenant at sick call the following day and I was eager to see what he had come up with. I was still doing a lot of physical therapy but nothing was working.

I was sitting in this cold hospital room in my PT gear waiting to see the lieutenant. He had just completed a physical on both knees and now they were throbbing. He said he would bring me back some ice packs after he looked over his report. It was already cold, I didn't know if I wanted any ice packs.

"Ok, Payton," he said as he sat in the chair across from the exam table that I was sitting on. "I do not see any improvement and I spoke to both of your physical therapists and they both said the same thing; the only option would be surgery."

"I don't want to have surgery on my knees. There has to be another option."

"The only other option would be to be discharged from the military. Any other job that you get will involve some heavy lifting, bending of the knees, and stairs. Anything that you did from this point would result in a stress on your knees."

When he said that, the only thing I could think of was Daniels telling me that once they set you up with TPU, then they have already made the decision for you.

"Ok. Well, I guess I have no other option."

"Which type of discharge did you want to choose?"

"Which one was the paid discharge, again?"

He smiled. "Medical."

"Well, medical it is," I said with a worried look on my face. I didn't expect to be getting out so soon. I had so many plans but now that I couldn't do the job that I had signed up for and from the sound of it, any other job, I had to get out. Talk about feeling useless, abandoned, and rejected. I didn't know what was next for me. I was still planning on doing another tour so that I could go shopping with the money that I had saved but now that went straight out of the window. I should have shopped till I dropped while I was there.

"The process will take a couple of months and you will continue to work at TPU until that time. We will begin processing all of the paperwork and you will have some mandatory appointments prior to your discharge date. You will need to take a Transition Assistance Program (TAP) class prior to being discharged so that you are aware of what happens when you transition from the military back to civilian life and the benefits afforded to you. I'm sorry that this happened to you but do you have any questions?"

"Not at this time."

"You will have an appointment with administration where they will go over the next steps and you can ask any questions you have at that time."

"Ok, thank you."

"You're welcome and good luck."

Luck, huh? You guys are kicking me out and you're wishing me good luck. When he left, I looked up at the ceiling and pondered on what I just heard. What am I supposed to do now? I knew being discharged was a possibility but now it was a real thing. I was getting out. I shook my head as I gathered my things and left the building. I didn't have anything else to do besides that appointment, so I headed home.

The following week, I had my appointment with administration and I had thought of some questions to ask. When she called me back into her cubicle, I sat in the chair across from her while she pulled out my file.

"It says here that you are receiving a medical discharge. Is that correct?"

I wanted to say, isn't that what you just read because I was still bothered that I had to get out but I decided to be nice.

"Yes, that's correct."

"What will happen next is you will have a series of appointments and then you will be scheduled to attend a TAP class. This class will assist you with how to transition out of the military. You will also take a career placement test to let you know what jobs best fit your personality in the civilian world. The entire process could take up to three months."

"So, I will be discharged completely in three months?"

"That's correct."

Wow! That was quick. You're in one minute and out the next. If you're no use to them, there's no need for you sticking around.

"Do you have any questions?"

"Yes. For the paid discharge, I mean medical discharge, what exactly does that mean besides that I get paid? And how much do I get paid?"

"Because you are being discharged for a service-connected disability, you will have certain benefits as a veteran with a disability. That's the purpose behind the transition class. You will receive a one-time severance payment once you are discharged and you will also receive a disability rating from the navy. Once you are back in your hometown, you can go to the Veterans Administration to sign up for benefits through them. That's all the information that I have."

"So, this pay is a one-time thing?"

"Yes. You will receive one severance payment based on your years of service."

The lieutenant made it sound like this was a life-time payment but nope. I get one payment and then its good riddance. I couldn't believe my navy career was coming to an end. On the one hand, so many things had happened to me that maybe I did need a change but on the other, I wasn't nearly done. There was still plenty I wanted to do, to see, to experience, but it was being taken away from me as quickly as it was given to me. I had to accept that within the next three months, I had to create another plan. What was I going to do? Where was I going to go? It was too much to think about as I sat there so I just signed the papers that she placed in front of me and headed back to TPU.

When I got back to TPU, there was no work for us so Daniels and I sat in the front office assisting those that came in needing directions.

"You were right Daniels."

"About what?"

"I'm getting out in three months."

"Yeah, it's only a matter of time when you get here."

"I didn't think it was going to be that soon, though."

"We are in the same boat because I'm getting out the same time as you."

"What are you doing when you get out?"

"I don't know yet; thinking about going back to Georgia. My family is there and they can help out with Tyre. Are you going back?"

"No!"

"Wow. Where did that come from?"

"I came here to get away from there. I don't want to go back, I really don't. I don't know what I'm going to do. I could easily stay here and get a job or go back to school. I like my apartment and I have a lot of friends here. Ah! So many decisions."

"I understand. It'll come in time. Just pray about it."

"I will."

When I got home, I just sat on the sofa trying to decide what I was going to do. Evans came over and I told him what had happened with my appointments. He stated that he had some news of his own. He was getting ready to go to A-school in Meridian in a couple of months so he was about to leave me too; just another thought to add to the others. I hated that the military took people away from you whenever they wanted to but as they say, that's what we signed up for. All of these reasons must be in fine print because I didn't sign up for any of this.

Evans and I had gotten closer and were even praying together. We weren't perfect by any means but we were perfect for each other. We had a lot of fun together and would still mess with Turner about not having someone to call his own. Turner was still coming over and raiding the fridge and messing with Pena and Max. I would joke with them saying how cute they were as a family. He'd look at me like I was crazy and I would burst out laughing. I was having fun in Virginia and I didn't want to leave.

The first Friday night in August, Daniels and I decided to go to the club. We hadn't been out in a while and we were both craving a night out. Daniels decided to meet me at my place and we'd ride together.

"Payton, the one night we decide to go out, it starts raining."

"I know. I saw that. It has been calming down. I say we wait a little longer and head out because we are going out tonight."

"I agree. We desperately need this night out. Tyre is with my cousin so momma is free to stay out as late as she wants."

"Look at you living it up."

We both laughed and I continued to get ready. After about thirty minutes, the rain had ceased and we decided to head out. I decided to drive to give Daniels a rest from having to drive to my place. I made a left out of my apartment complex and got to the first red light. We were talking about which club we wanted to go to when we heard tire screeching and then all of a sudden, BAM! My head hit the steering wheel, bounced off and hit the back of my seat, and was going back toward my steering wheel. Daniels's head lunged forward but the seat belt stopped her from going too far forward but she hit the back of her head on the headrest. I sat there dazed trying to figure out what had just happened. When I snapped out of it, I realized that the car behind us had hit us. I looked out of my mirror and I saw a guy get out of his car and he was walking toward my car. When he realized that we were moving, he ran back to his car and sped off. I just sat there frozen, not knowing what to do.

"Go! Go! Go!" Daniels screamed and we took off after him. He wasn't stopping at any stop signs or traffic lights and neither were we. He turned left into a grocery store and then sped out of the parking lot down this dark sketchy street. We knew better than to follow him down a street where we didn't know where it led. We decided to go to the CVS that was right next to my apartment complex and call the police. Daniels was able to write down the license plate and description of the vehicle before he got away.

"Hello, I'd like to report a hit and run!"

"What's your name and location?"

"My name is Yasmine Payton and I am in a CVS parking lot on the corner of Ralph and Main."

"Is anyone hurt?"

"No, I don't think so."

"Ok, we will have someone there as soon as possible."

"Thank you."

"Daniels, are you ok?"

"My head hurts but I'm ok. Are you ok?"

"Same. My head is throbbing."

"I can't believe he hit us and took off."

"I saw him get out of the car because he knew he hit us hard but when he saw that we were moving, he took off."

"The nerve of him. Did they say how long it was going to take?"

"No. They just said as soon as possible. To think that we were on our way to have a girl's night out."

"Right. We were right next to the apartment. We could have literally walked across the street and walked inside from your patio. I guess that was God telling us we didn't need to go to the club."

"Yeah, I'm sure He didn't want us to go anyway. What the devil meant for evil, God means for good."

We sat there for an hour and then another. What was taking them so long? I decided to call back to see if anyone was coming.

"911-what's your emergency?"

"Yes, I called two hours ago to report a hit and run and I'm still sitting at the CVS and no one has shown up yet."

"Sorry, ma'am. They said they will get there as soon as they can. They are dealing with more pressing matters at the moment. Just stay right there."

I hung up the phone. It had been two hours and I could literally walk back to my apartment and not have to cross the street. I was not going to sit there all night. Daniels and I decided to just call it a night. She got in her car and left and I went into my apartment. What a night. We only wanted to hang out and de-stress and now we both had headaches. This was not how we had hoped our night would end.

The next morning, I heard someone beating on my door. I got up and put on some clothes and there it went again. By this time, my body was out of shock and I was hurting all over. I answered the door with plenty of attitude.

"What?!" I looked up and it was a cop.

"Hi, are you Yasmine?"

"Yes," I said astonished that he was now at my door.

"Did you call in a hit and run last night?"

"Yes, I did."

"Why did you leave the scene?"

"I stayed on the scene for two hours. Why are you just now showing up?" At this point, I really didn't care if I got in trouble. Something had to have snapped loose when I hit my head as many times as I did because I was saying exactly what I was thinking.

"We had more pressing matters to attend to like murders and robberies."

"Well that's why I left. I can literally see the CVS parking lot from here so it made no sense for me to stay there when I could come home and rest."

He looked annoyed but I didn't care because I was annoyed too.

"Can we take a look at the damage of your vehicle?"

"Yes, let me get my keys."

I hadn't stopped to think to check the damage to my vehicle. I assumed my bumper was missing and that my back seat was now touching the front seat because of the impact of the crash but when we went to look at the back of my car, I was surprised to see that I only had a couple of scratches and even they were hard to see.

"Is this the car that was in the accident?" he asked.

"Why would I show you someone else's car? Of course this is the car."

"It doesn't look like you suffered too much damage. Was anyone in the car hurt?"

"My friend and I both have headaches because of the impact."

"You both need to be checked out as soon as possible. I will write up a report and you can call in a couple of days to get a copy."

"What about the person that hit us?"

"Did you take down the license plate number?"

"Yes, we did." I reached in the car and took the paper where Daniels had written down the information.

"I will add this to the report and see what I can find out."

"Ok."

"Do you have any more questions?"

"No."

"Ok, you have a good day."

I looked at him annoyed and walked back in the apartment. Why did I leave? Was he serious? Why did he show up the following morning? I called Daniels and told her that she needed to go get checked per the cop's request as soon as possible and I was going to get checked as well.

When I called sick call, they told me to come in as soon as possible. When I got there, they took me to get a CT and gave me an exam because I informed them that I was very sore and my back and shoulders were hurting. After the exam, the doctor left to wait on the CT results. When he came back, he informed me that I had a walking concussion and that I needed to rest. He said that he would prescribe me some ibuprofen and that I needed to stay hydrated and rest. He gave me documentation to take to TPU that informed them that I was to stay on bed rest for the next couple of days. That was fine by me because I was more irritated than usual. It was probably best that I didn't be around people.

The next couple of days, I was going through all kinds of emotions. I was sad, mad, then very angry. It was as if everything that had happened to me while I was in the military came flooding back all at once. I would sit and cry when I thought about the hit and run because, what if I had died and my family didn't know why or what if the ship that was coming toward us had actually hit us and we all died on impact or what if our ship got bombed? The questions kept swirling around in my head and I would get even sadder. I didn't know what to do with all these emotions so when it was time to go back to work, I buried them. I didn't want anyone to know what I was going through or what I was thinking because my thoughts weren't the greatest at this point in my life.

After a couple of weeks, my petty officers noticed a change in my behavior. My evaluations were always great but now I was acting out of character. I was being very short with people and would walk away and not come back for hours and didn't care about getting in trouble. I was angry all the time and would stare off into space when someone was asking me a question. I couldn't concentrate on a task long enough to finish it and when I sat too long, I would get dizzy but when I would try and get up in order to walk it off, I felt unstable. I didn't know what was going on with me but it felt like I was losing my mind.

One day, I showed up to work and my petty officer stated he wanted to have a talk with me.

"Payton, what's going on? You have not been acting like your normal self."

"Nothing."

"Nothing? You need to tell me something other than nothing because your career is at stake."

"What career? I'm getting out. My career is over! My life is over! Everything keeps happening. The hit and run, the ship, what if I die? Will my family even know that I died?"

It was like the flood gates were opened and I couldn't stop crying or talking. Everything that I was thinking was coming out of my mouth and I couldn't stop it from coming.

"Payton, Payton! Calm down."

"I don't know how to calm down. I can't think! I'm going crazy!"

By this time, I was hyperventilating, my heart was beating faster and faster and I couldn't stop crying. Petty Officer Ross gave me a brown paper bag from his desk.

"Payton, breathe in this and put your head between your legs. It will relax you and allow you to catch your breath."

I took the paper bag as I was sitting in my chair and did as he said. Slowly, my breaths started to return and my heart slowed down. I couldn't even pick my head up to look at him. This was not who I was. What had happened to me? I didn't even recognize this person anymore. I felt as if someone else had taken over my body and I had to go along for the ride.

"Payton, I'm going to sign you up for anger management classes. These classes, although called anger management, help with all kinds of issues. There will be a psychiatrist there moderating the class and I think this will really help you out."

Psychiatrist? Sounds about right. At this point, that's probably the only person that could help.

"I think you should start right away. I will let them know that you will be coming over starting tomorrow. When you arrive, make sure you give them this document. You can leave for the rest of the day. Report to building 5420 first thing in the morning."

I took the document, nodded my head, and left his office. I couldn't bear to look at him in his face. I wanted to go dig a hole, crawl into it, and sleep. I no longer felt like dealing with the world. It had done enough to me and I was over it.

The next morning, I arrived at building 5420. When I went inside, it felt like a ghost town. I wondered if I was the only person there. I checked in and was told to go down the hall and to room J. As I walked down the hall, I peeked inside of the other rooms and there were different group meetings being held in different rooms. I guess no one was in the lobby because everyone was held up in one of these classes.

When I got to room J, I opened the door and looked inside. The room was well lit as there were three big windows on the wall opposite the door. There was a long rectangular table with chairs on both sides. There were about eight people that were already there so I made nine.

"Come on in and have a seat," this woman said. When I looked over at her, I realized she was a lieutenant. I sat next to this guy who was leaning all the way back in his chair looking up at the ceiling.

"Price, lean up please," the lieutenant said. He smiled at her and then leaned up in his chair. I didn't know where I was but it felt like a different part of the military.

"You're Payton, correct?"

"Yes, Lieutenant."

"Since this is your first time here, you don't have to share why you are here if you don't want to. You can observe to see how the classes will go. From the looks of it, you will be here every day for two weeks."

"Ok."

She took her eyes off me and placed them back on the class. She was sitting at the head of the table and we were sitting across from each other. It was a very intimate setting for obvious reasons. I'm sure if these classes were any bigger, no one would feel comfortable talking about their feelings or why they were here in the first place.

"Today, we are going to talk about what makes you angry and some techniques on how to diffuse that anger in certain situations."

"I can't diffuse it. When the anger comes, it takes over," said this one guy and everyone chimed in, in agreement.

"Bennet, I understand but you have to try not to let it overtake you because if you don't start learning how to deal with your anger, it's going to lead you into a lot of trouble."

"But people get on my nerves. Sometimes, I just want to shoot everyone."

Again, everyone chimed in, in agreement.

"But what would shooting people accomplish? There will always be someone that is going to do something that you don't like. You can't go around shooting everyone. You have to learn to deal with the inner part of yourself. That's the only way you will be able to deal with others."

I was sitting and listening to everyone's story about what made them angry and why they were there and I was surprised to hear that they felt the exact same way I was feeling. I realized that there was a purpose for this class and hopefully it would help.

By the end of August, I had one more class to take. By this time, some people had to have their classes extended, while others were happy to finally be done. We had all opened up about why we were there and learned some techniques on how to deal with anger, sadness, depression, nervousness, and anxiety, to name a few. At the end of the class, almost all of us were signed off and ready to return back to duty. I didn't plan on coming back because I only had a couple of months left in the navy. I would have to deal with my issues on my own moving forward.

By early September, I had started my TAP classes. These classes were two weeks long and would go into depth on the process of being discharged from the military and what to do next. They were all-day classes and very boring. They reminded me of being back in Lieutenant Lewis's class. I knew we needed the information but they could have done better with their choice of instructors. I figured I'd need to pay attention since I had been notified that I would be getting out in December.

By Tuesday, September 11, we had only a couple more days to go. We had taken a test to see what jobs would better fit us and I got things in the hospitality industry. I found that bizarre seeing that I had gone to college for accounting. I knew I wanted to finish my accounting degree because my dad said that once I stopped going, I wasn't going to finish it and I was determined to prove him wrong.

The morning started off like any other morning with our instructor letting us know what topic we were going to discuss and what page to turn to in our TAP handbook when someone rushed into our class and headed straight for the instructor. We all stared at our instructor and noticed that her eyes got big as she was hearing the information being whispered into her ear. It reminded me of the USS Cole bombing. What happened this time? Was it another one of our ships? Were they heading this way? So many questions swarmed my thoughts but I tried not to freak out until I had something to freak out about. We all looked at each other trying to figure out what was going on. After less than two minutes, the person rushed back out of the classroom.

"If anyone has family in New York, you need to call them now. One of the twin towers was just hit by an airplane."

We were all stunned and for a moment it didn't sound real. Some people got up in a panic and started making phone calls and running out of the room. I had no idea what the twin towers were but it sounded serious. As I looked out of the window, I saw people frantically moving around the base and heard sirens going off. I froze not knowing what to do or where to go. I heard the instructor saying something but it sounded like it was muffled. I had blacked out and wasn't listening with comprehension. After I came through, I heard that they were locking down the base. They did the same thing with the USS Cole and I didn't want to be stuck on the base for who knows how long so I rushed to my car and headed toward my apartment.

I was able to get off base before word got around that the base was on lockdown. I got to my apartment and turned on the TV. They were showing the first tower being hit by an airplane and the explosion that it caused. I couldn't believe what I was seeing. A plane went into a building in New York. How could this happen? As I sat there watching the news, I felt my heart start to beat faster and faster and I felt my breathing start to change so I quickly turned off the TV and sat there staring at a blank screen with tears running down my face. It's happening again. We are under attack and who knows where they are going to attack next. They are going to send us to war especially our ship because we are a supply ship. We are going to be right there in the thick of it. The thoughts kept swarming through my brain and my heart wasn't calming down. I sat in front of the TV for a couple of hours not moving an inch. When I snapped out of it, I heard my phone ringing. It was Pena.

"Hello."

"Payton, thank God you answered the phone. Where are you?"

"I'm at the apartment. Where are you?"

"I'm stuck on the base. They shut the base down and won't let anyone on or off. They said one of the planes may be headed straight toward us!"

"Oh, no!"

"I don't know how long I'm going to be here. Can you pick up Max from school?"

"Yeah, I got you."

"Ok, I will keep you informed on what's going on here."

"Ok." I hung up the phone and went to pick up Max from school. The traffic was crazy because everyone was out and about and I was guessing that they heard the news and were trying to get their kids from school. My main objective was to grab Max and get back home as soon as possible.

Although Max's school was only two miles away, it took me an hour to get there and an hour to get back. It was crazy. When we got home, Max asked where his mom was and I had to tell him that she was at work and she would be back as soon as she could. He was fine with it. He went in my room and watched cartoons. Although we had a TV in the living room, he would always go in my room and watch TV while sitting on the floor. I didn't understand it but I'm sure he had his reasons. There were plenty of times I would go in my room to check on him because he was too quiet and found him asleep on my floor. Right about now, I would be happy to do the same.

Three days later, they released the lockdown on the base. I did not want to go anywhere near the base. I was fearful that something was going to happen. Just a couple of weeks before the twin towers were hit, I was having therapy sessions and now I felt like all of that work was for nothing. I was now sleeping with my gun under my pillow and would get startled at the slightest of noises. Insomnia had set in deeply and I was always looking behind me and checking my surroundings before I left the house. I was so paranoid that something was going to happen at any time.

Pena had made her way back home and was filling me in on the havoc that was going on in the base the past three days. I didn't know what was about to happen but I felt a change coming to the base. All I had to do was make it to December and I wouldn't have to go on the base any longer.

November had come and I was sitting in my apartment with a major decision to make—stay in Virginia or move back home to Georgia. Evans had already left for school and I was still distraught about that. Turner and I had taken him to the airport in October and I tried my best not to cry as we said our goodbyes. I felt like someone had taken my tattered heart and given him half of it and left me with the other half. How was I supposed to survive with half of a heart? I could tell that he was holding back emotions as well because he would look at me with sad eyes as to say, "Tell me to stay. I want to stay here with you," but he knew duty called and he had to go wherever the military told him to go.

When he got on his plane, I came back home and sat in the floor of my bedroom and cried for what seemed like hours. I felt like I was dying inside. I felt like the military had taken a part of me and left me with the other half to fend for myself. I had never felt a feeling like that before. I had never truly cared for someone as much as I cared for him. Besides Eric, I had never been in a long-term relationship before. I really didn't know what love was because I never had anything to compare it with but this surely felt like what I had heard love was and now he was gone. It felt empty in my apartment without him. I knew eventually he would be able to choose his orders and if I stayed, he could come back here. If I decided to move back home I knew what awaited me there; the same thing that I ran away from in the first place only this time I had a lot more issues. My once suicidal thoughts were now homicidal thoughts. I wasn't going to allow anyone to hurt me ever again and if I had to do something about it, I would. Was going back home the safest decision for me or was staying in Virginia something that I could do? My mom told me to call her when I had made my decision because my dad kept saying that coming home and being closer to the family was the best choice. I sat on the sofa for what seemed like hours until I felt the pressure to make a decision. I picked up the phone and dialed our house number and my mom picked up.

"Hi Yaz. How are you?"

"I'm fine. How are you guys?" I put on the "everything is ok" mask because I hadn't told them any of the things that I had gone through while I was in the navy. I didn't think they could really understand unless they were here. To them, I was having the best time of my life.

"We are good. So, have you made a decision?"

"Yes. I've been thinking about it for some time now and trying to weigh what would be the best for me and I believe I've come to a conclusion. I'm going to come home."

"That's great! We will come up there and help you get your things. When can you come home?"

"They said I can go now and wait on my discharge documents to be mailed to me."

"Ok, I'll let your dad know so we can plan on driving up. It's going to be good to have you home. Once I have all the details, I'll call and let you know."

"Ok."

"I love you and I will talk to you later."

"I love you too. Bye."

By the time I hung up the phone I knew I had made a bad decision. The only reason that I decided to go back home was because Evans was going to Meridian and that meant he would only be a three-and-a-half-hour drive away. I figured wherever he would be stationed next, I could move there. I couldn't bear to be in Virginia without him. I needed to be as close as possible to wherever he was. If that meant going back to a dysfunctional situation, then that's what I had to do. I'd figure everything else out later.

My parents came with a U-Haul and I got some of my friends to come over and help us load up the truck. My parents went ahead of me since it was going to take them longer to get there in the U-Haul than me in my car. I had to do a final walk throught with the apartment manager and turn in my keys. Once I got everything taken care of, I got in the car and headed toward Atlanta. As I listened to the radio, the questions started swirling in my head. What was I going to do when I got back? What was the plan? Was I going to school? Would I get a job? Where was I going to stay? I had no clue how to answer any of those questions. All I knew was that I was on a road; a road that would eventually lead me to Evans. All those questions didn't matter. I was headed home and he was waiting for me to arrive.

MESSAGE FROM THE AUTHOR

I am a navy veteran and I strive to help those that are also dealing with the remnants of military duty and wartime to get a better grip of their reality. Sometimes our scars are not seen on the surface. Sometimes they run deep; deep within the very souls of who we are. I'm here to let you know that you must deal with these issues or they will consume your life-thoughts, wills, and emotions until you are no longer you. You are not alone. There are resources out there that will allow you to shed some light on those dark areas we try so hard to hide; those events that we suppress because we feel like no one else could possibly know the extent of what we have had to endure. I was one of those people and I have suppressed events for many years and put on a happy face so that no one would ever know the pain that I was dealing with daily. I too received help and while it's a day to day process that may never go away, I can rest assured that I don't have to do it on my own.

Mental health is vital to living a satisfying life. If you need to speak with someone, do it! There is nothing to be ashamed about if you have to go outside of your circle to get mental help. The Disabled American Veteran (DAV) association is a good resource as other veterans also work for them. While the Veterans Administration (VA) varies from state to state, there are some good counselors out there that can help you get a grasp on your mental state and live a prosperous life. If you cannot locate a good VA representative, ask the VA to refer you to an outside clinic. While others outside of the military may not truly understand what we've gone through, they are here to help. Give them a chance because believe it or not, we care about you. I love all my veteran brothers and sisters out there and I want only the best for you, but you have to want it for yourself as well. Be blessed!

OTHER WORK BY THE AUTHOR

NEW LIFE, NO SEX, WHAT NOW?
Straight Talk About Sex and Celibacy

Lust and temptation are rampant in our world, but casual sex is no small matter. That is serious business!

Celibacy has become the road less traveled, but why? Why aren't more people—even Christians—willing to wait? And what about those who don't plan to marry? Is sex off limits to them forever?

Have you wondered about celibacy? Are you looking for a book that "tells it like it is"? Well, this is it! Nine women share their experiences with celibacy and answer the questions most people are too embarrassed to ask.

Although the book is an honest conversation of women, it is also very useful for men to understand why women act the way they do.

There is nothing sugarcoated in these pages. So strap up your boots and let's walk the path called *celibacy*.

www.ingramcontent.com/pod-product-compliance
Lightning Source LLC
Chambersburg PA
CBHW070300010526
44108CB00039B/1414